D1569423

San Antonio

San Antonio

A Historical

and Pictorial Guide

by Charles Ramsdell

Second Revised Edition by

Carmen Perry with

editorial contributions by

Charles J. Long

Foreword by

Maury Maverick, Jr.

University of Texas Press

Austin

Requests for permission to reproduce material from this work should be
sent to Permissions, University of Texas Press, Box 7819, Austin, Texas 78713.

Library of Congress Cataloging-in-Publication Data

Ramsdell, Charles.
    San Antonio: a historical and pictorial guide.

    Bibliography: p.
    Includes index.
    1. San Antonio (Tex.)—Description—Guide-books.
I. Perry, Carmen. II. Long, Charles J. III. Title.
F394.S2R3 1985 917.64'351'0463 85-13367
ISBN 0-292-77605-5 (pbk.)

To

Mary Vance Green

and

O'Neil and Wanda (Graham) Ford

champions of great traditions

and to those other members of the

San Antonio Conservation Society

whose courage and foresight have

saved for their city most of the

things worth writing about

Contents

Foreword

This book, written by Charles Ramsdell and revised by Carmen Perry, is the best of its kind on the City of San Antonio. Nothing can compare with it from the standpoint of scholarship, accuracy, and simplicity.

The late Charles Ramsdell was a friend of mine of many years and a civilized good fellow. I never saw such a researcher in all my life. Year after year I saw him poring over books in the Alamo Library; this book is the fruit of that labor.

Carmen Perry, another long-time friend, is a scholar who has won many academic honors. I first met her when she was the librarian of the Alamo Library. From there she went to St. Mary's University and then to the University of Texas at San Antonio. Born in Mexico to a German father, British grandfather, and a mother from Spain, her first language was Spanish.

My great-grandfather, Samuel Augustus Maverick, arrived in San Antonio in 1835, signed the Declaration of Independence of the Republic of Texas the next year as the representative of the defenders of the Alamo, and eventually gave the word *maverick* to the English language. With that background, I unhesitatingly recommend this book to you with the sure and certain belief that no tourist or newcomer (or oldtimer!) should be without it.

Maury Maverick, Jr.

Acknowledgments

To these the author offers his heart-felt though altogether inadequate thanks:

To Josephine Bramlette Ramsdell, who died December 2, 1957, and whose name, but for the exigencies of practical considerations, would be on the title page, next to the author's, where it belongs.

To the everlasting patience of Fred Schmidt, that rarest of birds, the photographer who is not a prima donna.

To super-librarians Minnie B. Cameron, Grace Philippi, Elizabeth McCollister, and Marg-Riette Montgomery, for their immeasurable help.

To photographers Dick McConnaughey, Richard MacAllister, Hal Swiggett, Gilbert Barrera, Charles Long and Joe Elicson, for the unstinted gift of their time and substance.

To Ted James for the use of his superb collection of rare old photographs.

To Gretchen Rochs Goldschmidt, Mrs. William Watson, and General J. R. Sheetz, for the use of their manuscripts, and to Frances Finlay for an introduction.

To Keith Elliott, of the Chamber of Commerce, and to Cal Williams, of the Civic Advertising Committee for advice and aid.

To Lois Burkhalter and to Margaret Carson for lessons in the value of antique art.

To Charles Kilpatrick and the Express Publishing Company for permission to use portions of articles published in the *San Antonio Express Sunday Magazine*.

To Jess McNeel and to the Edgar Tobin Foundation and to General J. C. Gordon, of the Lone Star Brewing Company, for assistance.

To Mrs. Virginia C. Koenigsberg and James Brown Associates, Inc., for their kind permission to condense a passage from *King News*, by Moses Koenigsberg.

C. R.

To these I offer my heartfelt though altogether inadequate thanks:

The Reverend Balthasar Janacek, for information on the Catholic missions in San Antonio.

The Reverend Benedict Leutenegger, O.F.M., for information on San José Mission and translations of the various mission records.

To super librarians Minnie B. Cameron, Elizabeth McCollister, Catherine McDowell, and Grace Philippi.

To Charles Kilpatrick and the Express Publishing Company for permission to use portions of articles published in the *San Antonio Express Sunday Magazine*.

My gratitude for their help also goes to the following: Mary Burkholder, Lois Burkhalter, Walter N. Mathis, General J. R. Sheetz, Susanna Shields, the Edgar Tobin Foundation, Mrs. William Watson, and Eric Steinfeldt.

Many organizations cooperated in providing information, including all the military bases, universities, and civic organizations, especially the San Antonio Conservation Society. Numerous individuals provided information, photos, and other help to bring this book up to date.

C.P.

San Antonio

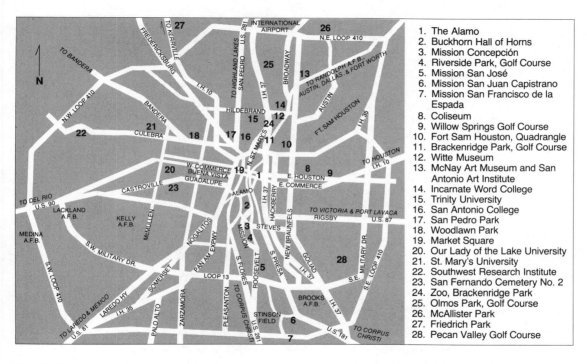

1. The Alamo
2. Buckhorn Hall of Horns
3. Mission Concepción
4. Riverside Park, Golf Course
5. Mission San José
6. Mission San Juan Capistrano
7. Mission San Francisco de la Espada
8. Coliseum
9. Willow Springs Golf Course
10. Fort Sam Houston, Quadrangle
11. Brackenridge Park, Golf Course
12. Witte Museum
13. McNay Art Museum and San Antonio Art Institute
14. Incarnate Word College
15. Trinity University
16. San Antonio College
17. San Pedro Park
18. Woodlawn Park
19. Market Square
20. Our Lady of the Lake University
21. St. Mary's University
22. Southwest Research Institute
23. San Fernando Cemetery No. 2
24. Zoo, Brackenridge Park
25. Olmos Park, Golf Course
26. McAllister Park
27. Friedrich Park
28. Pecan Valley Golf Course

Map 1. *Greater San Antonio*

1. Chamber of Commerce
2. St. Joseph's Catholic Church
3. Joske's Department Store
4. Menger Hotel
5. Lady Bird Johnson Fountain
6. Alamo Cenotaph
7. The Alamo
8. Long Barrack
9. Federal Building
10. Municipal Auditorium
11. St. Mark's Episcopal Church
12. Travis Park
13. St. Anthony Hotel
14. Travis Park Methodist Church
15. Consulado General de México
16. Gunter Hotel
17. Majestic Theatre
18. Republic Bank Plaza
19. La Mansión Motor Hotel
20. St. Mary's Catholic Church
21. St. Mary's School
22. Aztec Theatre
23. Flood Gate
24. Alamo to River
25. Reconstructed Springs
26. Paseo del Río
27. Nix Hospital Building
28. Hyatt Regency Hotel
29. Commerce Street Bridge
30. "Casa Río" Restaurant
31. River Extension
32. Hilton Palacio del Río Hotel
33. Convention Center
34. Tower of the Americas
35. Maverick Plaza
36. Palasadoed House
37. HemisFair Plaza Gate 1
38. Institute of Texan Cultures
39. Old Beethoven Hall
40. National University of Mexico
41. USO
42. German-English School Site
43. El Cuartel
44. St. John's Lutheran Church
45. La Villita
46. Villita Assembly Hall
47. Little Church of La Villita
48. Conservation Society Headquarters
49. Cos House
50. Arneson River Theatre
51. City Water Board Plaza
52. Hertzberg Circus Collection
53. Groos National Bank
54. Old First National Bank Site
55. M Bank Alamo
56. Public Library
57. Tower Life Building
58. Flood Channel
59. Casa Reales Site
60. Menger Soap Works Site
61. Main Plaza
62. St. Anthony Statue
63. Main Flood Gate
64. *U.S.S. San Jacinto* Ship's Bell
65. Bexar County Courthouse
66. San Fernando Cathedral
67. Frost Bank Tower
68. Frost Motor Bank and Money Museum
69. Roosevelt Monument
70. City Hall
71. Moses Austin Statue
72. Spanish Governor's Palace
73. County Jail
74. Navarro House
75. Alameda Theatre
76. Rosa Verde Medical Center
77. Santa Rosa Medical Center
78. Ben Milam Statue
79. Old Cemetery List
80. Market Square
81. Farmer's Market
82. El Mercado
83. Museum of Art
84. Fiesta Plaza

Map 2. *Walking Tour of San Antonio*

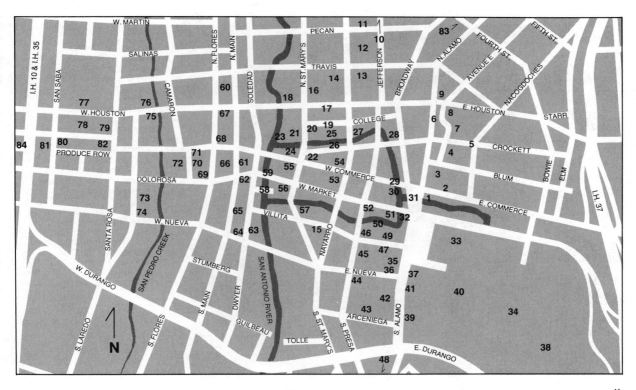

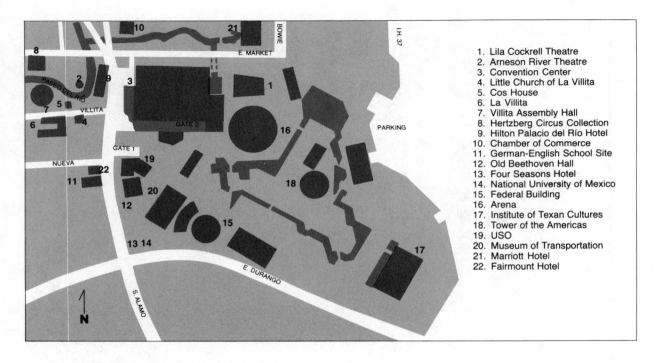

1. Lila Cockrell Theatre
2. Arneson River Theatre
3. Convention Center
4. Little Church of La Villita
5. Cos House
6. La Villita
7. Villita Assembly Hall
8. Hertzberg Circus Collection
9. Hilton Palacio del Río Hotel
10. Chamber of Commerce
11. German-English School Site
12. Old Beethoven Hall
13. Four Seasons Hotel
14. National University of Mexico
15. Federal Building
16. Arena
17. Institute of Texan Cultures
18. Tower of the Americas
19. USO
20. Museum of Transportation
21. Marriott Hotel
22. Fairmount Hotel

Map 3. *HemisFair Plaza*

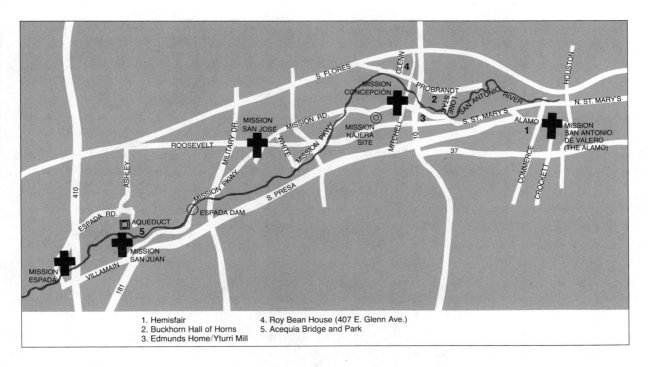

S. FLORES
GLENN
MISSION CONCEPCIÓN
PROBRANDT
2
MISSION SAN JOSÉ
MISSION RD.
WHITE
MILITARY DR
ROOSEVELT
MISSION PKWY
MISSION NÁJERA SITE
LONE STAR
SAN ANTONIO RIVER
S. ST. MARY'S
N. ST. MARY'S
HOUSTON
MISSION SAN ANTONIO DE VALERO (THE ALAMO)
ALAMO
1
3
MITCHELL
10
37
COMMERCE
CROCKETT
410
ASHLEY
ESPADA RD.
MISSION PKWY.
S. PRESA
ESPADA DAM
AQUEDUCT
5
MISSION SAN JUAN
MISSION ESPADA
VILLAMAIN
181
4

1. Hemisfair
2. Buckhorn Hall of Horns
3. Edmunds Home/Yturri Mill
4. Roy Bean House (407 E. Glenn Ave.)
5. Acequia Bridge and Park

Map 4. *The Mission Trail*

1

The Spell

*Entrance to the Spanish
Governor's Palace*

The easy pace of life, the lilt of the Spanish tongue, the bronze Indian laughing away centuries of pale dominion, sunburnt landscapes, secluded patios, the remembering river, time-stained walls—things of the past in a setting of present-day America, and the sense of exciting things to come—these give San Antonio, in Texas, its indefinable charm.

But *charm* is not, perhaps, the right word. It suggests a neat, well-ordered place, like Taxco in Mexico or many a European town, a cozy arrangement of natural beauty and architecture.

San Antonio is not well ordered, not wholly beautiful, not wholly anything. It is, and has been always, a meeting place, on the verge, between France and Spain, between Spain and England, between the Indian and the white, between the South and the West, the old and the new.

What fascinates the visitor—and the long-time resident as well—is the amazing variety of the place, its startling contrasts.

San Antonio is gaudy but not neat.

This city of nearly three-quarters of a million people, who are themselves a piquant scrambling of races and cultures, sprawls where three diverse geographic areas join. Fertile rolling prairies stretch to the north and east. Limestone hills dotted with junipers rise as far as the High Plains to the northwest, the Rocky Mountains to the west. The brush country, the thorny chaparral, reaches the Gulf of Mexico on the south and continues beyond the Rio Grande on the southwest.

The flora of these different regions grow within view of the city streets. In the spring you may find, blooming near together, wild plum and redbud, buckeye and Texas mountain laurel, and the spiney fragrant acacias: huisache and cat's-claw.

From a precipitous rocky hill on the north side of town you can

1

drive in a car on the expressway just a few minutes, then look around on a flat and seemingly limitless plain.

The weather, too, is variable. Summers are hot and dry. Spring and fall are mostly delightful, winters generally mild, except when a blue norther strikes; then it blusters out in three days. About once in every four years a light snow thrills the young. Nobody dares to predict the weather; the official forecasters are butts of popular humor.

In the words of Sidney Lanier, the poet, who came here as a consumptive seeking health in the winter of 1872/73, "the thermometer, the barometer, the vane, the hygrometer, oscillate so rapidly, so lawlessly, and through so wide a meteorological range, that the climate is simply indescribable."

Lanier found no healing in this climate, but he did find enchantment in the town.

"It stands with all its gay prosperity on the edge of a lonesome, untilled belt of land one hundred and fifty miles wide, like Mardi Gras on the austere brink of Lent." He was drawn to the river, "the lovely windings of the green translucent stream," and to the street life, "a bizarre exhibition of sights and sounds, arising from the crushing conflux of Americans, Mexicans, Germans, Frenchmen, Swedes, Norwegians, Italians . . . all manner of odd personages or 'characters.'"

San Antonio, not one town, but a collection of towns, is still easygoing, festive, cosmopolitan, far from any other oasis. The river is still lovely, although it is no longer green or translucent. And, thanks to the influence of the Latin spirit, which does not wane but grows and subtly pervades the entire populace, it is one of the few cities in the United States where life on the streets is diverting. "Characters" still abound. People stroll on the downtown walks or the riverbanks for enjoyment's sake. They are not necessarily going anywhere—unless it is Saturday afternoon. Then everybody beams with anticipation, with the air of looking forward to some kind of delightful evening.

"Relaxed and playful" is a good three-word description of San Antonio by Texas writer Walter Prescott Webb.

Where else does a hotel guest wake before dawn to Spanish song and bursts of laughter from the crew of a garbage truck, who beat out the rhythm, like timpanists, with a clatter of lids on pails?

There is much that is new and attractive: homes and gardens, stores and shops, unique museums, a model zoo, excellent hotels (and motels), good restaurants.

Youth is everywhere, the fresh faces of airmen from the flying fields, boys from Iowa, Vermont, Holland, Peru.

But this remains an old town. Not many of the ancient buildings stand—the brooding Alamo, the Spanish Governor's Palace, the missions, a house here and there. But

2

Convention Center and Tower of the Americas, HemisFair Plaza

any way you turn, there are vestiges of the past, walls that have the worn, mellow, somehow pathetic look that walls get when they have been very close to a whole lot of human living for a very long time.

If a street jogs, or veers abruptly for no apparent reason, maybe it follows the course of a vanished irrigation ditch built by mission Indians, under the supervision of Franciscan friars. Or maybe a cattle pen stood here, and the trails went around it. You tread, unknowing, in the footsteps of men who died more than a century, two centuries ago.

And yet, San Antonio is, in many respects, a young town, still gawky and growing fast. It has not attained its full stature. You feel that. It is becoming a more civilized town, a meeting place of the Latin and North American minds, a garden spot where the arts are flowering.

2

A Backward Look

It was water—cool, abundant, life-giving—that first drew men to the San Antonio valley.

The San Antonio River "burst from the earth in one mighty gush of sparkling water," and a few miles westward the tributary San Pedro Springs, less copious, purled from a bank of limestone in the shade of spreading oaks and tall pecans.

The Indian came gratefully to the shade, the streams jumping with fish, the pecans, the mulberries, the arbors of wild grapes. He came so often and camped so long, archeologists have gotten the notion that a settlement here covered an immense reach of riverbank over a period of ages.

How many thousands of years ago it was that man first smiled upon this oasis, we do not know. Perhaps the first to taste these waters was the hunter of the mastodon: bones of the huge beast were dug up, in the 1880's, when a city street was being put in. Perhaps the first was that hunter who left the scrap-er of chipped flint found underneath the bones of a giant tiger in a cavern a few minutes' ride north of San Antonio, along with the bones of the dire wolf, the Colombian elephant, an extinct horse—all animals that lived here at the time of the last Ice Age, or more than ten thousand years ago.

Whether this early man was an Indian, or of some as yet unlabeled breed, we may never know, unless his bones are unearthed, and that is not likely. About the beginning of this century, the skeletons of "a race of giants," together with stone implements, were found in a cave in the northeast corner of San Pedro Park. The cave was stopped up with a big rock, we are told, to keep children from getting lost in it; what happened to the skeletons we are not told, but they would appear to be of the earliest type so far discovered in Texas: tall and longheaded. Whatever the race of the first visitor to this valley, he was a true man, *Homo sapiens*, no more apelike

Commerce Street, looking west, about 1868

than you or I. He could marry your sister or mine, and our nephews would be no more apelike than our sisters are.

The Indians camping in the San Antonio area when the Spaniards came were wandering tribes of a family called by scholars "Coahuiltecan," after the southernmost tribe, which gave its name to the Spanish province of Coahuila, now a Mexican state. These tribes were scattered out over a vast region stretching from far below the Rio Grande on the south and west to the Guadalupe River on the east. The hill country on the north was the lair of their mortal enemy, the bloodthirsty Apache. The Coahuiltecan tribes hunted and fished; they had no agriculture and no pottery; they lived as in the Stone Age. They were among the Indians described by Cabeza de Vaca, who was with them about 1535. But he did not, evidently, get as far north in this part of Texas as San Antonio, despite historians of the Chamber of Commerce school.

The Spanish Effort

Not until 1691 did a Spaniard gaze on this valley, so far as we know.

The landing of the Frenchman La Salle on the Texas coast in 1685 had aroused Spanish officialdom to the importance of the immense blank on the map between the rich mines of northern Mexico and the Mississippi River, where the French were taking hold. An expedition under Alonso de León in 1689 found La Salle's fort destroyed by Indians, a few scattered survivors. The next year, to bolster Spain's claim, a mission was founded in East Texas and called San Francisco de los Tejas. To strengthen this outpost, a governor was appointed for the new province and sent, with fifty soldiers and thirteen priests and friars, to found more missions and a fort, in 1691.

The first governor of Texas, Domingo Terán de los Ríos, and his ecclesiastical aide, Father Damián Massanet, both kept diaries of the expedition and recorded their impressions of the place that historians have assumed was precisely the same spot where the modern city of San Antonio was founded in 1718. But they do not mention San Pedro Springs, or the creek, or the head of the river. They journeyed only five leagues, or thirteen miles (a league is 2.6 miles), from the Medina River to the San Antonio. But later travelers (Alarcón in 1718, Aguayo in 1721), going straight northeast from the Medina, measured six leagues to the San Pedro and seven to the head of the river. Terán must have crossed the Medina near the present Laredo Highway (U.S. 81); then, going east by northeast, he would have reached the San Antonio River about where Mission San

Juan Capistrano was located in 1731. The woods along the river at this spot have always been lovely—at least until 1958, when acres of groves were destroyed by ditch-happy engineers. The beauty of the location is actually mentioned in the Spanish title to the lands of Mission San Juan.

One other site may have been the Indian camp Yanaguana that was christened San Antonio de Padua: this is Acequia Park at Espada Dam. Here we find a ford, a beautiful grove, even "small hills with large oaks" west of the river. But the site could not have been any farther north than this, or the Spaniards, on their forward journey, would have encountered instead of "level lands without woods" the rugged, even now impassable bluffs along Salado Creek.

Governor Terán's diary for June 12, 1691, tells of discovering "a new road" and reaching a stream which, at various points, on previous trips, had been called the Medina. Here were great numbers of buffalo:

On the 13th our royal standard and camp proceeded in the same easterly direction. We traveled five leagues over fine country—broad plains, the most beautiful in New Spain. We camped on the banks of a stream adorned by a great stand of trees. . . . I named it San Antonio de Padua because we reached it on his day. Here we found an encampment of the Payaya tribe. We observed their actions, and I concluded that they were docile and affectionate, naturally friendly, and very well disposed toward us. I saw the opportunity of using them to form missions: With one at the Presidio of Rio Grande, and another at this point, the tribes in between could be persuaded.

Father Massanet's diary for June 13 gives their direction as "NE, a quarter E," and goes on:

We passed through some low hills covered with oaks and mesquites. The country is very beautiful. We came on a plain which was easy for travel and continued on our easterly course. Before reaching the river there are more small hills with large oaks. The river is bordered by many trees: cottonwoods, oaks, cedars, mulberries and many vines. There are lots of fish, and prairie hens are numerous on the high ground.

On this day there were such droves of buffalo, the horses stampeded. We found at this place the encampment of the Indians of the Payaya tribe. This is a very large tribe, and the country where they live is very fine. I named this place San Antonio de Padua because it was his day. In the language of the Indians it is called Yanaguana.

June 14 was Corpus Christi Day, so the padre had a cross set up and an arbor of cottonwood branches built, and, placing his altar in front of it, said High Mass. The Indians attended. When the Host was elevated, the Spaniards fired a salute with all their guns. Next day they "left San Antonio de Padua and traveled East, a quarter Northeast, over level lands without woods."

They crossed the "level lands" where Brooks Air Force Base has its flying field today and traveled five leagues, camping on an intermittent stream where they saw alligators; this was the string of sloughs later named Chupaderas.

They went on nearly to Louisiana, founded more missions among the Indians called "Tejas." The missions were not a success. The Indians died by hundreds from the white man's diseases. The soldiers, mainly bachelors and other low characters, molested the Indian women. The Spaniards were firmly shown the road home in 1693. The

vision of the farsighted Governor Terán was not made real at once. But it was made real.

The Second Naming, 1709

There had scarcely been a Spaniard in Texas for sixteen years when, in 1709, two Franciscan friars stationed in the north of Mexico obtained leave to go meet the Tejas Indians, who, it was rumored, had come halfway to the Rio Grande, seeking the return of the missionaries. The friars found no penitent Indians; they did, perhaps accidentally, find a lovely spot for a new mission.

They were Father Antonio Olivares, elderly and determined, and Father Isidro Espinosa, young and enthusiastic. They secured a military escort under Captain Pedro de Aguirre. On April 13, 1709, according to Espinosa's diary, they explored the terrain where the city of San Antonio is today:

Crossing a broad plain, we entered a growth of mesquite with some motts of live oaks in it. We came upon an irrigation ditch full of water and very well wooded, which was sufficient for a town, and all along it were places to tap the water, for the ditch was on high ground, and the land was sloping. We called it the Water of San Pedro. And at a short distance we found a great shady grove of very tall pecan trees, cottonwoods, elms and clumps of mulberries, which are irrigated by the water of an abundant spring.

This [last] river had not been named by the Spaniards so we called it the River of San Antonio de Padua.

Well! Did someone remember subconsciously that the river *had* been named by the Spaniards for St. Anthony? Or was this second naming pure coincidence? In 1691 the river was reached on St. Anthony's Day, June 13. Did they now

View of San Antonio, 1840

Mission San José (opposite); *Mission Concepción, by Herman Lungkwitz, 1855*

name the creek for Captain Pedro de Aguirre's patron saint, and the river for Father Antonio Olivares's patron saint?

When Father Espinosa called San Pedro Creek an "irrigation ditch," he was indulging in an exuberance of rhetoric characteristic of him. He was simply hammering in the point, all-important to officials schooled in the problems of arid Spain, that the site was ideal for irrigation.

In 1716, Espinosa again visited the site, on his way to East Texas with the expedition of Domingo Ramón, and this time he recommended it for a mission. By the year's end Father Olivares had obtained the authorization of the viceroy (and the necessary funds) to abandon his mission, quite literally a dry hole, below the Rio Grande and to found a new mission on the San Antonio.

The Founding, 1718

Father Olivares refused to accompany the new governor of Texas, Martín de Alarcón, to the San Antonio, being irked at the officer's failure to give him all the assistance he required, but followed him a few days later, arriving on May 1, 1718.

On that same day Alarcón formally founded the Mission San Antonio de Valero. It was situated, according to one witness, "three-quarters of a league down the creek" from San Pedro Springs, or nearly two miles; according to another witness it was near the springs and "half a league from a high ground," which would put it a little more than a mile down the creek, or near the present-day Chapel of the Miracles (at North Salado and Laredo streets). Like the chapel, it was on the west bank. The mission was founded, says a document dated in 1787, at *los adovitos*—the "little adobes"; the first

name for Laredo Street was "Street of the Little Adobes."

On May 5 the Villa de Béjar (or Béxar, a variant spelling of the identical name, pronounced Bā´ här, almost like "bear") was founded. "In this place of San Antonio there is a spring of water which is about three-fourths of a league from the principal river. In this locality, in the very spot on which the Villa de Béjar was founded, it is easy to secure water [for irrigation], but nowhere else. The governor, in the name of His Majesty, took possession of the place called San Antonio, establishing himself in it and fixing the royal standard with the requisite solemnity, the father chaplain having previously said Mass, and it was given the name of Villa de Béjar." Thus the father chaplain himself.

"The place in which we find ourselves," writes another diarist on the same day, "is very pretty because of the woods near the spring."

Father Olivares was building a hut for his mission down the creek, near a grove of live oaks.

The governor's camp was moved on May 17 "across the creek, between the creek and the river." This indicates that the original camp, at the "place called San Antonio," was a little below the San Pedro Springs, on the west bank. The Spaniards crossed over and built huts and corrals and made gardens. This was the actual beginning of the city of San Antonio.

The tag "de Valero" to the name of Mission San Antonio was in honor of the Marquis of Valero, viceroy of Mexico at the time. And the *villa*, or town, of Béxar was named in honor of the viceroy's brother, the Duke of Béxar, who had died at the defense of Budapest against the Turks, fulfilling his vow to "live like a Christian and die like a soldier." He was one of the great heroes of Spain.

Early History of the Alamo

The errors of historians, both amateur and professional, who have written about Mission San Antonio de Valero, ultimately famed as the Alamo, have been served up so many times, condensed, scrambled, and garnished, no one would dare to suspect that the original recipe was based largely on blurred vision and spots before the eyes.

The commonest error is the statement, long accepted as fact, that Mission San Antonio was founded in 1718 on the same site where the Alamo stands today. Another error is the statement that the mission was founded in 1716, or anyhow before Alarcón arrived. The evidence on both these points is quite clear, as we have seen.

Father Olivares, in one of his letters denouncing Governor Alarcón, complained that the mission was founded with just a pair of Indians, and these he had brought with him from below the Rio Grande. He went all the way to East Texas and returned early in 1719 with two carpenters from Louisiana; then the governor made him send the Frenchmen back. Meanwhile, Father Olivares erected a temporary structure, made of brush, mud, and straw. By the end of the winter of 1718, numerous Indians of the Jarame, Payaya, and Pamaya tribes had come to the mission. When Olivares had labored at the site west of San Pedro Creek for about a year, one day he was crossing a bridge of timbers covered with dirt which was near the mission, and, to quote his former companion, Fray Isidro Espinosa (whose *Chronica apostólica* was published in 1746): "The beast on which he was riding got its foot stuck, and the blow of the fall broke the father's leg. He was in grave danger, and it was necessary to send to the missions of the Rio Grande for a confessor." A soldier saved his life with rustic remedies.

*The Alamo: first photograph, about 1868; (opposite) Main Plaza, the
Alameda, San Pedro Springs, and the "New Bridge," by Herman Lungkwitz, 1851*

15

"He had to stay in bed a long time but was entirely cured. When quite well he moved his mission to the other side of the San Antonio River, because the location was more advantageous."

It certainly was more advantageous: the best land was on that side of the river. And it could be irrigated. This second location was very near today's Alamo, about where the Alamo Ditch would cross East Commerce Street, where the Alameda, the avenue lined with cottonwoods, would be laid out in 1805, and where St. Joseph's Church stands.

Here Father Antonio Margil, regarded as a saint by his contemporaries, lived with his fellow fugitives in grass huts after the French chased the Spaniards out of East Texas in the summer of 1719. The padres, retreating by slow stages, arrived late in the year and remained until March, 1721, when the Marqués de Aguayo appeared with his magnificent cavalry of five hundred and escorted them back to their disrupted missions.

Father Margil, a truly creative man, consoled and occupied himself during his term of exile by founding a new mission, which he named in honor of his friend José de Azlor, Marqués de San Miguel de Aguayo. He founded Mission San José y San Miguel de Aguayo for his college of Zacatecas over the protests of Father Olivares, his host, who belonged to the rival college of Querétaro, in February, 1720.

In 1724 a hurricane destroyed Mission San Antonio de Valero, which consisted of huts and a small stone tower, and it was moved to the final site on what is now Alamo Plaza. According to an inspection in 1727, it contained 273 Indians. A convent of stone had been started, but not a church; services were held in a hut. All energies had been expended on a ditch more than two and a half miles long.

A terrible epidemic in 1738 devastated the missions. In San Antonio de Valero, out of 837 Indians that had been baptized, only 182 were left alive. By 1740, however, fresh tribes had been brought in from the wilds; there were more than 500 souls in the five missions then clustered at this point, and more than half of them were in Mission San Antonio, which, so claimed the father minister, was in better shape than the fort or presidio (on Military Plaza), and the Indians were cleaner and better clothed than the soldiers.

In 1744 the first stone church for the mission was commenced. This was not—although we have the statement of several historians that it was—the same church that we know today as the Alamo. Not in the slightest part was it the same. The documents are quite clear. In 1745 the inspector Fray Francisco Xavier Ortiz said the first stone church was then being built. In May of 1756 he said it had fallen down entirely, and a second one had not yet been started. The date 1758, which is inscribed above the door of our present Alamo, tells us when this façade was erected. In that very year Governor Jacinto de Barrios reported progress on the second church: of cut and chiseled stone, with two towers, nave, and transept, it was capacious enough for a very large town. In 1762 an inspector said: "The church of this mission, although it had been completely finished, with a tower and sacristy, fell to earth because of the poor skill of the architect, and another is being built, of harmonious design, with quarried stone which is found almost on the spot and has the solidity and perfection required for beauty and for the support of the vaults."

The church was never finished. A series of epidemics depopulated the mission. By 1778 there were not enough Indians to work the fields. In 1793 San Antonio was the first of the Texas missions to be secularized. Its rich lands were par-

celed out to various applicants. According to the inventory made then, the church lacked a dome and the vaults of the transept, little else. The gap in the roof was evidently covered with beams and shingles. Anyhow, the building was used as a church then, and earlier and later. From 1801 until the disturbances of 1813, and even after that from time to time, it was used as a chapel by the troops who were quartered in the Alamo.

The name *Alamo*, which means "cottonwood" in Spanish, can be traced to a particular tree that grew (perhaps it still grows) at a spring some thirty miles west of the city of Parras, in the Mexican state of Coahuila. A ranch was named El Alamo for this tree, and a town built on the spot in 1731 by Tlaxcaltecan Indians from Parras was called officially San José y Santiago del Alamo de Parras—commonly shortened, of course, to El Alamo. It is now called Viesca. A "flying" (mobile) company of cavalry, re-

cruited there in the 1780's, took, as custom required, the full name of the town. By 1801 the "Flying Company of San José y Santiago del Alamo de Parras," having been moved about from one place to another, was stationed at the erstwhile mission of San Antonio de Valero, where it remained for twelve years at a stretch. The old compound became known as El Alamo. When the American Lieutenant Zebulon Pike was escorted through San Antonio in 1807, the place was pointed out to him as "the station for troops"; he did not know it had ever been a mission. Neither did the Texans and Americans who died there in 1836.

The statement, oft-repeated, that the church of the Alamo, at the time of the battle in March, 1836, was "a ruin filled with the debris from its two towers, its dome and its arched roof, which had fallen in 1762," is a gross error. What really happened to the church, and when, is told by Samuel Maverick:

"I was myself a prisoner in the hands of General Cos. Upon the approach of the first Texian army under Austin, Cos commenced putting the Alamo into fort fashion. During the month of November '35, with great labor, he threw down the arches of the Church which now [1847] lie embedded with the earth in order to make an inclined plane to haul cannon on top the Church."

The ruin that now stands along the northeast walk of Alamo Plaza was reduced to this condition by no exigency of war, but by commercialism, sometimes known as the March of Progress, about 1913. It is all that remains of the convent of Mission San Antonio de Valero. Begun before 1727, it was in 1762 a two-story building with cloisters of arches above and below, forming a square about 140 feet long each way and enclosing a patio. This patio, with the installation of troops, became a corral. A smaller patio on the north of the convent was originally faced by the weaving room and other workshops of the Indians; it too became a corral.

The convent was never—despite popular fancy—aswarm with "monks." Two Franciscan friars and one lay brother were assigned to San Antonio de Valero because it was headquarters for the missions in Texas run by the college of Querétaro. There were never more than two friars in any other mission. In San José, headquarters for the missions run by the college of Zacatecas (which ran them all after 1773), there were two missionaries, Father Agustín Patrón and Father Miguel Núñez. Rooms for guests, who were often persons of high rank, had to be provided in these convents. At Mission San Antonio in 1762 this main building contained "rooms for the habitation of the ministers, a porter's lodge, a dining hall, kitchen and offices, all religiously adorned." By 1793 the convent had diminished to a couple of wings. Here the first hospital in the city of San Antonio was installed, from 1807 to 1812. The building, still of two stories, was called by the Texans and Americans in 1836 the "Long Barrack." Many of them died defending it.

More of them died in the plaza that it faces. In mission days this was the plaza of the Indians. Their stone houses with *portales* of arches lined the walls; a water ditch ran between willows and fruit trees; there was a well with abundant water "so they should not lack for it in case of attack"—no doubt one of the wells used by the defenders in 1836.

The "Low Barrack," as they called it, in the south wall, originally the mission's granary, with flying buttresses, had been made into a guardhouse by Spanish soldiery, who had put a gate through it. Before the city demolished it in 1871, in order to join together the two halves of Alamo Plaza, it served as a police station, known as the Gallera, or "cage for fighting cocks."

The mission owned a ranch house and a chapel, both of stone, at a distance of a hundred yards, where East Commerce Street is today. Father Ortiz in 1756 described the chapel "on the site where the mission was in the time of the Venerable Father Margil, in which a Most Holy Cross of Stone has been placed, which is greatly venerated. And here the faithful repair to pray for the relief of their troubles." He said a "large crucifix" at the mission was carried in the Descent from the Cross, on Good Friday. This crucifix is first mentioned in his report of 1745. But it may well have adorned the rude church that was on the second location of the mission (on East Commerce Street), and it may just as well have adorned the hut on the first location, west of San Pedro Creek.

In any case, it can be seen now in the tiny, unsanctified Chapel of the Miracles, which is near the first location and which is the survival of a long-forgotten chapel once near the second location, where people went to pray "for the relief of their troubles." What strange interaction of things real and impalpable!

1722: The Fort of San Antonio de Béxar

When the Marqués de San Miguel de Aguayo arrived with his splendid cavalry, in March, 1721, to chase the perfidious Frenchman from East Texas, the war was already over. A man of vigor and intelligence, he set about putting the vast wild province in order. He began by moving the garrison of San Antonio de Béxar from a spot south of San Pedro Springs to the present Military Plaza, on a line with Mission San Antonio de Valero, then at its second location. The river in between was crossed by a wide ford slanting from present Navarro Street to Villita Street. The bend of the river protected the soldiers' horses from thieving Apaches; it was called for

generations El Potrero ("the Horse Pasture").

The *marqués* had a presidio, or fort, built of adobes. He had an irrigation ditch dug from San Pedro Springs. He wrote the king that Spain could never expect to hold Texas unless the country was settled. He proposed that 400 families be brought to settle this, the most fertile province in the Americas: one permanent family would do more to hold it than a hundred soldiers. He suggested that two hundred families be brought from among the Indians of Tlaxcala, deep in Mexico; they had been successful settlers of the northern frontier (Saltillo, Parras) since 1591; the additional two hundred could be brought from the Canary Islands. The king, in 1723, decreed that this plan be carried out.

But officials who had learned that the best way to get promotion was to talk economy frustrated this and every other plan that was ever offered for the development of

Ford to La Villita, about 1876

20

Texas. A military inspector recommended in 1727 that the San Antonio garrison be reduced and that the one in East Texas be abolished (leaving, however, the one at Los Adaes, "capital" of Texas, then a cluster of huts, now a pasture in Louisiana). This was done. The friars of the college of Querétaro decided to move their three missions in East Texas to San Antonio, where a fresh supply of Indians was available, with soldiers to keep them in line.

During the 1720's there were about two hundred Spaniards at San Antonio: fifty-three soldiers and officers with their families, and four civilians with their families. There were about six hundred Indians in Mission San Antonio and Mission San José. The total population barely reached two thousand by the end of the century: as the number of Spaniards increased, the number of Indians diminished.

The Marqués de Aguayo did not succeed in saving Texas for Spain.

The viceroy wrote the king in August, 1730, that the first few families of Canary Islanders had been sent forward to Texas; they should also be the last, despite the pleas of the *marqués*, who merely wanted to bolster his own estates in the north. And they were the last.

1731: The Town of San Fernando

At eleven o'clock on the morning of March 9, 1731, a weary procession of fifty-six Canary Islanders (sixteen families, counting a single man as a family) came straggling into the stockade at San Antonio de Béxar. They were cared for, until they could build huts, by the soldiers and settlers. A town was laid out for them west of the fort, but for lack of water it was shifted to the river side; the Plaza of Islanders (now Main) began to build up; they were given land; they were soon raising Cain with their neighbors.

The first town council in Texas was appointed to office (by the captain of the presidio) in August. As "first settlers of a new city in the colonies," the islanders received, in accordance with the Spanish "Laws of the Indies," the title Hijos Dalgos (literally "Sons of Something") or Hidalgos, the lowest order of nobility, roughly equivalent to the English "Gentlemen." The governor of Texas offered to name the city after the viceroy, who craftily declined and named it San Fernando, in honor of the heir to the throne of Spain, later Ferdinand VI. It was to be the capital of the province of Texas, although the governor was still stationed, as captain of the presidio of Los Adaes, far to the east, until 1773.

The title, said Father Agustín Morfi, swelled the simple islanders' heads, and they refused to work. This is, perhaps, unfair. They found themselves in a tight squeeze. There was no way to make a living except by cattle ranching, and the father missionaries had pre-empted all the land. The only available pastures were to the west and north, domain of the Lipan Apaches, now suddenly turned furious.

The Apaches' rage, like the islanders' discontent, was aggravated by the removal to San Antonio of the three missions that had been founded in East Texas by the college of Querétaro. On March 5, 1731, four days before the islanders arrived, the missions of Concepción, San Francisco de la Espada, and San Juan Capistrano (its name changed from San José for an obvious reason) were established close to the town, the closest—Concepción—being less than three miles away, and each was given a huge grant of land. Since the missions of San Antonio and San José already possessed huge grants, the islanders had a right to feel hedged in. As for the Apaches, they saw the new missions serving as refuges for tribes that had always been their mortal enemies.

The Apaches took out their rage in bold assaults on the town at least twice; in 1745 only the prompt succor of the Indians from Mission San Antonio saved it. But the Apaches took out their rage more often against the Indians of the missions. One example will do: they killed their victim on the road between Concepción and town and drank his blood, "catching it in a pouch which they made for that purpose, and they stripped off his flesh, leaving only the bones."

The islanders expressed their discontent in lawsuits and petitions. In one of their innumerable petitions they asked the viceroy to (1) combine the missions, so there would be only two; (2) require the mission Indians to help them in their fields; and (3) forbid the missions to sell any produce to the military. They also squabbled interminably with the missions over water rights and grazing rights. The viceroy's auditor in Mexico City lost patience once in 1745:

The 14 families from the Canary Islands complain against the reverend fathers of the five missions, against the Indians that reside therein, against the captain of the presidio and against the other 49 families settled there, so that it seems they desire to be left alone in undisputed possession. Perhaps even then they may not find enough room in the vast area of the entire province.

The islanders were, however, brave men and proud. They fought unfriendly Indians and tried to keep friendly Indian blood out of the family. "All these pioneer families," wrote J. M. Rodríguez, one of their descendants, "were connected by consanguinity or affinity, and it was a Godsend that so many army officers, attracted by the beauty of the San Antonio girls, married them." Within the past hundred years or so, descendants of the islanders have come to have, more and more, English or German or Irish surnames.

Every morning of March 9 there is a solemn requiem in the Cathedral of San Fernando to honor the memory of those pioneers who came on that day in 1731 to carve a city out of the wilderness. Some of their many-times-great-grandchildren are there, and the women—outlandish names and all—still cover their heads with the mantilla of Old Spain.

1749: Peace with the Apaches

In August, 1749, the Apaches, frightened by the Comanches, made peace with the Spaniards.

On August 16 a sumptuous feast was served to the chiefs of the Apache nation on Main Plaza. The next day Mass was said in San Fernando Church. The third day was the big one.

A great hole was dug in the center of the plaza, and in it a live horse was placed, and also a tomahawk, a lance, and six arrows. Then the captain of the presidio and the four principal Apache chiefs, joining hands, danced three times around the hole. Then the Indians danced with the reverend fathers of the missions three times around. Then with the councilmen of the town. Then, at a signal, they all rushed to the hole and rapidly buried the horse alive, together with the weapons. The Indians whooped. The Spaniards yelled, "Long live the King!"

1768: A Warm French View

An interesting glimpse of San Antonio in the mid–eighteenth century, just before the Comanches became the lords of the open country, can be found in *Travels round the World*, "by Monsieur Pages," published, in English, at Dublin, Ireland, in 1791.

Pages, a Frenchman, visited Texas in 1768, crossing the province from Louisiana to Texas. When he reached San Antonio, he was surprised to see immense swarms of cranes along the banks of the river. He described the place as a "Fort" in an oblong bend of the river. The approaches to the settlement were defended by palisades, while the houses built all around the Fort (Military Plaza) served the purpose of walls. The defenses were weak, however, because the settlement was "of considerable extent," and many of the houses were in ruins.

The Fort was also "much incumbered from without by several miserable villages" (one of these, perhaps, was La Villita?), which served as an attraction for marauding Indians. The space enclosed by the bend of the river was "crowded by a multitude of huts," which were occupied by immigrants from the Canary Islands. But the settlement was "pleasantly situated" on the bend, "sloping gently to the river and commanding an agreeable prospect over the opposite grounds." There were about two hundred houses, two-thirds of them built of stone. Upon the roof was a kind of earthen terrace, which, owing to the dry, temperate climate, lasted a long time.

Monsieur Pages was repelled by the cold, haughty character of the Spaniard, but found the Indian lovable.

At San Antonio I lived in the family of an excellent Indian, for whom, by reason of his faithful, disinterested, and patient services in the course of my travels from Adaes, I contracted a most sincere friendship. The good people were in hopes that I might be disposed to settle in this country. My naïve, *decent, and temperate behaviour might have inclined them to approve of my falling in love with one of their daughters. Besides, as we all ate and slept in the same apartment, no man could have fairer opportunities than myself of observing the shapes, or of obtaining the affections and consent. . . . But however sensible I might be to the charms of their women, the amiable qualities of their minds, and the beauty and fertility of the surrounding country, the strong partialities I still retained for my native soil, were not to be subdued.*

1778: A Haughty Spanish View

Early in 1778 two very great dignitaries paid San Antonio the honor of a visit: the Caballero de Croix, two years earlier appointed as *comandante general* of the Interior Provinces, an office created for the purpose of dealing with Indian problems on the frontier and subordinate only to the king, and the Franciscan prelate, Father Agustín Morfi, who would become one of the first historians to write about Texas.

Like all the intelligent Spaniards who saw the country at first hand, they were deeply impressed with the possibilities of development and cried out for colonization. They saw Texas at a time when the Comanche Indians on the warpath had paralyzed ranching, the only industry there was. The Lipan Apaches, at peace with the Spaniards, were devouring their cattle at the rate of nearly two thousand a year. The Indians in the missions were dying off. In 1780, only two years later, the Spanish inhabitants begged for permission to pack up and leave the country altogether. It was hardly fair of these grandees to sit in haughty judgment on a people so beleaguered. But they did. Some of the sour notes in Father Morfi's comment may be due to the bad feeling between the townspeople and the missions, all administered by the college at Zacatecas, a feeling which interminable litigation over water rights, lands, and cattle had kept raw.

San Antonio, said Morfi, was a mean city. It had fifty-nine little houses of stone and mud and seventy-nine frame huts (jacales). Most houses had only one small room. All were low, with dirt floors, and without comforts or any attempt at good appearance.

The streets were without regularity and were so poorly cared for that whenever it rained one had to mount a horse in order to leave the house.

The barracks (on Military Plaza) were uninhabitable, not fit even for stables. The residence of the governor, Barón de Ripperdá, was the *cárcel* (jail), and his wife gave birth to a child in the *calabozo* (lockup). It was the most comfortable room and the best shelter, so she had her bedchamber there.

The church, which was built at the expense of the king, was large enough, but, though quite modern, it was already threatening to fall into ruins.

The Canary Islanders, said Morfi, were not ashamed to depend for their subsistence on the Indians of the nearby missions, from whom they begged food. Writing to the viceroy, Croix said:

The first jurisdiction [in Texas] is the Presidio of San Antonio de Béxar, in whose shadow was established without any boundary or separation the town [villa] of San Fernando. . . . For this establishment were brought fifteen families from the Canary Islands at a cost of 72,000 pesos . . . and thirty more families of Creoles or natives of these colonies were aggregated. And they all live in wretched poverty to this day because of their laziness, trifling ways, squabbling and lack of steadiness—defects which they display at first meeting, and, therefore, it does not take very long to know them for what they are.

But, with all these wretched circumstances, they are governed by two alcaldes, *six councilmen, one high sheriff and one secretary, who make up the most ridiculous town council, because they are all ignorant, and because they have committed any number of stupid and absurd acts. Knowing that any recourse to their superiors would be very distant, it has not been difficult for them to make a mystification of everything, reducing to suits and legal entanglements whatever they would rather not have cleared up.*

The population of San Antonio in 1778 was 2,060, counting the Indians in the missions. The population of all Texas, not counting the "wild" Indians, was only 3,103.

An Uneasy Lull

The faithfulness of the Lipan Apaches, who had never, since their pledge of peace in 1749, given "the slightest reason for suspicion," was embarrassing to the Spaniards. The faithful friends did more than hang around the settlements and eat the cattle: they brought down upon the Spaniards the wrath of the terrible Comanches. By hanging around the settlements, however, they exposed themselves to the succession of smallpox epidemics which struck between 1778 and 1781, just about finishing off the missions and reducing the Apaches to such small numbers that their faithfulness was no longer important to the Spaniards, who, in 1785, made peace with the Comanches. The Apaches, feeling themselves betrayed, nearly succeeded in assassinating the governor of Texas in 1789 but were slaughtered by General Ugalde in the Sabinal Canyon (seventy miles west of San Antonio) a few months later.

For twenty years Spain had peace in Texas and might have had prosperity if there had been enough Spaniards to colonize it. But a stupid king let Napoleon diddle him out of Louisiana, and Napoleon sold Louisiana, in 1803, to the United States. Where the Mississippi Valley went, Texas, tied to it by geography, would eventually go.

For a time, however, there was a kind of factitious prosperity in Texas, brought about by increased numbers of soldiers sent to guard the frontier against the aggressive Americans, by peace with the Indians, and by enlightened governors.

1807: Yank's Peek

A glimpse of San Antonio in perhaps its brightest day under Spanish rule, just before the deluge, is given us by Zebulon M. Pike, who in 1807 was twenty-eight years old and a lieutenant in the United States Army.

The young officer had volunteered to head an expedition seeking the headwaters of Red River; had made a side trip to the famous peak that bears his name (he tried, and failed, to climb it); and, after suffering frightfully, along with his men, from cold and hunger, had crossed the mountains into New Mexico, where the Spaniards nabbed them all. While a careful watch was kept over Pike by the Spaniards, escorting him to the United States border by way of Santa Fe, Chihuahua, and Texas, they treated him with the utmost courtesy.

When he reached San Antonio, on June 7, 1807, he was given a royal welcome. From a ranch on the Medina his party proceeded to Mission San José, where they were received in a friendly manner by the priest and others. About three miles out from San Antonio they were met by two governors—Cordero, of Coahuila and Texas, and Herrera, of Nuevo León—taken in a coach to the governor's quarters, treated "like their children," and offered money if they needed it. Governor Cordero vacated his house for Pike and prepared one "immediately opposite" for the men. In the evening there was a levee, attended by all the officers and priests, and after supper they went to the "public square [Main Plaza], where might be seen the two governors joined in a dance with people who in the daytime would approach them with reverence and awe."

When Pike left San Antonio, after seven days and several parties, he described it as being in a flourishing and improving state. This prosperity, he said, was owing to "the examples and encouragement given to industry, politeness and civilization by the excellent Governor Cordero and his colleague Herrera."

Among things Pike saw that were not so polite was a show given by a company of traveling acrobats or tumblers. The dialogue, it seems, would make a sailor blush.

The population of the city was about two thousand souls, most of whom resided in miserable mud-daubed, grass-roofed houses. To the east, across the river, was the station of the troops (the Alamo). By 1807, it is obvious, no one thought of it any more as a mission. Pike counted only three "formerly pros-perous" missions, which, for solidity, accommodation, and even majesty, he said, were surpassed by few he had seen in Mexico.

The resident priest at Mission San José, who was respected and loved by all who knew him, treated Pike with the kindest hospitality. He made a "singular observation" about the Indians who had composed the population of the missions. Pike asked him what had become of the natives. He replied that, it appeared to him, they just could not exist under the shadow of the whites.

A Decade of Disaster (1811–1821)

In January, 1811, the revolution, started in Mexico by Father Miguel Hidalgo on September 16, 1810, spread to Texas, where the revolutionaries were actually trying to find refuge. A not-very-bright officer named Juan Bautista Casas raised the standard of revolt in San Antonio, only to find himself duped and Hidalgo betrayed. Casas was sent to Mexico in chains; his head was soon sent back to be displayed on Military Plaza, but it spoiled.

In March, 1813, a motley army of Americans, insurgent Mexicans, and Indians whipped the Spaniards at what is now Goliad, and then at the battle of the Rosillo Crossing on Salado Creek, nine miles from San Antonio. The city was taken, and a few days later fourteen Spanish officers, including Zebulon Pike's friend, Governor Simón de Herrera, were taken out and butchered by Bernardo Gutiérrez.

On June 17, 1813, Ignacio Elizondo, a Spanish general, was surprised and routed on Alazán Creek, where he was preparing to attack the city.

On August 18, General Joaquín de Arredondo, with a large army for that day, perhaps four thousand

San Antonio de Béxar, Mission San José, Mission Concepción, Mission San Juan Capistrano, and the Alamo, by Herman Lungkwitz, 1851

men, drew the Americans and Mexicans and Indians into ambush just south of the Medina River and cut them to pieces in a gory rout. In San Antonio, he imprisoned three hundred men in a granary on the north side of Main Plaza; eighteen suffocated. Others he sent to the firing squad. The women he imprisoned in a building known as the Quinta (east of the present Courthouse) and forced them to grind corn for the soldiers. For years San Antonio was a well-nigh deserted town. There was a long drought, followed by pestilence, followed by a flood, in 1819, that nearly finished it off.

In December, 1820, Moses Austin, a Connecticut Yankee who had long been a Spanish subject, came to see the governor. He succeeded in obtaining permission to settle Americans in Texas. And in 1821 Mexico declared itself independent of Spain. A new era started.

Under Mexico (1821–1836)

Stephen F. Austin carried out his dead father's plan, which was ratified by the new government of Mexico, and colonized Texas with Americans. In San Antonio all was quiet until September, 1835, when the tyrant Santa Anna sent his brother-in-law, General Martín Perfecto de Cos, to San Antonio with an army to quell the spark of revolt in Texas. Instead of quelling it, the presence of the troops set off the explosion.

After a skirmish at Gonzales, Stephen F. Austin marched with an army of frontiersmen on San Antonio. On October 28, James Bowie, with an advance guard, fought and won a battle near Mission Concepción. After that, Austin took a position at an old mill north of town and sat down to wait, while his army dribbled away. There was the "Grass Fight," to no purpose, on November 26. On December 5, Ben

Milam led about three hundred men into San Antonio. They fought from house to house, down present Soledad Street and Main Avenue to Main Plaza. Milam was killed in the yard of the old Veramendi House on December 7. But the Mexicans surrendered on December 10, and next day the articles were signed in the Cos House, at La Villita (see Chapter 5). Most of the Americans hastened southward to take part in the idiotic Matamoros expedition, but a few stayed, and died in the Alamo.

Under the Republic of Texas (1836–1845)

San Antonio was again almost a deserted town. Jack Hays, who became the first captain of the first Texas Rangers, and a handful of his "boys" were all the protection the town had from thousands of hostile

Indians and Mexican troops.

On March 5, 1842, General Rafael Vásquez took the town without resistance and held it for two days. It was then John Twohig blew up his store on Main Plaza to keep his munitions out of enemy hands.

A more serious invasion, by General Adrian Woll with about sixteen hundred Mexican soldiers, on September 11 of the same year, met with a spray of lead on Main Plaza, where Samuel A. Maverick and other citizens fired from his roof (at the northeast angle of the plaza) into a vanguard of musicians who were marching in and killed some of them. The Texans, overwhelmed, had to surrender. On September 15 they were taken off to the dungeon of Perote Castle, deep in Mexico. On September 19 a Texas force drew the Mexicans into battle on Salado Creek, east of town, and whipped them decisively. But a company of volunteers led by Captain Nicholas Dawson, attempting to join the main body, were cut off;

thirty-three out of fifty-nine were massacred. Woll retreated to the border, but women and children did not return to San Antonio until Texas became the twenty-eighth state of the Union, on December 29, 1845.

1844: An Immigrant's Notes

Until Henri Castro founded the village of Castroville, twenty-five miles west of San Antonio, in 1844, there was not an inhabited house between this town and the banks of the Rio Grande. Here is a memoir of Auguste Frétellière, one of his colonists, as recorded in Julia Nott Waugh's *Castro-ville and Henry Castro*:

We made our entry into San Antonio on the thirtieth of March, 1844. We had a letter of introduction to the vice-consul of France who received us very cordially, and through his intermediary rented for my tutor and me a little jacal at the rate of two piastres* [Note: About $2.00] per month. . . . An abundance of meat was to be had for five cents, and we could choose the most delicate cuts. Sweetbreads, calves' flesh and head not being appreciated by the Mexicans, they gave them to us for nothing. Corn and beans were the only vegetables cultivated, for others were not as yet known in the charming country.

The city of San Antonio had at that time about 1,000 inhabitants, nine-tenths of whom were Mexicans, and the Spanish language was generally spoken. The Americans living there spoke it rather correctly, and the city ordinances were published in the two languages. The city was made up of two parts: the business section where the Catholic Church and the courthouse were situated; and the Military Plaza, to the west of the church, which extended from one plaza to the other.

San Pedro Springs, about 1878

From these squares nine streets radiated, three to the north, two to the east, two to the south and two to the west. The whole lay between the San Antonio River and the San Pedro Creek. The longest street, Flores, was scarcely more than three hundred varas, and the others were much shorter. The one which is now called Commerce Street then bore the name of el Potrero ["the Horse Pasture"]. On it were about twenty Mexican houses, that is to say buildings of rock and adobe with flat roofs of mortar and gravel. They were one-storied and had usually only one door, and two windows with iron grills. A man might think himself in Palestine. These were the best houses. The others were jacales made of mesquite sticks [posts] more or less chinked with clay, with roofs of tules, a kind of rush that grew very abundantly in the San Pedro. These roofs made a good shelter from the rain, and above all from the sun, but also served as a refuge for scor-pions, spiders, centipedes and other animals, whose company no one likes. Three quarters of el Potrero was a field of nopals [prickly pear] where we went to shoot rabbits which were very plentiful. My mentor spoke Spanish very well, so I made rapid progress and in a little while I understood much better the Mexican character, which pleased me infinitely—they were very polite, always gay and very obliging. In those days there was no thievery, the police were noticeable by their absence. The sheriff and his constable and a single justice of the peace were more than sufficient to maintain order. I remember especially taking a walk in the middle of the night, most of the houses had their doors open and people were sleeping on rawhides before the jacales. A company of rangers was commanded by Captain Jack Hays, a brave and delightful officer. His men, for the most part Americans, were rendering a great service to the locality, for without them the Indi-ans would have given us a bad time.

We had the Lipans, the Comanches, the Mescaleros, and other tribes whose names I have forgotten. They came into the town to exchange Buffalo hides, deerskins, wolfskins, and other game. Sometimes they numbered more than one hundred, but usually they retired to their camp to spend the night. They disappeared for a month, then returned anew. They are usually large and well made, but they give but little care to their persons, even the Indians with most vermilion who paint their faces. They overlay or anoint themselves with any grease whatsoever, for they smell not as the rose. . . .

Although our expenses were light my money was exhausted, and I was obliged to exchange the objects I had brought from France. For example, for one pair of pistols that had cost six piastres in Paris, I obtained a magnificent bay mare, a milch cow and her calf, a sow with eight little pigs, in addition to a

33

measure of corn and a bushel of frijoles. *We continued to live on exchanges from my sack of salt. It was a great aid to me, since for a ridiculously small amount of salt I could have two chickens, or three dozen eggs, or butter. All in all, we managed. About a month after our installation, there arrived in San Antonio another expedition for the Castro colony, among them a young Parisian artist called Théodore* [This was Théodore Gentilz].* He came to lodge and board with us, which was very agreeable to me. We were congenial and our ages were about the same. He was a good swimmer, and as we lived on the river we went every day for a plunge into that charming stream.

We had often heard of the fandango. We resolved, Théodore and I, to go to one, and toward ten o'clock of a certain evening we walked over to Military Plaza. The sound of the violin drew us to the spot where the fête was in full swing.

It was in a rather large room of an adobe house, earthen floored, lighted by six tallow candles placed at equal distances from each other. At the back, a great chimney in which a fire of dry wood served to reheat the café, the tamales and enchiladas: opposite, some planks resting on frames, and covered with a cloth, formed a table on which cups and saucers were set out. A Mexican woman in the forties, with black hair, dark even for her race, bright eyes, an extraordinary activity, above all with the most agile of tongues—such was Doña Andrea Candelaria, patroness of the fandango. At the upper end of the room, seated on a chair which had been placed on an empty box, was the music, which was a violin. That violinist had not issued from a conservatory, but on the whole he played in fairly good time. He was called Paulo [Pablo] and being blind, played from memory. The airs, for the most part Mexican, were new to me. The women were seated on benches placed on each side of the room. The costumes were very simple, dresses of light colored printed calico, with some ribbons. All were brunettes with complexions more or less fair, but generally they had magnificent black eyes which fascinated me. As for the men, they wore usually short jackets, wide-brimmed hats, and nearly all the Mexicans wore silk scarfs, red or blue or green, around their waists. The dance I liked the best was called the quadrille. It is a waltz in four-time with a step crossed on very slow measure. The Mexicans are admirably graceful and supple. When the quadrille is finished, the cavalier accompanies his partner to the buffet, when they are served a cup of coffee and cakes. Then he conducts the young lady to her mother or chaperon to whom the girl delivers the cakes that she has taken care to reap at the buffet. The mother puts them in her handkerchief, and if the girl is pretty and has not missed a quadrille, the *mama carries away an assortment of cakes to last the family more than a week. Finally we went home, very content with our evening, and promising ourselves to return another time.*

. . . .

On a certain evening toward four or five o'clock, I had gone to look for my mare which I had put out to pasture in a meadow situated where the convent of the Ursulines now stands. I returned leading my horse by its halter, with difficulty making a passage through the tall weeds. Suddenly I heard a noise resembling the charge of a regiment of cavalry, accompanied by a sound strange and strident. An instant after I saw pass, at about one hundred paces from me, an immense concourse of people rushing along, and several individuals entirely nude exciting them by their cries. They were on foot but bounded like deer. I continued on my way, but I met shortly some Mexicans on horseback who demanded whether I had seen los Indios. *I gave the information that they demanded, and when I got home I was told that those Indians had killed the three cowboys who guarded the stockade. I thanked Providence for having escaped that terrible affair.*

The Missions in Mid-Nineteenth Century

The notion was widespread, a century ago, even among educated people, that the Anglo-Saxon race, so-called, was vastly superior to any other race. It was destined to carry its blessings to the dark corners of the earth. And if those blessings had to be rammed down the throats of the benighted natives, it was, after all, for their own good.

This was the viewpoint of many Anglo-Americans who came to Texas both before and after the war with Mexico (1846). They glowed with a sense of "manifest destiny." And they were inclined to belittle the civilization which had preceded them—which had crossed terrible deserts and had built solid monuments of stone in a savage land.

When John R. Bartlett, one of the United States commissioners who surveyed the new boundary with Mexico, came to San Antonio in 1850, he remarked (*Personal Narrative*) with approval that modern American structures had for the most part superseded the massive Spanish buildings on the plazas, although some few remained, "seeming lost and out of place in the company of their smart-looking neighbors." The newcomers in town, he noted, were "rapidly elbowing the old settlers to one side."

"The greatness of Bexar," according to *Gleason's Pictorial Drawing-Room Companion*, in 1854, "is being developed under the brighter auspices of Anglo-

Ruins of Mission San José

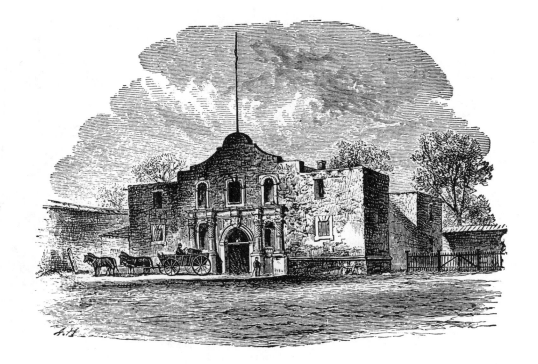

The Alamo

American energy and enterprise. And, although the Spanish idioms and customs are still tenaciously maintained among the Mexican population here, the chapeau vies with the sombrero, and the chaste attire of the American ladies presents a not unpleasing contrast to the mantilla and rebozo of the dark-eyed senoritas."

"The Mexican," it was predicted, "will soon disappear altogether."

There seems to have been a general feeling that all things Latin were on the way out.

What, then, did these bustling men from the North think of the Spanish missions?

As for the rude frontiersman, clothed in deerskins, who had seldom seen any building more dignified than a log cabin—what he thought when he first gaped at the imposing walls of stone, we can only guess.

But fortunately we have the notes of several travelers who were all civilized men, and all impressed by the magnificent ruins.

The great journalist George Kendall, of the *New Orleans Picayune*, passed through San Antonio in 1841, on his way to the horror of the Santa Fe Expedition. He reported (*Narrative of the Texan Santa Fe Expedition*) that the missions were all most substantially built, the walls were of great thickness:

The Mission of Concepción is a very large building with a fine cupola, and though plain, magnificent in its dimensions and in the durability of its construction. It is here that Bowie fought one of his first battles with the Mexican forces, and it has not since been inhabited.

The Mission of San José consists also of a large square, and numerous Mexican families still make it their residence. To the left of the gateway is the granary. The church stands apart from the other build-

ings in the square but not in the center. The west door is surrounded with most elaborate stone carving of flowers, angels and apostles. Though the Texan troops were long quartered here, the stone carvings have not been injured. The church has been repaired and Divine service is performed in it.

Here we have an interesting contrast with Bartlett's account of 1850, when, he said, the statues in front of the church had been greatly damaged by the United States soldiers, who had used them for target practice. What was it that led the rough Texas woodsmen to respect works of art which disciplined United States soldiers would not respect?

Kendall describes the church of Mission San Juan as a plain, simple edifice with little ornament, forming part of the side of the square. The adjacent buildings were poor and out of repair. The granary stood alone in the square, and on the northwest corner were the remains of a small tower.

Espada, like San Juan, was inhabited. The church was in ruins. Two sides of the square consisted of mere walls; the others were composed of dwellings.

Kendall was the only one of our travelers who made the trip to Espada. The other three missions, apparently, were a full day's tour for a man on horseback.

In 1846 the German scientist Ferdinand Roemer toured the missions. He found Concepción quite well preserved, although large cactus plants grew on the cupola, doors and windows had long disappeared, and he could ride into the interior of the church. The building had evidently been abandoned long before. The walls had given shelter from the cold northers to the half-wild cattle that roamed about.

The walls around San José were partially intact. Some Mexicans were living there in huts. There were still traces of gaudy colors on the statues.

At San Juan the church (not the chapel now in use but the building, still in ruins, on the east side of the enclosure) could be traced only by its foundations. The encircling walls, with Indian houses leaning against them, were almost perfectly preserved.

Bartlett says of San José:

This was the largest and wealthiest Mission and its buildings were constructed with greater display of art and still remain in better preservation than the others. The principal doorway [of the church] is surrounded by elaborate carving, which includes numerous figures.

The action of the weather has done much to destroy the figures, and the work of ruin has been assisted by the numerous military companies near here who, finding in the hands and features of the statues convenient marks for rifle and pistol shots, did not fail to improve the opportunity for showing their skill at arms. That portion of the front of the church not covered with carving was ornamented with a sort of stencilling in colors, chiefly red and blue. But few traces of this had withstood the rain.

The interior presents but little of interest. The damp has destroyed the frescoes upon the wall and the altar has been stripped of its decorations. It is now seldom used for religious purposes.

The convent in the rear, he notes, was in a tolerable state of preservation and was inhabited by an American, who cultivated the surrounding crop lands.

San Juan was in worse shape. In the church he found the remains of "exceedingly rude painting," and the earthen floor was broken up in several places, where graves had recently been made. As for Concepción:

The two towers and dome of the church make quite an imposing ap-

Mission San Francisco de la Espada, about 1868

pearance when seen from a distance, but, on approaching it, we found it not only desolated but desecrated, the church portion being used as an inclosure for cattle, the filth from which covered the floor to a depth of a foot or more. Myriads of bats flitted about, which chattered and screamed at our invasion of their territory; and we found nothing of interest within the church to repay us for encountering their disagreeable presence.

Finally, in 1854, we have the report of Frederick Olmsted (*Journey through Texas*), who laid out Manhattan's Central Park. He gives no details. "They are in different stages of decay, but all are real ruins, beyond any connection with the present—weird remains out of the silent past."

This is the verdict of an intelligent man: the missions had no future except decay.

Mission San José, before the storm of 1868

North side of Main Plaza, about 1857

North side of Main Plaza, 1886

United States Frontier (1846–1861)

After the excitement of the war with Mexico, San Antonio began to prosper. In 1846 the German scientist Ferdinand Roemer, in Texas from 1845 to 1847, estimated the population of San Antonio as only 800. In 1850 it was 3,448. In 1860 it was 8,235.

The influx of Germans began. One immigrant, Viktor Bracht, who wrote a book in German, *Texas in the Year 1848*, was enthusiastic:

One of the taverns in San Antonio has two billiard tables, and adjoining is a reading room where a German newspaper of St. Louis is kept. Women pay more attention to dress in San Antonio than they do in New York or in the large cities of Europe. We have balls and revelries. Men, thank God, are not so particular; they appear in shirtsleeves or woolen jackets.

There were two magnificent buildings, the Plaza House and the house of the French consul, Guilbeau.

Before the Civil War [writes Vinton James, in Frontier and Pioneer*] San Antonio was fast becoming a prosperous city, supported by a rapidly developing country stocked with vast herds of cattle and many sheep. Protection from Indian raids by the U.S. troops, who occupied frontier posts, promised security and confidence for the future. Farmers and stock-raisers settled along the beautiful streams.*

Suddenly, like a bolt of lightning from a clear sky, came the firing on Fort Sumter, which shattered all the bright prospects of San Antonio. Everything was turned to ruin and despair.

Major Ben McCulloch

44

In the Civil War (1861–1865)

Two dramatic events occurred in San Antonio at the outset of the Civil War, both on the same day: the surrender by General David E. Twiggs of all the United States equipment in Texas to a committee of local secessionists backed by a large force of volunteers and Rangers under Major Ben McCulloch on the morning of February 16, 1861, and the decision of Colonel Robert E. Lee to follow the course of Virginia. This was two months before the firing on Fort Sumter, which triggered the secession of Virginia from the Union.

At about two o'clock that afternoon, an army ambulance drew up in front of the Read House on Main Plaza. Its sole passenger was Robert E. Lee. As he got out he was surrounded by Rangers with grim faces. "Whose men are these?" he asked of a fellow officer's wife who happened to be crossing the plaza.

"McCulloch's. We are prisoners," she replied.

"Has it come so soon as this?" His eyes filled with tears. He went to his room in the hotel, changed his clothes, and reported to military headquarters, where secessionists told him to resign his commission and join them; otherwise he would have to go to Washington without his baggage. He answered hotly that he owed allegiance to Virginia and to the Union, but "not to any revolutionary government of Texas." All that night he paced the floor of his room in the Read House. He left without his baggage. He never saw it again, although he asked for it repeatedly. He never saw Texas again.

A committee of vigilantes, during the war, specialized in "necktie parties" for desperados, horse thieves, and Union men; the most spectacular of these parties was in honor of a cowboy named Bob Augustine, who was hanged from an oak on Military Plaza.

Up from the Slough (1866–1877)

After the Civil War [writes Vinton James] business was at its lowest ebb, there being no money to make improvements or to keep the city clean. Real estate was a drag, its value destroyed by taxes. The gas works, completed in 1859, was idle, there being no funds to run it. The streets at night were dark. The plazas during the rainy weather were quagmires; people who went abroad at night carried lanterns to avoid mud puddles. The trash and garbage was thrown into the back yards. Drinking water was obtained from shallow wells and irrigation ditches, and this water became contaminated from outhouses, and typhoid fever and malaria were prevalent. Livery stables did a big business, while the grain waste and garbage harbored thousands of rats and millions of flies, which were the principal inhabitants of San An-

West side of Main Plaza, 1886

46

South side of Main Plaza, 1886

tonio in those gloomy days. Where there is one rat in San Antonio now there were thousands then; they fought the dogs and killed the cats.

In 1866 a cholera epidemic carried off many of the leading citizens and scared the rest. San Antonio started to clean up.

One great help to local business was the United States Army, with headquarters here. It gave protection from the Indians by resuming command of the posts in West Texas. The ranchmen and farmers again became prosperous. The settlers, returning to their ranches, found their herds had immensely increased during their absence. Then commenced the great cattle drives to Kansas, where good prices could be got.

Southwest Texas [writes Vinton James] was inhabited by owners of vast herds that roamed the plains. The cattle drives to Kansas in the later sixties and seventies brought the owners wealth. The cattle barons were a meat-eating people and generally hard liquor drinkers. Inured to the rough life of the frontier, they spent their time fighting Indians, rounding up and branding their increase. This sudden accumulation of wealth made them great spenders when they visited San Antonio. They came to have a good time, and they had it, regardless of cost. They and their friends visited every amusement in the city, both good and bad, generally ended all by having a great time eating and drinking. During these festivities quarrels and disagreements sometimes occurred, and homicide took place.

Wool sold on the San Antonio market in 1873 for 40 cents a pound. Every acre of land in West Texas, except along the water courses, belonged to the public domain. Free range and the high price of wool caused such a boom, there was a rush of capital to invest in land and ⸺ *ep, and a rush of immigrants. San Antonio, to complete its prosperity, only awaited the advent of the railroad.*

1877: The Iron Horse

"Only the snort of the iron horse," declared an editor of the *Express*, away back in 1868, "can save us from our barbarism." And he went on to deplore the primitive aspect of the city's market on Military Plaza, where small piles of produce were displayed on the ground.

It was the general conviction of the populace that, after the glorious day when the railroad should arrive, there would be oodles of money in every pocket, beer and champagne for the men, and the latest modes, straight from Paris, for the ladies.

Sure enough, the transformation of the old Spanish town of San Antonio from a rude Spanish outpost to a modern city was pretty well achieved in the space of ten years following the arrival of the first train, in 1877.

After many delays the tracks of the Galveston, Harrisburg, and San Antonio railroad (also known as the Sunset Lines and now the Southern Pacific) reached the city. The first train was due to arrive on February 19, 1877. The town went wild with excitement. Shoes had been shined and carriages had been greased the night before. The citizens had their breakfast early that morning. Everybody from all around was there when the train came in.

The band struck up a lively tune. The locomotive whistled. The people cheered. Two horses, not of iron, ran away with their human freight. Shrieks of dismay added to the uproar.

The engine was the model whose smokestack looked like a stovepipe with a washtub set on top. The rest of the train consisted of a baggage car and one passenger coach, which carried officials of the railroad and a number of other gentlemen who, at that particular hour, were important. The train was covered with flags and bunting, and the cowcatcher displayed a huge framed portrait of the president of the line. A great man, indeed!

That night eight thousand men took part in a jubilant torchlight parade.

The citizens fairly sweated optimism. Their town, cosmopolitan already, would soon be tremendously big and rich, wallowing in luxuries and festooned with refinements.

Not everybody got rich after the railroad came. But some did. And San Antonio became a city.

1877: A Woman's-Eye View

A romantic picture of San Antonio as a city of gardens is painted by a lady writer (Harriet Prescott Spofford, in *Harper's Magazine*) who, arriving at the brand-new railroad station on Austin Street, in 1877, felt "soft wafts of balmiest fragrance" saluting her. As her carriage rolled into Alamo Plaza, she was "conscious of being in a world of flowers." She goes on:

As you alight at the Menger, enter a narrow, unevenly-stoned passage, and come out upon a broad flagged courtyard, surrounded on three sides by open galleries, with the stars overhead, and the lamplight flaring on a big mulberry tree growing in it below, you feel that you are in the heart of old Spain.

On a more enchanting spot the eyes of poet never rested. There is probably nothing like it in America.

As you go about you find the town one wilderness of roses, a very vale of Cashmere. Blush and creamy and blood-red:

The delicate little Scotch rose, the superb Marshal Neil, the shining Lamarque, the beautiful great tearose, hundred-leaved and full, spot-

49

North side of Main Plaza, about 1868

less, waxen-white and damask, the heavy-headed Persian rose itself. They hedge gardens by the quarter of a mile together, lattice every veranda, climb and lie in masses of bud and blossom on every roof. It is a long red roof, usually, that, bending slightly, forms also the roof of the veranda.

Most of the houses beneath it are long and low and narrow, of a single story, and but one step from the ground, built of a cream-colored stone that works easily and hardens in the air, and so placed that the south wind or the east shall blow in every room. . . . the winds that blow all day long from the Gulf, and make the fervent heat itself a joy. There is no vestibule: You enter the salon from the door, and the other rooms open on either side of that, and as they all open on the veranda, that is used as a hall. Over them rise the tall cottonwoods and the huge spreading pecans, and before them or behind them, almost invariably, flows a swift, clear, artificial stream of water some four or five feet wide, the banks now stoned in, now covered with a lush growth of blooming cannas and immense arrowheaded leaves the size of an African warrior's shield, and now bridged beneath honeysuckle arbors.

These charming dwellings stand with little regularity or uniformity, but here and there, facing this way and that, just as the winding roads wind with the winding river, and always half buried in a sweet seclusion of leaf and blossom.

Not roses only, but all the other flowers under heaven: lilies and myrtles and geraniums make the air a bliss to breathe. . . .

There are groups of bananas, with their huge arching leaves; there are walls of the scarlet pomegranate, one blaze of glory; lanes lined with the lovely leaved fig-tree, where the fig is already large; and the comely mulberry tree, grown to enormous size, is dripping with its blackening and delicious fruit.

Sometimes there are summer houses at the gate almost half the size of the dwelling, entirely covered with vines, and the whole spot so sequestered behind mimosa and cacti and huge-leaved plants that it seems only a tropical tangle that you might hesitate to enter. But, pushing your way through, you will find, behind broad porches, lofty rooms with polished floors and rugs, books and pictures and vases and costly furniture, inhabited by lovely white-clad women whose manners have peculiar grace.

This is the San Antonio of the irrigating ditches—the acequias—"swift, clear, artificial" streams of water.

In 1878 the new water works began to pump water from the river. Soon after that, the first artesian wells were drilled. The days of lush gardens were over.

Market area on Military Plaza, looking northward, about 1883

1877–1887: "A Decade of Progress"

In 1878 San Antonio began to build. The most exciting pastime of that year was a ride on the first streetcars. Drawn by fat little Mexican mules, they bounced from Alamo Plaza to San Pedro Springs. The permanent army station at Fort Sam Houston (called Post San Antonio) was started. Stone crossings were placed on the unpaved downtown streets.

By 1881 gas lights, which had flickered feebly in the streets since 1866, were found in the houses of the more prosperous citizens. "Our streets are lighted at night," bragged the city directory, "and the pedestrian avoids falling into the irrigation ditches of the early Spanish settlers by the light afforded by 19th century gas." In that same year a second railroad, the International and Great Northern, wittily known as the "Insignificant and Good for Nothing," entered the city from the

Bird's-eye view of San Antonio, 1873

northeast. And the first telephone exchange was opened. In 1882 there were two hundred subscribers, and Gould's *Guide* said, "It is not thought the list will stop short of four hundred, even should the population of San Antonio not go beyond 25,000, a limit at which no one thinks it will stop."

In 1882 the first electric lights were introduced (on a hangman's post, one citizen said it looked like) on Main Plaza, but they sputtered dismally. Not until 1887 was a successful light plant started. Then the town really lit up.

Indians raiding up into the hill country from Mexico murdered their last victims—the last in all Texas—in 1882, a fifteen-year-old boy and a ranchman's wife, near Leakey, a Sunday afternoon's motor ride from San Antonio today.

And in 1886 the first really plush theater in San Antonio, the Grand Opera House on Alamo Plaza, was opened with fanfare and programs printed on silk.

The contrast between the new San Antonio and the old was set forth in the rare *History and Guide* of 1892 by an anonymous newspaperman who attended a state press convention here in 1886:

Twenty-five years ago we visited this city. Then it was little more than a collection of hovels. The howl of the coyote and the whoop of the Comanche could be heard almost from the plaza. The festive cowboy held high carnival in all the public places. Murder, robbery, rape and villainy were of nightly and almost hourly occurrence. The adobe house, the Mexican cart, and the walking arsenal met the gaze on every side. The beautiful river wound its way through ugly, filthy, uncouth streets, and was spanned by a few old rickety wooden bridges, and a peaceable man, not to mention a decent lady, dreaded to walk the rough cobblestone, muddy streets in daytime, let alone at night. But twenty-five years have passed,

the magic wand of civilization has touched the city and "presto, change!" has been pronounced. Where stood the old adobe huts, magnificent iron, stone and brick buildings are to be seen. Instead of the yell of the Comanche you hear the scream of the locomotive all around the city. Where the unsightly Mexican cart met the gaze, you see now the beautiful and convenient street cars, with their sleek, fat mules and their jingling bells. In the place of the mesquite thicket, where the coyote held his nightly revels, you see fine, broad avenues, lined on either side with beautiful and stately residences, surrounded with magnificent groves of shade trees and lovely gardens of flowers. Tall spires, piercing the skies, now mark the places where pious people assemble to worship God. The same spot was then occupied by the ravenous wolves that made the night hideous with their weird howls. The little old rickety wooden bridges have disappeared, and in their stead

Market area on Military Plaza, looking northwestward, in the 1880's

Menger Hotel, about 1868

Grand Opera House

a hundred magnificent iron bridges now span the beautiful stream. Instead of the "andele, andele!" of the Mexican cartman, with the yoke strapped to the horns of his oxen, the fine carriage, the commodious omnibus, drawn by beautiful teams of fine horses, meet you on every corner. Instead of the filthy, drunken wenches who thronged the streets, you meet on all sides, the beautiful, well-dressed lady, whose sweet smile of "welcome to our hospitable city," makes one feel as if he had met a morning zephyr which had just passed through a grove of magnolias. Where you then met the walking arsenal in the shape of a drunken cowboy, or the murderous desperado, you now meet the sober, courteous, polite policeman, with his club and badge of office, who is ever ready to give you any information you want. As for his protection, you don't seem to need that.

The cobblestone sidewalks have given place to the beautiful, broad, smooth artificial stone, and the rough cobblestones of the streets have been crushed and filled until they are as smooth as the shell streets of Galveston. Many manufacturing establishments have been inaugurated. They now have a population of 40,000, with three flourishing daily newspapers, and everything else in proportion.

The population of San Antonio was actually 37,673 in 1890—which means that it had tripled since 1870, when it was 12,256, and had nearly doubled since 1880, when it was 20,550.

1887–1900: An Era of Elegance

The flush, hectic boom of the middle eighties marked the end of a boisterous era in the history of San Antonio and the beginning of an elegant one.

Those were days of immense progress, to be sure, in the physical aspect of the city. But they were also the days—and nights—when shootings were still common on the plazas, when lurid vaudeville theaters and gambling halls flourished. The killing of Ben Thompson and King Fisher in the disreputable old vaudeville theater on the corner of Main Plaza and Soledad, March 11, 1884, was about the last act in the Götterdämmerung of the desperado. The place burned down in 1886, the year the opera house was opened, and a fancy, deluxe French restaurant, the Elite, moved in.

It was not only the favorite resorts of the rip-roaring cowboy that gave way to progress. The open

range was cut into small pieces by barbed wire. The fence cutters fought a losing war in 1883, '84, and '85, and a convention of cattlemen at San Antonio, December 12, 1884, lamented that their national trail had suffered ruination from railroads and land sharks.

On February 2, 1887, the *Express* published an exultant piece called "A Decade of Progress." A few days later, Sarah Bernhardt, pausing at the Sunset depot on her way from Mexico to the East, declared that San Antonio was the "art center of Texas."

In 1888 San Antonio had a chance to see both Edwin Booth and Joseph Jefferson.

In 1890 the New Year was ushered in by receptions at which (said the *Express*) "young men wore attire giving the impression of having burst into bloom all at once, with vests, shirts and even the edge of their collars covered with tiny blossoms, embroidered forget-me-nots being the favorite motif."

But, on the material side, the great event of 1890 was the trip made by the first electric streetcar from Navarro Street to the International Fair Grounds (now Riverside Golf Park). Everybody who amounted to much went along for the ride. At the park there was a sumptuous repast, music by a band, and a merry fusillade of champagne corks, while Sam Maverick, Jr., stood up on a table and made a speech.

San Antonio was, no doubt, a little drunk with progress and prosperity. "We have the most populous city in Texas," chants Corner's *San Antonio de Bexar* (1890): "Three railroad lines, a perfect system of waterworks, the purest water, wood block-paved plazas and streets, several electric streetcar systems, the prettiest Opera and Civic House in the South, beautiful public buildings, good electric lighting and gas systems, good hotels, a lovely river, a climate second to none."

1898: The Rough Riders

At Riverside Golf Park, in May, 1898, the Rough Riders were organized. Such a colorful and miscellaneous assortment of men as the First United States Volunteer Cavalry (which was their official name) has probably never been mustered into any army before or since.

The occupations of some of the men were listed as dancer, football player, steeplechaser, golfer, gourmet, oarsman, old soldier, policeman, fireman, miner, cowboy, down-and-outer, gambler, musician, and bad man. Since most of the men were enlisted in Arizona, New Mexico, and Indian Territory, cowboys were naturally in the majority. Texas was well represented, of course.

Among the westerners were some who had changed their names. Many more went by nicknames, like "Rocky Mountain Bill," who had lost a piece of his ear in a fight with a bear and who gave the impression that he was "constantly loaded for bear, with hilts of knives and butts of revolvers sticking out of every pocket and from every angle of his anatomy."

There was "Broncho George" from Skull Valley, Arizona, with a record of five men to his credit. "This means," wrote a possibly jocose reporter, "he has dropped that many in righteous causes, for cattle stealing, cheating at cards, incivility to women, etc. Broncho George's patriotism is undoubted. When the stage driver brought him word that Roosevelt had issued a call for troopers, he got up from dinner, jumped on his wildest broncho and set off, bareback, through Devil's Gate and Dead Man's Gulch and over the mountains to the nearest recruiting station."

There was "Dead Shot Jim," from Albuquerque, New Mexico, who could bring down Indians when they were so far off nobody else could see them. Not to speak of "Lariat Ned," "Fighting Bob,"

"Cherokee Bill," "Happy Jack," and "Rattlesnake Pete."

There were a number of full-blooded Indians and one ex-marshal of Dodge City whose ear had been bitten off, not by a bear.

But the "swells," the athletes from Harvard and Yale and the "dude millionaire clubmen" from Fifth Avenue, attracted even more attention, in their standing collars, patent-leather shoes, and hard-boiled hats, than the flamboyant characters from the West in high-heeled boots and chaps.

For instance, Hamilton Fish, Jr., who was soon to die in the forefront of a charge in Cuba, was described by a reporter as "a young man of great strength and misguided energies," who had "hitherto distinguished himself by fighting policemen and causing trouble in public. He once threw an ottoman at a music hall singer as a mark of his esteem. A favorite sport of his was to ride furiously on the back of a cab horse." The certificate required of

the recruiting officer, who had to state that the volunteer "was entirely sober when enlisted," was "peculiarly desirable in the case of Mr. Fish."

Another swell who was viewed with some acrimony by the press was William Tiffany, who was "noted as a leader of cotillions and for his taste in fine raiment." The "millionaire recruits" were described as submitting gracefully to discipline, for the most part. The first morning in camp,

Woodbury Kane was detailed to dig a ditch and swung his shovel cheerfully and unflinchingly. Craig Wadsworth helped to bring hay to the horses and Reginald Ronald helped to make a mess fire to cook dinner on. Nearly all of them already seemed to be inured to the hardships of camp life and in high spirits. The only one who seemed to be dissatisfied was William Tiffany. He seemed to find camp life a good

Main Plaza, 1868

deal more disagreeable than he expected and was in a state of distress. He found the camp fare nauseating and was also especially distressed over the lack of a hot bath. He escaped any ditch digging or wood carrying and spent most of the afternoon in writing letters home.

But it may be that the reporter's feelings were hurt by Mr. Tiffany's refusal to pose for him.

"What do you want the picture for, one of those horrible newspapers?" he exclaimed indignantly. "It's an outrage the way newspapers are treating us. They write about us as if we were a bunch of wild animals. Why don't they let us alone?"

But, with the exception of these few instances, the Rough Riders got a very good press indeed.

The newspapermen were especially delighted with the democratic intermingling of the eastern swells with the cowboys. "The club men and college athletes are getting along famously with their cowboy com-

rades," one reporter tells us.

The *Express* grew eloquent:

These millionaires and the wild cowboys of the plains are one homogeneous mass of patriotism and pluck, representing and illustrating our fierce democracy where every man is equally a sovereign and where crowns must be won before they are worn. Here the rough frontiersman, daring but uncouth, and the cultured collegiate, genteel but full of spirit, stand upon a common level and mingle in a common purpose. This is democracy as Washington, Jefferson and the other fathers of the republic dreamed of and gave their best thought and best blood to establish, and this is the democracy for which the highest and the lowliest, the rich and the poor, the young and the old, are ready to fight side by side.

Their commander was the highly efficient Colonel Leonard Wood, an army surgeon who had been seasoned in a grueling campaign against the Apache chief Geronimo. He arrived in San Antonio on May 5, 1898, two days in advance of the first trainload of recruits. Wood had been chosen to command the regiment by Theodore Roosevelt, who had refused the post himself because he lacked military experience. It was Roosevelt's original idea, however, to raise a cavalry regiment in the West to fight the Spaniards in Cuba. He resigned his post as assistant secretary of the navy to become a lieutenant colonel under Wood.

By May 15, when Roosevelt arrived, Wood had already done a thoroughgoing job of organization. But the colorful Teddy attracted the spotlight at once.

When he drilled the troops he "looked very handsome mounted on his dun steed." After the drill he treated them all to beer at the saloon which had been opened at the entrance to Riverside Golf Park, where the regiment encamped.

The men drilled intensively. On one occasion, some of them escaped to town, which they proceeded to paint red. But the offenders were so disciplined, we are told, that there was no repetition of the offense. On their last Sunday in camp virtually the entire city of San Antonio turned out to visit the men. The ladies, especially, were intrigued by these splendid specimens of manhood in their romantic uniforms. There was a military concert by Carl Beck's famous band.

The Rough Riders were so popular, indeed, that it was necessary to post guards to keep people from swarming continuously over the camp.

Little by little they received their horses and equipment. Finally, on May 29, the long trains rolled out to Florida, bearing over a thousand of "Teddy's Terrors," as they were now also called.

New Orleans received them with wild enthusiasm.

One San Antonian named Maverick wrote home: "We certainly keep to our name as we go along. Nothing is sacred. No law goes unbroken that we can break. In Alabama at one place as we passed along one of the boys threw a lariat with such precision as to rope a half-grown hog. Amid much cheering and squealing he was drawn on board unhurt and is now installed as mascot of Troop H."

Less than a month later the Rough Riders were fighting Spaniards in Cuba. They fought gallantly and many were killed or wounded. After the fighting was over, they had to face a much more formidable enemy: disease. The survivors were shipped up to Long Island, where they were mustered out, after barely three months' service.

3

The Alamo

Alamo Church

History is almost indispensable here. The hurried visitor, however, can leaf ahead to

Alamo Enclosure

(Alamo Plaza)
Entrance: through Alamo Church or gates on either side.
Open: weekdays, 9:00 A.M. to 5:30 P.M.; Sunday, 10:00 A.M. to 5:30 P.M.
Admission: free

The Alamo Battle

Alamo Plaza is an airy, cheerful place, buzzing with leisurely tourists and shoppers.

In this pleasant concourse, only the brooding church of the Alamo itself and the ruined walls adjacent remind us that here was once a scene of frightful slaughter.

What happened here was drama beyond senseless spilling of blood. What happened here was high tragedy.

The Reasons

Some quarter of a million people each year move through the doorway of a Spanish mission church to stand on the ground where fewer than 200 men died generations ago. These men are remembered not because they were brave. Men no less brave killed them and were killed by them, and are not remembered. These men are remembered because they died in the hope that their death would give to fighters for freedom in Texas a breathing space, and to fighters for freedom everywhere, heart.

They were not at war against another nation or another race of men. They were not struggling to hold or to gain anything. Most of them owned nothing in Texas. Perhaps 7 were native Texans, of Spanish or Mexican descent. The officers, and very few others, were colonists, who had settled in Texas under the Mexican flag and so had a home or a piece of land. To the short roll of colonists were added the 32 men (and boys) of Gonzales, who made their way into the walls a week before the end.

But most of the men were, like David Crockett, freedom-loving pioneers from the United States. Their fathers and their grandfathers had fought in the Revolutionary War and in the War of 1812 against the British king.

And yet, they were not all Americans. Settlers who fought and died included 12 natives of England, 4 Scots, 1 Welshman, and 12 Irishmen. There were also 2 Germans and a Dane.

To understand why these men were in the Alamo, it is necessary to understand the spirit of the times. Men were fighting for freedom, and against tyranny, the world over, wherever the ideas of America had reached, wherever the languages of Europe were spoken.

The president of Mexico, General Antonio López de Santa Anna, had stamped out the liberties of his own people. He had savagely crushed, with rape and murder, the revolt of Zacatecas, in May of 1835. There could be no doubt of his determination to crush the revolt of the 20,000 colonists, mainly from the United States, who had settled in Texas since 1821 at the invitation of Mexican governments. Santa Anna was a dictator, of the stripe that has often been seen since, and can be seen today, in Latin America and elsewhere.

The men of the Alamo may have come to Texas to get land, to make a fortune, to escape debt, or for any number of reasons. But they had also come to fight despotism. Anyhow, they stayed to fight despotism. To them it was an utterly intolerable thing.

They valued freedom higher than they valued life.

Space as Enemy

To understand the plight of the small band—fewer than 200 men, women and children—who were besieged in the Alamo from February 23 to March 6, 1836, when all the men were killed, we must see them as surrounded not only by about 2,500 hostile Mexican troops, but also by vast, unfriendly space.

On every side was waste land, the howling wilderness. On every side, and for thousands of miles to the north, murderous savages roamed the hills and plains. Westward the desolate thorny brush stretched 150 miles to the Rio Grande—Mexico.

To the east and south, beyond reaches of uninhabited wilds, were friends in small numbers. At Gonzales, 70 miles east, with scarcely a cabin in between, men were gathering, but slowly, in driblets, from tiny settlements scattered at weary distances over the roadless land. At Goliad, 100 miles southeast, was a small army of about 400 Americans. To them the men in the Alamo looked for help, and to them messengers rode out, risking their lives, to no avail. The volunteers at Goliad were mostly eager boys, poorly supplied, badly led. Stalked by an invisible, agile, overpowering foe, they could help no one. They were themselves doomed.

The space to the west, the thorny desert, had served for a time as a barrier, a safeguard for the Americans who had taken San Antonio by storm early in December, 1835.

Among these victors had been leaders of great ambition and short sight, who regarded this thorny barrier as a hurdle, easy to vault. By December's end they had persuaded some 200 hotheads at San Antonio to follow them to the coast, as the first move in an utterly mad plot to

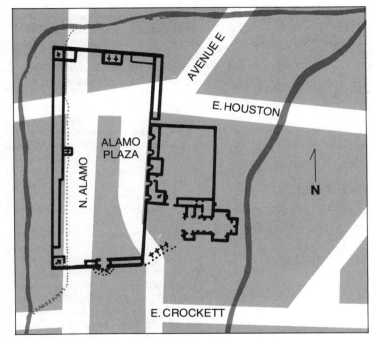

Map 5. *Alamo Plaza*

Colonel William Barret Travis

capture the Mexican port of Matamoros, at the mouth of the Rio Grande. They took with them all the horses they could get hold of, including those that were the mainstay of the Mexican herdsmen and ranchers. They took the food, the clothing, the blankets, the medicines. They waited at the coast for supplies that never came. Of course they met with disaster. And their folly invited the disasters at the Alamo and at Goliad.

What was left of the garrison at San Antonio was further reduced by the number of Texas colonists who simply went home. There was no reason why they should stay. No enemy faced them. It was winter. They were not paid. They could get no clothing to keep them warm. Their families needed them. Indians lurked about the fringe of the settlement. Soon it would be plowing time. By mid-January, 1836, Colonel J. C. Neill, commanding at San Antonio, warned that the garrison was down to 80 men.

On January 17 the ablest military leader in Texas, General Sam Houston, then at Goliad, sent Colonel James Bowie with about 30 men to San Antonio. Bowie carried orders for Neill to destroy the fortifications "in the town" (on Military and Main plazas); Houston also recommended—but did not order—abandoning the town and moving the munitions to Gonzales or the coast.

But the provisional council of Texas, a passel of mediocrities who had been appointed, along with the governor, at the Consultation held by the colonists in November, 1835, was committed to the idiotic Matamoros expedition. The governor appealed to the council for aid to the men at San Antonio. The council snubbed him. He insulted the council. It deposed the governor, stripped Houston of his authority, and ignored the men of the Alamo.

Bowie arrived on January 19. Like the commander, Neill, he knew how perilous the position was.

Like Neill, he begged for men and supplies. He pointed out that San Antonio was the only fortified place between the Rio Grande and Louisiana. "We will rather die in these ditches than give it up to the enemy," he wrote.

On February 3, Colonel William Barret Travis arrived with about 30 men. A few days later David Crockett arrived from Tennessee with 12. When Neill left for home, on the eleventh, because of sickness in his family, Travis and Bowie fell out over rank but made up their differences within twenty-four hours and assumed joint command. Meanwhile, Travis wrote to the governor, as Bowie and Neill had done before him, that San Antonio was certain to be attacked. "We are determined to sustain it as long as there is a man left," said Travis, even if no reinforcements were sent. And if it should fall, he declared, he would be "buried beneath its ruins."

Of the 150 men who made up the garrison in late February, many

were young and reckless. They naturally found lighthearted ways of passing the time—playing cards, watching cockfights, dancing at fandangos, "sleeping when and where they pleased." There were older men, sober and earnest. But all were equally devoted to freedom, or they would not have been there. They knew what the risk was. They knew the Mexican army was bound to come. They knew their position could not be held without reinforcements. They gambled that their friends could reach them across the space to the south and east before their enemies could reach them across the space to the west.

Travis expected an invasion about the middle of March. Even after a native scout informed him, on February 18, that a Mexican army had crossed the Rio Grande, he still believed it would be slow to make its way through the arid brush country. But he reckoned without Santa Anna's hunger for revenge.

The Mexican dictator spurred his

Alamo Cenotaph

army to traverse, in six days, without adequate food or water or medicine, the thorny barrier between the Rio Grande and the Medina, 20 miles from San Antonio, where he camped on the night of February 21. He learned the Texans were attending a fandango on the evening of the twenty-first. He planned to attack them in the early hours next morning. But a cloudburst brought a flood. He could not get his men across the river.

On the morning of the twenty-third unrest was noticed among the Mexicans of the town. Many were packing their household goods in carts. They said they were "going out to prepare for the coming crop." Travis, not satisfied by this answer and hearing, from a native, that the enemy cavalry had spent the night on Leon Creek, only eight miles west, posted a sentinel in the tower of the parish church (where San Fernando Cathedral is now) on Main Plaza, with orders to ring the bell if he saw any suspicious signs.

At noon the sentinel rang the bell. He shouted that the enemy was in sight. Those who climbed the tower saw nothing out of the ordinary and accused the sentinel of "a fake alarm." He swore he had seen the glitter of lances. At this point Dr. John Sutherland proposed to ride out west of town; John W. Smith agreed to go with him. They told Travis that, if they came back at a run, he could be sure they had seen the enemy. When they reached the top of a slope a mile and a half from town, they saw, within 150 yards, some 1,500 Mexican cavalry, "their polished armor glistening in the rays of the sun, the commander riding along the line, waving his sword, as though giving orders."

The Americans wheeled their horses and made for town; Sutherland's horse slipped in the mud and fell on him, breaking his leg. When they reached Main Plaza, Travis had already moved his men into the Alamo. Sutherland saw only the first hours of the siege; because of his broken leg he was sent to Gonzales as a messenger.

The space on the west, which they had hoped would serve as a barrier, had betrayed the men in the Alamo. Now they looked with hope to their friends beyond the space on the east and south.

Into the Alamo

Two survivors of the holocaust at the Alamo were an American woman and a Mexican boy. Strangely enough, their stories jibe.

The only American who had his family with him in San Antonio was Captain Almeron Dickinson of Gonzales, in charge of artillery. For some reason (perhaps they were brother Masons), Ramón Músquiz, the political chief of Texas, when he left with the Mexican army in December, turned over to him his town house at the southeast corner of Commerce Street and Main Plaza. Young Dickinson (he was twenty-

Storming of the Alamo

six), with his wife (twenty-one) and their fifteen-month-old daughter, set up housekeeping there and boarded a number of the Americans. Among them were Dr. Sutherland and David Crockett.

On the afternoon of February 23, Dickinson galloped up to the door, called his wife, and said to her, "Give me the baby, jump up behind me, and ask no questions."

She handed him the child, leaped up on the bare back of the horse, took the child and cradled it with her left arm, and clung to her husband. They galloped to the ford (where Navarro Street Bridge is today) and splashed through. They saw the Mexican soldiers filing into Main Plaza, and they felt the spray from bullets that cut the water.

They galloped through La Villita and up the street that leads to the Alamo. There all was in an uproar. Nat Lewis, local merchant, ran for cover to the fort and later described the scene to Reuben M. Potter.

Bowie with a detachment was engaged in breaking open deserted houses in the neighborhood and gathering corn, while another squad was driving cattle into the inclosure east of the long barrack. Some of the volunteers, who had sold their rifles to obtain the means of dissipation, were clamoring for guns of any kind; and the rest, though in arms, appeared to be mostly without orders or a capacity for obedience. No "army in Flanders" ever swore harder. But one officer seemed to be at his proper post and perfectly collected. This was an Irish captain, named Ward, who though generally drunk, was now sober, and stood quietly by the guns of the south battery ready to use them. Yet, amid the disorder of that hour, no one seemed to think of flight.

No one, that is, but Lewis. He fled on foot.

Enrique Esparza, a native of San Antonio, a boy of twelve, was playing with some other children on Main Plaza when Santa Anna's vanguard rode in.

Santa Anna's personal staff dismounted on Main Plaza in front of San Fernando church. I saw him dismount. He did not hitch the horse. He gave his bridle reins to a lackey. He and his staff proceeded immediately to the house on the northwest corner of Main Plaza. I will never forget the face or the figure of Santa Anna. He had a very broad face and high cheek bones. He had a hard and cruel look and his countenance was a very sinister one.

When Santa Anna and his soldiers came up we ran off and told our parents, who almost immediately afterward took me and the other children of the family to the Alamo. My father was a friend and comrade of William [John W.] Smith. Smith had expected to send my father and our family away with his own family in a wagon to Nacogdoches. We were waiting for the wagon to be brought to town. My father and Smith had heard of the approach of Santa Anna, but did not expect him and his forces to arrive as early as they did. Santa Anna and his men got here before the wagon we were waiting for could come.

My father was told by Smith that all who were friends to the Americans had better join them in the Alamo. Smith and his family went there and my father and his family went with them.

It was twilight when we got into the Alamo and it grew pitch dark soon. All of the doors were closed and barred. The sentinels that had been on duty without were first called inside and then the openings closed. Some sentinels were posted upon the roof, but these were protected by the walls of the Alamo church and the old convent building [the "Long Barrack"]. We went into the church portion. It was shut up when we arrived. We were admit-

ted through a small window.

I distinctly remember that I climbed through the window and over a cannon that was placed inside the church immediately behind the window. There were several other cannon there. The window was opened to permit us to enter, and it was closed immediately after we got inside.

We had not been in there long when a messenger came from Santa Anna calling for us to surrender. I remember the reply to this summons was a shot from one of the cannon on the roof of the Alamo. Soon after it was fired I heard Santa Anna's cannon reply. I heard his cannon shot strike the walls of the church and also the convent. Then I heard the cannon within the Alamo buildings fire repeatedly during the night. I heard the cheers of the Alamo gunners and the deriding jeers of Santa Anna's troops.

The Siege

The men in the Alamo knew they could not last long unless friends in force came to their aid. They had twenty-one cannon, mostly captured from the Mexican troops driven from San Antonio in December. With help, they could hold off a fair-sized army. Without help, they could inflict staggering losses before the inevitable end. Victory, as Travis prophesied, would be worse for Santa Anna than a defeat.

It was a sprawling mission compound made into a fort—more than four acres of it—that they had to cover. When you stand at the northmost tip of the tree-shaded park in Alamo Plaza, you are well within the large open yard that was on the west side, and several yards north of the main gate on the south. The west wall was parallel to, but behind the front of, the shops across the street to your left. The northwest corner was beyond Houston

Street, beyond an alleyway which angles off northwest, following the old north line, before it turns straight west. Eastward, the north line would cut through the post office. The ruined walls that stand today, with arches in them, just east of the tall marble shaft, the cenotaph, were first the convent of the mission and then the "Long Barrack" of the fort. This building made up the middle third of the east wall. But behind the Long Barrack was a pair of corrals, with a wall on the east reaching from present-day Houston Street to the Alamo Church, at the west line of the transept, just left of the side door.

A vast, bare area for 150 men to cover.

On February 24, Travis sent out his appeal for help. "I will never surrender or retreat," he wrote. "*Victory or Death!*"

The Mexican General Cos had unroofed the church of the Alamo in December, "throwing down the arches" to build an earthen artillery ramp to take cannon up to the top of the back wall. A wooden platform over the pillars served as roof and gun emplacement.

A ball rolling from this platform struck Bowie. On the night of February 25 a cold norther blew. Bowie, already suffering from tuberculosis, came down with pneumonia. Travis was now sole commander.

For the first four days of the siege the defenders made forays, burned houses outside the walls, fought skirmishes. After that they were hemmed in. They got water from two wells. They ate beef and cornbread. Powder and ammunition ran low.

David Crockett played his fiddle to entertain the men. "I think we should march out into the open," he said. "I don't want to die penned up."

Messengers could come and go at will. John W. Smith made several trips, the last one, out. James Bonham made a trip out and a last one in.

On March 1 a band of 32 colonists from Gonzales made their way in.

On March 3, Travis sent out his last messages. So far, he said, his men had been "miraculously preserved." But a pair of nine-pounders in the town were tearing holes in the Alamo walls with every shot.

On this day he is said to have drawn a line on the ground with his sword. According to Mrs. Dickinson, he invited all who wanted to leave the Alamo to cross it. According to the story told by Moses Rose, all who would stay in the Alamo were to cross it, and all but himself did so, and he escaped. Esparza confirms this story. The stories agree that Bowie asked his comrades to carry his cot over the line.

Travis spoke to his men and said he had now lost hope of aid from Goliad or from anywhere else. They understood what they had to do.

General Antonio López de Santa Anna

The Assault

Santa Anna had been receiving almost daily reinforcements. When he had 2,500 men, he ordered an assault on the Alamo, to begin at 5:00 A.M. on March 6.

The troops, in position at 4:00 A.M., lay on their bellies in the dark. One of them later wrote home: "Whew! It was cold!" A bugle shrilled from the north.

The assault was to be a surprise. But the soldiers in one of the charging columns yelled hurrahs for Santa Anna, and the twenty-one cannon in the Alamo turned on them a blasting fire. The soldier who wrote home saw 40 men fall about him. A second charge was shattered. There was a pause, to regroup the ranks. Santa Anna, watching from the north, called up the reserves.

This time, the columns on the east and west turned northward and, massed with the column on that side, rammed through a breach that had been made by artillery in the north wall. Travis fell on the cannon there, with a single shot through the forehead. "They poured over the walls like sheep."

The defenders turned "a small cannon on a high platform," near the middle of the west wall, against the oncoming mass. But just then a Mexican column on the south, "taking clever advantage of the protection offered by some little huts with walls of mud and stone which were near the southwest angle, by a daring move seized the cannon embrasured in that angle, and through the gap entered the plaza of the fort." Meanwhile, the troops who had come over the north wall turned the cannon on that side against the doors of the Long Barrack, "in which the rebels had taken refuge, and from which they were firing on the troops that were climbing down from the parapet into the plaza. And within those doors, by grapeshot, musketshot and the bayonet, they were all killed at last."

David Crockett

Mrs. Dickinson, with her child, was in a "small, dark room with arched ceiling [the sacristy] at the rear of the church." Smoke and the roar of battle filled the room. A boy she had known well in Gonzales, Galba Fuqua, sixteen years old, came to her. He was pale and haggard and had both jaws broken by a bullet and blood flowing from his mouth. He made several attempts to tell her something, but she could not understand him. Holding his jaws together with his hands, he tried to talk but could not. He shook his head and went out to the walls.

The battle had been going on for two hours when Dickinson rushed into the room where she stood holding the child, and exclaimed: "Great God, Sue! The Mexicans are coming over the walls! We are all lost. If you are spared, save my child." He drew his sword and ran out. At this moment Bowie, in the smaller room next door, attempted to rise from his cot and follow but was restrained by his Mexican nurse.

Soon after he left me [*Mrs. Dickinson related*] *three unarmed gunners who had abandoned their useless cannon, came into the church where I was, and were shot down by my side. One of the men, named Wolfe, asked for quarter, but was instantly killed. He had two little boys, aged 11 and 12 years. They ran into the room, where the Mexicans killed them, and a man named Walker, and carried their bodies out on their bayonets. I saw four Mexicans shoot Walker and stick their bayonets into his body and raise him up like a farmer does a bundle of fodder with a pitchfork when he loads it onto a wagon.*

When the Mexican troops poured into the room, Mrs. Dickinson closed her eyes and knelt in prayer, clasping her baby in the folds of her husband's Masonic apron.

"There was much noise and confusion as they crowded round Bowie, and the poor man met his death fighting to the last breath."

A Mexican officer then came into the room and said in English: "Are you Mrs. Dickinson? Then follow me." She did so. A rifle ball wounded her in the calf of the leg. As she went out of the church, she saw heaps of dead and dying men. "I recognized Colonel Crockett lying dead and mutilated between the church and the two-story barrack building, his peculiar cap by his side."

Enrique Esparza confused the thunder of Travis's artillery with the enemy bombardment, which had ceased before the attack:

After all had been dark and quiet for many hours and I had fallen into a profound slumber, suddenly there was a terrible din. Cannon boomed. . . . Then men rushed in on us. They swarmed among us and over us. They fired on us in volleys. They struck us down with their escopetas [*muskets*]. *In the dark room our men groped and grasped the throats of our foemen and buried their knives into their hearts.*

81

By my side was an American boy. He was about my own age but larger. As they rushed upon him he stood calmly and across his shoulders drew the blanket on which he had slept. He was unarmed. They slew him where he stood and his corpse fell over me. My father's body was lying near the cannon which he had tended. My mother with my baby sister was kneeling beside it. My brothers and I were close to her. I clutched her garments.

They took my mother, my brothers and me to the church's southwest corner, the small room to the right of the large double door as one enters it. There were other women and children all huddled. Another of the women had a babe at her breast. This was Mrs. Dickinson.

Before he was taken out of the church, Enrique Esparza saw the corpse of Bowie "in one of the smaller rooms on the north side." It was "riddled with bullets."

After the soldiers of Santa Anna had got all the women and children huddled in a corner, they stood still and fired into the darkness in the eastern end of the church. It was pitch-dark there. They kept firing on the men who had defended the Alamo. For fully a quarter of an hour, and until someone brought lanterns, they kept firing on them, after all the defenders had been slain and their corpses were lying still.

The last I saw of my father was when one of Santa Anna's men held a lantern above his corpse and over the dead who lay about the cannon he had tended.

Alamo Enclosure

As you stand before the Alamo Church, the ruins of the "Long Barrack," scene of great slaughter in the Battle of the Alamo, are to your left.

Alamo Church

This, the second stone church of Mission San Antonio de Valero, was commenced in 1756, the first one, begun in 1744, having fallen down. Above the doorway is the date 1758 and the monogram "A[ve]M[aria]." The niches once held images of saints. The original church had twin towers.

The Alamo: Interior

Several months before the Battle of the Alamo, during the siege of San Antonio by the Texan and American volunteers who took the city in December, 1835, the Mexican army put the old church into a state of defense, throwing down the arched roof to build a ramp from the doorway to the rear, in order to raise cannon to the top. This ramp was covered with a platform of heavy beams. The church was in this condition when it was occupied by the

Alamo Church

men with Travis and Bowie.

In the small room to the right, the women and children were huddled after the battle.

In the small room to the left, the powder and shot were kept.

In the next room to the left, James Bowie was confined to his cot. Here he fired on the Mexicans with his pistol until he was "riddled with bullets," according to Enrique Esparza, who saw his body.

In the vaulted room, next to the left, Mrs. Dickinson and her child, and the friendly Mexican women with their children, waited out the thirteen-day siege and the two-hour battle. Mrs. Dickinson could see Bowie from her room. This was once the sacristy of the Mission San Antonio de Valero and was a much longer room. It opened into the courtyard behind the Long Barrack (which had once been the convent of the mission). In this sacristy, in 1778, was an altar where an image of St. Anthony was venerated. Al-

Colonel James Bowie

84

though small (says Father Morfi), it served as a church until the large edifice could be ready.

The door now opening to the left in the north transept would have opened outside the east wall of the compound and was certainly sealed off during the battle, if it was there at all. The east wall was a projection northward of the wall between the transept and the sacristy.

There was definitely a door, or arched window, in the south transept, however; it is shown in old drawings. This is the window through which Enrique Esparza was hoisted into the Alamo on the evening of February 23, 1836, and the window where he said his father's cannon was stationed. There is little sign of an opening now.

In the south transept can be seen the original doors of the historic Veramendi House, formerly on Soledad Street, where Ben Milam was killed during the siege of San Antonio on December 7, 1835.

Numerous paintings on the wall represent scenes from the Battle of the Alamo.

Alamo Museum

Out the door of the north transept is a walk to the 1936 museum building. The exhibits consist of Texas history vs. Alamo history. They include historic artifacts, including guns. Souvenirs are the focal point.

Alamo Gardens

Perhaps the loveliest gardens in San Antonio surround the historic church on three sides. A remnant of the old Alamo Ditch, running directly behind the church, feeds aquatic plants. The gardens are in bloom most of the year, with an almost uninterrupted succession of flowers. The roses and the chrysanthemums, in their season, are glorious.

Alamo Library

In the southwest corner of the gardens is the attractive library, rich in Texana. It is intended especially for students in history. But the pictures alone are worth anybody's time. Most rewarding are the thirteen small enamellike paintings by Théodore Gentilz of early San Antonio scenes. Gentilz came to Texas in 1844 with the Castroville colonists. His contribution is unique, having value both as art and as history. (See also the Frételliere diary [Chapter 2].)

The adjacent Alamo Hall is the meeting place of the local chapter of the Daughters of the Republic of Texas. The state organization of the DRT is the custodian of the Alamo and its grounds.

Later History of the Alamo

The first American to see the Alamo after the tragedy was Dr. J. H.

Barnard, who was spared from the massacre at Goliad and brought to San Antonio, where several hundred wounded soldiers of Santa Anna were in bitter need of medical help. He saw the fire the troops set in the church as they left town after Sam Houston's victory at San Jacinto, saw it consume the "platform extending from the great door to the top of the wall on the back side."

The first drawing made of the church after the tragedy is probably Mary Maverick's (in *Samuel A. Maverick, Texan*); she came here as a bride in 1838. It shows statues in the four niches of the façade and an arcade along the convent. A traveler in 1837 remarked on the "life-sized statues of some of the apostles" on either side of the church door (according to the inventory of 1793 these were St. Dominic and St. Francis); in the first picture of the Alamo ever published (title page, William Ikin's *Texas*, 1841) the images are shown; in 1842 William Bollaert, English traveler, found them lying in weeds near an old house on East Commerce Street.

Litigation over Alamo property raged between the Catholic Church, which finally won most of the suits, the United States Army, which refused to budge until it was ready, the city of San Antonio, and squatters. Samuel A. Maverick, who escaped death because the men of the Alamo chose him as their delegate to the Convention that declared independence on March 2, 1836, was obsessed by a desire to live on the spot. He was the first to prove that the Alamo had been a mission, not a fort, and so was not subject to preemption by the army. In 1849 he got F. Giraud, like himself a gentleman from South Carolina, to survey the site; Giraud obliged his friend by cutting off a northwest corner and the entire corral on the northeast, and making the boundary the inner line of the buildings around the walls instead of their outer line, and emphasizing the ecclesiastical character of the compound. His map was published in Yoakum's *History of Texas* (1855) and is still widely accepted; the metal markers now in the ground are on his corners, but the two on the north fall short. Maverick's house was built in the northwest angle, well within the old walls.

For fourteen years the ruins of the Alamo were untouched. Then, in 1850, the United States Army, leasing from the Catholic bishop, restored the church and convent on their original walls and used them as a quartermaster's depot, to store hay and grain. The familiar line of the parapet was designed by architect John Fries. After the Civil War the army resumed its use of the buildings, although the bishop wanted the church for his German Catholics (they built St. Joseph's instead). But in 1878, when a depot was provided at Fort Sam Houston, the army moved out. A merchant bought the convent, revamped it into a store, and built wooden galleries bristling with wooden cannon all around. He leased the Alamo Church and used it for a warehouse. In 1883 the state of Texas bought the church; in 1885, turned it over to the city. A custodian was employed to keep vandals from carrying the shrine off, stone by stone. He boasted, in 1885, that he received about twenty visitors a day; he had acquired a portrait of David Crockett. In 1906 the state of Texas bought the convent and gave custody of the site to the Daughters of the Republic of Texas, who have charge of it today.

Alamo Church, 1904

4

The Bridge and the River

Paseo del Río

Commerce Street Bridge

(Commerce and Losoya streets)
The best approach to Paseo del Río
(the River Walk). Also to the boat
landings. A variety of boats can be
hired here, from paddleboats for
one or two persons to launches for
as many as thirty, with a sliding
scale of prices.

Arneson River Theatre

On the River Walk;
entrance also on Villita Street
by the Cos House.

Commerce Street Bridge

Commerce Street Bridge is not an
imposing monument, nor was it
ever a scene of decisive action. But
across the river at this point a stream
of life has been flowing, quiet or festive or tragic, since the first enduring
settlements were built by the Spaniards two centuries and more ago: a
fort and a mission—one on each
side of the river—clusters of huts
that became a city.

If you stand on the bridge that is
over the San Antonio River on Commerce Street, just off Alamo Plaza,
either way you look there is a pleasant view. Trees shade the banks, cypresses that turn rusty with fall. An
oak arches above the water. The
river curves, each way, between
walks bordered with kept grass,
adorned with cannas, banana plants,
and bright flowers in season.

The trees shadow and cover parts
of the varied walls that rise. Some,
of mellowed stone, have been there
many years. Some, of superficial
stuff, have not been there long and
will not be there after a few tomor-
rows.

In the light of the moment, in
the noise of the traffic, among the

89

Commerce Street Bridge, by Herman Lungkwitz, 1854

shifting figures crossing, you may not be aware that, of all this lively scene, only the river itself, from our point of view—or a gnat's—is eternal. It was flowing here, in this same gentle curve, before there were men to see it. And the trees are old. The oldest have been here since the day of the Spaniard, although they were then only saplings.

The Padre's Bridge

After the Mission San Antonio de Valero, later called the Alamo, was definitely placed in the year 1724 where its church and ruined convent remain, the shortest way to reach it from the fort (Military Plaza now), a distance of half a mile, was by the path called Royal Street (later Commerce), which led here to the river.

But the water ran deep. A man on horseback must cross farther down, at the ford below La Villita (where Navarro Street Bridge is now). This was a semicircular way around. But there was, at first, no crossing on the short way.

In 1736 a temporary bridge was laid here, by order of the padre at the mission. It consisted of six large beams, to be used later for the roof of a new church.

A colony of Canary Islanders had been planted (in 1731) around Main Plaza, one block east of the military post. These people had no church of their own. They could attend Mass in a room of the fort, a makeshift for a chapel, which threatened to collapse at any minute. And it was bare of adornment. Civilians and soldiers alike preferred to hear Mass at the mission. There, too, the chapel was a makeshift: the padres had never been able, owing to the lack of artisans on this extreme frontier, to build a proper church. But they did have splendid images. And, according to a report on the mission made several years earlier by a pair of inspecting friars, "the spiritual needs of the soldiers and the citizens are met absolutely without charge. This is well known to all and it has always been the custom." The padre had a bridge placed here for a strictly religious purpose.

But the townspeople traipsed over to the mission on weekdays as well as Sundays. What was worse, the soldiers molested the Indian women, or so the padre was told. He ordered the beams removed.

The governor of Texas, who then resided in San Antonio, was a hard-boiled Spanish army officer. He had small use for friars. The removal of the bridge without his authorization vexed him. He sent the padre word that the beams must be put back. For answer, he got an argument. The governor sent back word that he needed some Indians for a job. The padre, suspicious, asked if the Indians were needed for military service. Otherwise, he could not spare any: they were all either sick or at urgent work in the fields.

The governor was furious. He sent a squadron of soldiers to the mission's fields. They collared some Indians, made them put back the beams. The governor exulted. But not for long.

The stubborn padre set Indian guards at the forcibly restored bridge.

"No one, *but no one*, is to pass," he ordered, "not even the governor himself."

Of course, this news reached the governor. His rage was spectacular. The Indian guards at the crossing must have had a fearful moment when they saw, and heard, the red-faced governor and his retinue come galloping up. The governor and his retinue passed over.

The padre, in his office at the mission, was enjoying a chat with a fellow friar when they heard a terrific commotion outside. The governor burst in, shouting and brandishing his cane. He swore, among other things, that he would send the padre packing to Mexico on a mule.

The guards were removed. After a few years, the governor was removed. Pretty soon, no doubt, the bridge was removed.

Santa Anna's Bridge

For almost a full hundred years, history has little to say about any bridge across the river at this point. In 1803 the Spanish governor ordered the townspeople to build one; it was doubtless destroyed by the flood of 1819.

In the winter of 1836 there was a footbridge of planks. After the capture of San Antonio by the Texas volunteers early in December, 1835, some 200 hotheads among them made off for the coast, with the mad scheme of attacking the port of Matamoros, at the mouth of the Rio Grande.

Only 104 men stayed at their post in San Antonio. This nearly naked band had to garrison "two distinct fortresses"—Military and Main plazas west of the river and, east of it, the Alamo, which had long been abandoned as a mission but still was not a proper fort. Between these two centers of activity, half a mile apart, the men were con-

Paseo del Río near old St. Mary's College

stantly passing, to prepare the Alamo for defense and to amuse themselves in the town with card games, cockfights, and fandangos.

They crossed the river by footbridge. A few had horses, but these were kept several miles to the east, on Salado Creek, where water and grass were abundant, as there was no forage in town.

Some of the men whose homes were in the distant settlements of Texas took leave. By mid-January only 80, mostly Americans fresh from "the States," remained. But, a month later, after Texas Colonels James Bowie and William Barret Travis had each brought with him to San Antonio 20 to 30 men, and after David Crockett had arrived with 12 from Tennessee, the number stood at 150.

The army of General Antonio López de Santa Anna, president and dictator of Mexico, appeared west of town shortly after noon on February 23. The Texans left the plazas undefended, according to

Restaurant along Paseo del Río

93

plan. The few men who had horses splashed through the ford at La Villita; the others ran across the bridge to the Alamo walls.

Santa Anna marched his troops into the plazas. He had a blood-red flag run up on the tower of the parish church (now San Fernando Cathedral). It meant *no quarter*. Travis, in the Alamo, replied with a cannon shot.

Then (says Dr. John Sutherland's account) watching eyes in the Alamo spotted "a white flag . . . descending Commerce Street." A pair of officers were sent "to meet it and confer with its bearers. This meeting took place on a small foot bridge which led from the Alamo to the city. An unconditional surrender was demanded."

This much is certain: After Travis fired the cannon shot, someone informed Bowie that the enemy had asked for a parley. Bowie sent Green B. Jameson, the Alamo's engineer, to the Mexican officers with a note and a white flag.

It may be the demand was delivered "on a small foot bridge" at the Commerce Street crossing.

This bridge was of strategic importance to Santa Anna. He spent the first days of the siege feeling out the defenders, trying to approach the walls. Some of his men came too close. Their bodies were not retrieved.

The bridge was in easy range of the Alamo guns. Santa Anna's secretary reports: "During one of our charges at night, His Excellency ordered Colonel Juan Bringas to cross a small bridge with five or six men. He had no sooner started to carry out his instructions than the enemy opened fire and killed one man. In trying to recross this bridge, the colonel fell into the water and saved himself only by a stroke of good luck."

This, it seems, was the night of February 24. The next day Santa Anna succeeded in planting batteries across the bridge, and in the days that followed he hemmed the Alamo

in with gun emplacements. But messengers were sent out by the besieged. And on March 1, 32 Texans from Gonzales rode into the walls. By March 3 he had artillery belching iron on the defenders. On the afternoon of March 5 he issued orders for the assault.

The next morning before daylight, Santa Anna "took his station, with a part of his staff and all the bands of music, at a battery near the bridge" (according to Reuben M. Potter's not very reliable version); the signal for the attack, a bugle blast from the Mexican camp north of the Alamo, "was followed by the rushing tramp of soldiers. The guns of the fort opened upon the moving masses, and Santa Anna's bands struck up the assassin note of *degüello*, or no quarter . . ."

A small official group huddled in an entrenchment where the public library used to be. They were the local bigwigs: Francisco Antonio Ruiz, the alcalde, or mayor; Ramón Músquiz, political chief of Texas; Refugio de la Garza, parish priest, who had come to administer extreme unction.

These officials knew well the men in the Alamo. Músquiz had turned his residence over to Captain Almeron Dickinson and his wife, who had boarded David Crockett and several others. De la Garza had read the marriage rites for Bowie and Ursula Veramendi, daughter of the vice-governor and dead three years of cholera, with both their children. Ruiz's father, José Francisco, had been sent as a delegate to the convention at Washington-on-the-Brazos, and four days earlier (although none of them here knew it) he had signed the Texas Declaration of Independence. These officials were here by order of Santa Anna. They were here to take care of the wounded and the dead. Ruiz says, in his account, "Travis's artillery resembled a constant thunder."

The first assaults were repulsed with frightful slaughter. Santa Anna called up his reserves. He could see his mass of troops—nearly 2,500 against fewer than 200—pour over the southeast corner of the Alamo compound. Then (he says in his report) "the brisk fire of musketry illuminated the interior of the fortress, the walls and ditches." Says Ruiz:

As soon as the storming commenced, we crossed the bridge on Commerce Street . . . and about 100 yards from the same a party of Mexican dragoons fired upon us and compelled us to fall back on the river and the place we occupied before. Half an hour had elapsed when Santa Anna sent one of his aide-de-camps with an order for us to come before him. He directed me to call on some of the neighbors to come with carts to carry the [Mexican] dead to the cemetery and to accompany him, as he was desirous to have Colonels Travis, Bowie and Crockett shown to him. . . . The dead Mexicans of Santa Anna were taken to the graveyard, but not having sufficient room for them, I ordered some to be thrown into the river, which was done on the same day.

The route to the graveyard west of town (where Santa Rosa Hospital is now) was by way of the bridge. Here, no doubt, the bodies were dumped, and the river ran red.

The bodies of the Texans—Ruiz counted 182—were burned, some distance to the northeast of the Alamo, after being arranged in order: first a layer of wood, then a layer of bodies, a layer of wood, another layer of bodies . . .

Not until many months after the Texans won victory and independence at San Jacinto (near present Houston, April 21, 1836) did a detachment of their tattered army take possession of the town and bury the bones of the defenders of the Alamo. No one knows just where.

Approach from the East

San Antonio was nearly desolate during the nine years of the Republic of Texas. Under constant menace of attack by Mexican armies or by marauding Indians, many native families moved away. Very few Americans moved into the vacant houses. Very little building was done. A bridge built in 1842 at the Commerce Street crossing was evidently bashed in by the first flood that came along.

Some bold Europeans came to seek their fortune on the wild frontier. A young *boulevardier* of Paris was among those brought over in 1844 by Henri de Castro for a colony twenty-five miles west of San Antonio. Auguste Frétellière recalls in his memoirs: "At that time there were no bridges, the foot travelers crossed the river on a tree uprooted by some great flood, which reached to the other bank. I made my way over that little bridge and rejoined my companion who had crossed at the ford."

In 1846, the first year after Texas's annexation to the United States, there was a footbridge, and skylarking young people would cross it to visit the Alamo, a dismal ruin in the mesquite brush, but no longer frightening, now that the United States troops were near. One of the boys unearthed a cannon ball and rolled it merrily down "the hill," which had been the Texans' artillery ramp at the rear of the church.

In the 1850's, a low wooden bridge welcomed visitors from "the States" and immigrants from beyond the sea. A German artist left a painting of it. Frederick Law Olmsted, designer of Central Park, tells in his *Journey through Texas* how he crossed it in 1856: "We descend to the bridge, which is down upon the water . . . of a rich blue and pure as crystal, flowing rapidly but noiselessly over pebbles and between reedy banks. One could lean for hours over the bridge rail. From the bridge we enter Commerce Street, the narrow principal thoroughfare."

Lanier's Bridge

In 1870, the masonry was laid for a new bridge, which would be Sidney Lanier's favorite spot when he visited San Antonio in the winter of 1872/73, hoping to find in this climate a cure for his consumption. He wrote home:

"Presently I stood, before I knew it, on a bridge over the San Antonio River which flows directly through the heart of the city and my surprised eyes ran with delight along the lovely windings of the green translucent stream, flowing beneath long sprays of weeping willows and playing incessantly with the swaying stems of the water grasses." Again: "After the siesta a stroll to the bridge, where I stand and gaze on the pleasant pale-green water, the

queer canvas-covered bathing houses, of which each riparian owner seems to have one,—and upon the long swaying tufts of a grass which grows in the middle of the stream and lies along the surface and laves itself forever in the smooth fresh current."
In his oft-quoted "In San Antonio de Bexar," he writes:

One may take one's stand on the Commerce Street bridge and involve oneself in the life that goes by this way and that. Yonder comes a long train of enormous, blue-bodied covered wagons, built high and square in the stern, much like a fleet of Dutch galleons, and lumbering in a ponderous way that suggests cargoes of silver and gold. These are drawn by fourteen mules each who are harnessed in four tiers, and that next the wagon of two. The "lead" mules are wee fellows, veritable mulekins, the next tier larger, and so on, to the two wheel-mules who are always as large as can be procured. Yonder

fares slowly another train of wagons, drawn by great wide-horned oxen, whose evident tendency to run to hump and foreshoulder irresistibly persuades one of their cousinship to the buffalo.

. . . .

Presently, one's gazing eye receives the sensation of hair, then of enormous ears, and then the legs appear, of the little roan-gray burros, or asses, upon whose backs that Mexican walking behind has managed to pile a mass of mesquite firewood that is simply astonishing.

. . . .

And now as we leave the bridge in the gathering twilight and loiter down the street, we pass all manner of odd personages and "characters." Here hobbles an old Mexican who looks like old Father Time in reduced circumstances. There goes a little German boy who was captured a year ago by Indians. Here is a great Indian fighter . . . there a portly, handsome buccaneer-looking cap-

tain—and so on through a perfect gauntlet of people who have odd histories, odd natures or odd appearances.

The Iron Span

Lanier's bridge was replaced, in 1880, with an iron one, brought in by railway. The Sunset Lines reached San Antonio in 1877.

This iron span rests now on quiet Johnson Street, in the neighborhood of King William, down the river, where it vibrates only to an occasional passing car. But for thirty-four years, while the town was changing from a frontier outpost to a modern city, this was the Commerce Street Bridge, and everybody crossed it, again and again. Even after traffic had shifted north to Houston Street, with its ample width for mulecars, then for trolleys, then for automobiles, this remained a vital ligament between the city's halves.

The iron bridge bore a warning in three languages—English, Spanish, and German—"Walk your horse, or be fined $1 to $25."

This was a standing invitation to the cowboy headed for the coastal range to fire a salvo from his pistols, then spur his horse hell-for-leather beyond the reach of the constabulary.

"Commerce Street, which crosses this bridge," says a book published in 1883, "is the chief thoroughfare of the city, and most of the principal business houses are on it. When one vehicle passes another there is hardly room for the dog to escape."

The iron bridge, now so quiet on Johnson Street, reverberated with all the traffic of the time. But many a soul who was heavy-laden sought it as the bridge to peace. In 1883 a young man, not identified, leaped to the rail and let himself go with a mighty splash. The body was never found. A hoax was suspected.

In 1895, Stephen Crane, dallying on his way to Mexico, dived from a bridge—this one?—to save a drowning girl.

In 1894/95, William Sydney Porter made frequent visits to San Antonio from Austin, where he resided, on the pretext of business.

O. Henry's Bridge

The narrow, crooked, pullulating Commerce Street of the past has been widened and straightened several times. Finally, in 1914, the present concrete bridge was placed here, many buildings were demolished, and some on the south were pushed back twenty feet.

But if the W. S. Porter who became known later as O. Henry could return now, he would still recognize the crossing where the iron bridge used to be. Surely he found the spot attractive (though he nowhere in his writings says so), throbbing with life as it was and directly between the newspaper offices and the jollier saloons.

On the west bank, the buildings are about the same now as then, for a block. On the north, at the river, a Renaissance *châtelet* bears, carved above the door, the date 1893. Next is the front of the old Schultze hardware store. Next is the former H. Rilling "Leather & Findings" shop, founded in 1868. Next, behind a slick, modernized front, is the shell of Harnisch and Baer's confectionery, where, it is said, the ice cream soda was invented. Here, among banana plants and elephant ears, customers of all ages sipped cool drinks and nibbled cookies. This was a favorite rendezvous for courting couples, and young men, according to a newspaper wit, would pay back in summer refreshment what they had cost their girls' daddies through the winter in fuel for the parlor stove. Next, under a stone coping, the name "F. Heye" is carved. This was a famous saddle shop (now moved), patronized by discriminating horsemen from the whole Southwest and by Theodore Roosevelt in

O. Henry

1898, when he outfitted his Rough Riders.

On the east bank of the river O. Henry would recognize only the Dullnig Building, shorn of its turrets now, but with the iron steps still leading up to its corner door still open on Losoya Street.

O. Henry would miss the vanished *Express* building that stood where Losoya, then just an alley, now meets the bridge. He is said to have hawked feature stories there. The *Light*, chief rival of the *Express*, was housed in a cubbyhole, catercorner, across East Commerce Street. The short-lived *News* (no kin to a later *News*) was officed several blocks west on Commerce. A good picture of the old *Express* building—and of the times—is in the book by M. Koenigsberg, *King News*.

Koenigsberg was, in 1893, a precocious reporter of fifteen and the entire staff of the *News*. His editor, "Majah" Harris, was feuding with William C. Brann (later "the Iconoclast"), then editor of the *Express*.

One evening Harris tanked himself up with mint juleps and set out along Commerce Street to challenge his foe. Says Koenigsberg:

Locking arms with me, "the Majah" adopted a jaunty gait. . . . The three blocks beyond St. Mary's seemed to me the longest walk I had ever taken. The west side of the Express *building formed an angle with the Commerce Street Bridge. Twenty windows lighted each of the three floors. That meant sixty openings through each of which we might be potted. Harris' approach had cleared the street of pedestrians. Innocent bystanders won little sympathy in San Antonio.*

In the middle of the bridge, Harris released my arm. He stepped to the rail. His right hand on the gun holstered under his left arm while he looked up to the windows of the Express, *Harris lifted his stentorian voice.*

"William C. Brann, stand forth!" The call echoed down the river and

through the surrounding blocks.

There was no response. Twice again at full minute intervals, Harris repeated his shout. The intervening pauses were oppressive. Whether by design or accident, a strange quietude prevailed in the newspaper building. Faces could be seen furtively pressed against window-panes. Harris waited fully three minutes after his last summons. Then, turning to me, he spoke as if addressing an audience. "We have offered the craven cur an opportunity to behave like a gentleman. We have discharged our duty to him and to ourselves. Let us proceed." Once more locking arms, he led me to Scholz's garden on Losoya Street around the corner.

Brann, who shortly resigned from the *Express* because of another feud, went to Austin, where he founded a magazine, the *Iconoclast*, sold it to a bank clerk, William Sydney Porter, and thence to Waco, where he was shot to death in a final feud.

Porter turned the magazine into a humorous sheet, the *Rolling Stone*, and took as partner Henry Ryder Taylor, who was the staff of the *San Antonio News* and had previously been the staff of the *Light*. A top-hatted Englishman, he had once been the secretary of Charles Dickens. The pair did not make a go of the *Rolling Stone*, which they tried to publish simultaneously in Austin and in San Antonio, but the enterprise gave Porter a pretext for his frequent visits here.

One of O. Henry's most moving stories, "A Fog in San Antone," tells of a doomed consumptive who stands "upon a little iron bridge . . . under which the small tortuous river flows." And the tragic final scene takes place in the Scholz Palm Garten (long vanished in smoke), which had an entrance on Alamo Street, and a concert hall "set plentifully with palms and cactuses and oleanders," and an orchestra that played Wagner and Von Suppé, and galleries that extended above Losoya Street and overlooked the river.

At the Moment

Everyone who has been important, for a time, and who has honored the city with his presence has been conveyed, by horse or carriage or limousine, across the river at this point.

Past here the solemn parades have blared, the gaudy, the flamboyant.

The soldiers of eight wars have marched this way.

If you stand on the bridge now, in the light of the moment, in the noise of traffic, among the shifting figures crossing, you may not be aware of the vast company that joins you here. And yet it is with you, even in the stillest hour.

Paseo del Río

Paseo del Río is accessible at any bridge downtown. It follows the immemorial windings of the river, sometimes on one bank, sometimes on both. The United States Army engineers, who have converted the river into a drainage ditch at many other places, have been thwarted here by the town, which has built up solidly for centuries along the bend of the stream and cannot be ignored. A cutoff, crossing Commerce and Market streets half a block east of Main Plaza, has been provided to make the river a straight line in time of flood.

The walk winds for about a mile north of Commerce Street Bridge and about half a mile south of it. The planting is attractive, and there are many fine old trees, mainly cypresses and weeping willows, as far north as Travis Street and as far south and west as the cutoff beyond the Hilton Hotel, where the walk ends.

Paseo del Río

The beautification of the river-banks downtown was done as recently as 1939/40. A few years earlier, some go-getting businessmen conceived the idea of covering the river over, making a sewer of it, and converting the space above into a thoroughfare. For many years, as a matter of fact, the river was hardly better than a sewer. It was a dismal, sluggish trickle between banks festooned with weeds, adorned with dead cats, slain bottles, and other unsightly objects. The flow of the stream has been greatly diminished by the drilling of numerous artesian wells. By the 1890's the day was long gone when "swimming everywhere along the river was common," as a *History and Guide* of the times laments, "and the ecstasy of beholding long tresses and females of fine form and figure were hourly enjoyed."

Convention Center from Paseo del Río

The Arneson River Theatre

The Arneson River Theatre, a bit more than two blocks down the river from the Commerce Street Bridge, is officially a part of La Villita (see Chapter 5). But it is also a part of the San Antonio River promenade and the center of many festivities held on the riverbanks.

The River Parade of Monday evening in Fiesta Week is reviewed by the current King Antonio from its stage. In the River Art Shows, spring and fall, the prize-winning canvases are set out along the tiers of seats on the opposite side of the stream. The whole theater is used for the Fiesta Noche del Río, or "Party Night on the River." (These events are described in Chapter 14, under "Fiesta San Antonio," "Paintings and Crafts," and "Theater," respectively.)

Arneson River Theatre

PLAZA
JUAREZ

CRAFTSMEN • ARTISTS
SHOPS • RESTAURANTS

5

La Villita

(Villita Street)
Entrance: from Alamo or South
Presa streets; a gate is open sometimes on Nueva Street, and from the
River Walk one can climb up and enter via the Arneson River Theatre.
Open: daily, about 6:00 A.M., but
the stores and shops begin their day
about 9:00 A.M.; some parts are
locked up at 10:00 P.M. unless
some special event is in progress.
Admission: free.

This was the site of a small village
during the Battle of the Alamo. The
only thing left from this 1836 period
is the Cos House. Other buildings in
the area were built from approximately 1840 through the 1880's. A
few buildings were added in 1905
and then La Villita seemed to enter
a period of rest and disintegration. In
the 1940–1950 period the area was
partially cleared and buildings were
added to make it a community and
tourist area.

La Villita, in Europe, would be
known as a "quarter," in Spain or
Mexico as a *barrio*—indeed, it was
so designated in Spanish times.
Most of the buildings are now occupied by artists and various working
craftspeople and their studios.

La Villita now covers the entire
block bordered by Alamo Street,
South Presa Street (some parking),
Villita Street (no auto traffic), and
Nueva Street (some parking).

Fund-raising events take place
here from time to time, during which
all or part of the area may be closed
to the general public.

La Villita Enclosure

La Villita Enclosure (Villita Street)
is an attractive walled area, gay,
most seasons of the year, with a bizarre mingling of lush tropical plants
like the banana and the bougainvil-
lea, and the sedate hollyhock, the

La Villita: Plaza Juárez

prim petunia and baby's breath.

The enclosure is ordinarily a quiet place. The best time to see it is while a Mexican celebration is going on or at "A Night in Old San Antonio," during Fiesta San Antonio (see Chapters 14 and 15).

A number of little Spanish-Mexican houses, some of them with German trimmings, have been preserved here. Others were swept away to make Plaza Juárez, a space for dancing and other open-air festivities in the northwest corner of the area.

On the south side of the enclosure stands a two-story building intended to represent a United States Army headquarters on the Texas frontier in the 1850's. It is called Bolívar Hall and is the largest building in La Villita. The office of the complex is upstairs and the rest of this building is very flexible in purpose and use.

In La Villita

Villita Craft Shops

When La Villita was restored by the National Youth Administration in about 1939 one of the main goals was to encourage the arts and crafts. Since that time the shops and galleries have housed working artists and their creations. Many of San Antonio's leading artists have some of their works for sale here. It is a good art hunting ground.

Along Villita Street

There is no auto traffic but this is the main thoroughfare of the little village. On the north side is the Villita Assembly Hall and the entrance to the Arneson River Theatre and the Cos House.

The city block across the street is split by King Phillip V Street. Each of the two side areas has a large plaza and can be divided for group use. The largest program that utilizes all

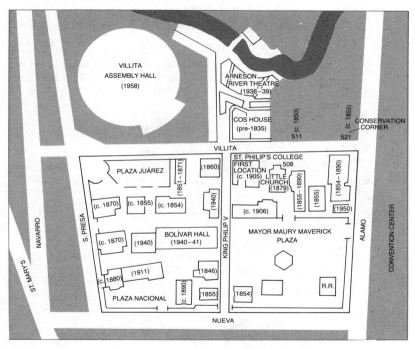

Map 6. *La Villita*

107

Little Church of La Villita

the facilities is the "Night in Old San Antonio" staged by the Conservation Society.

South to Nueva Street the historic buildings have been rented to private studios. Most of these buildings are old, and interesting as architecture.

Number 508

Number 508 is the Little Church of La Villita, so-called since 1957, when it was opened as a nondenominational chapel, after having been abandoned for several generations. Originally the German Methodist Church, built in 1879, it is not the site where John Wesley Devilbiss, pioneer Methodist preacher, installed his bell in 1847 (see Chapter 13)— that was across the alley from the Cos House (below), on a lot overlooking the river. The chapel is kept open during the day. Vespers are held daily at 6:00 P.M.

On the north side of the street, beginning at the northeast corner:

Number 521

Number 521, Conservation Corner, two stories of stone, was built in 1855. About 1860, according to deed records, it was inhabited by Viktor F. Bracht, author of *Texas in the Year 1848* (published in Germany) and by "other Germans." For at least half a century it was a saloon, The Old Stand. In 1950 it was acquired and refurbished by the San Antonio Conservation Society. It is now leased to the Little Rhein Restaurant.

Number 511

Number 511, Casa Villita, is a charming New Orleans–type cottage, perhaps built by François Guilbeau about 1850.

The Cos House

The Cos House (no number) is an ancient adobe, much restored. It is the only spot in La Villita on which anyone has been able to pin a major historic event: according to the reminiscences of old-timers, the surrender of General Martín Perfecto de Cos, commander of the Mexican forces besieged by the Texans during the fall of 1835, was signed here December 11, 1835. This seems logical, as the house was halfway between Main Plaza, which had just been captured by the Texans, and the Alamo, which was still in Mexican hands.

The house, a part of the La Villita project, has a lovely patio shaded by small live oaks; it is often used for entertainments.

Arneson River Theatre

Arneson River Theatre, also a part of the La Villita project, can be reached by a passageway just west of the Cos House. Its tiers of grassy seats descend to the river's edge; the stage is on the bank opposite. Really a part of Paseo del Río, its uses are mentioned in Chapter 4, detailed in Chapter 14.

The Assembly Hall

The Assembly Hall at the corner of Villita and South Presa streets, designed for the San Antonio Public Service Board in 1958 by architect O'Neil Ford, is a splendid example of a modern structure built to blend with surrounding mellowed walls.

Cos House

History: La Villita

Just when the village which has been called "La Villita" since Spanish times, and which is now very near the heart of sprawling San Antonio, was first built on the bluff where it sits today we do not know for sure.

But, certainly, it was an offshoot of the Mission San Antonio de Valero, whose church is now known as the Alamo. And it was built on lands belonging to that mission, which were bounded on the west by the river.

It may have been one of those "miserable villages" which the French traveler Pages described, in 1768, as lying on the outskirts of the city and weakening the defenses of the fortress because they were a sort of standing invitation to marauding Indians, who, it seems, could not resist the temptation to raid these settlements and carry off any stray horses or goats or pigs or children.

It was probably the village described by a Spanish inspector in 1792 as having sprung up outside the walls of the abandoned San Antonio de Valero to house the families of the soldiers who already were using the buildings and corrals of the mission.

Anyhow, although there may have been a cluster of wretched huts on the site many years before, not until after 1793, when the Alamo was secularized—when it ceased officially to exist as a mission and became a military post and its lands were parceled out to individuals— did the little town really begin to grow.

The only ford between the Spanish town, centered on Main and Military plazas, and the Alamo was where Navarro Street Bridge is now. Villita Street was called the "Street of the Crossing." And South Alamo, "the road to the missions," was lined, on both sides, with small houses and small gardens, as far as the ancient mission compound, on what is now Alamo Plaza.

For many years La Villita or, rather, the "Town of the Alamo," even had its own alcalde, or mayor.

Then, in 1819, came the great flood which swept through the city and carried with it so many houses that, as the governor wrote to his superiors in Mexico, very few of the inhabitants would have escaped if they had not been, most of them, superb swimmers, who had spent a good deal of their time in the river.

Many Spanish families who, it appears, had looked down their noses at the sleazy settlement across the river, decided to move to the higher ground there. The bluff was soon solidly built up.

In the stirring events of the Texas Revolution against Mexico, La Villita had an important role. There the capitulation of Mexican General Cos to the Texans was signed on December 10, 1835, in a house that still stands.

When Santa Anna took his terrible revenge, in March, 1836, a battery was trained on the defenders of the Alamo from this strategic position, which commanded the only ford across the river.

The second chapter in the history of La Villita began with the end of the Texas Republic, when people of all nations came to live under the protection of the United States flag, in the modest homes along the narrow streets of the little town.

Until recent years there was still one Mexican jacal, or hut, made of posts driven into the ground, tied together with rawhide and chinked with mud. But the more substantial houses of adobe and caliche began to look like European cottages, as immigrants from Germany and from France moved into them and put their Old World touches on them.

These were solid, honest people, who paid their taxes and their debts. But they lived simply, in a few rooms with chaste white walls, ceilings painted blue, and straw mats instead of turkey-red rugs on the floors. There were no baronial castles—none of the opulent gingerbread that adorned the castles of the wealthy merchants of German descent who built their homes, in the 1870's and 1880's, on King William and its neighboring streets. But they did go in for fancy hand-sawed furniture, whatnots, and the like.

Strangely enough, La Villita, through the years of middle-class German respectability, was also the center of artistic endeavor in San Antonio. The air was laden not only with the smells of coffee cake from a little bakery on South Alamo and of the candy made in Mr. Duerler's factory, but also with the resinous odor of oil paint being applied to canvas. And there were the sounds of music—the squeaks of practice, the harmonies of attained artistry.

After the First World War the little town went through a period of decay. The respectable people moved out, the old houses crumbled, the place became a slum. When the Great Depression reached its lowest point, in the early thirties, the area was an eyesore, squalid and shabby.

It was then that some good citizens had the inspiration of making La Villita into a place that would be not only a monument to its own colorful history, but also a workshop for the arts and a social center dedicated to friendship between this country and all the countries of Latin America. The late Maury Maverick, Sr., as congressman and as mayor of San Antonio, was the moving spirit behind the Villita project.

The city of San Antonio and the federal government worked in partnership on this. As a result, San Antonio has conserved a number of its fine old houses and has built a place to honor our neighbors who live to the south and their mellow culture, from which we have learned so much—and have so much to learn.

6

Heart of
Béxar

Spanish Governor's Palace: patio

San Fernando Cathedral

(Plaza de las Islas—Main Plaza)
Open: daily, 6:00 A.M. to 5:00 P.M.

Spanish Governor's Palace

(Military Plaza)
Open: Monday through Saturday,
9:00 A.M. to 5:00 P.M.; Sunday,
10:00 A.M. to 5:00 P.M.
Admission: adults, 50¢; children,
25¢.

The two plazas now known as Main and Military have been the pulsing heart of Béxar and San Fernando and San Antonio since the first huts began to rise along the sides of a vacant square. From these plazas, trails or cowpaths opened into the brush and became streets or roads. The huts lining the plazas were replaced with staunch houses of stone and mud. Along the clear-flowing San Pedro Creek and along the irrigation ditch, no less clear, that was cut from the creek, rose the jacales of the poor, made of mesquite stakes chinked with mud and roofed with reeds. But the people met in the plazas. There all the really important things happened: the fiestas, the announcing of great events, the whispering interchange of news and gossip, the marriages, the funerals.

Plaza de las Islas (Main Plaza)

No plot of ground this size on the continent, north of Mexico City, has been the scene of such varied pageantry as this plaza. Now the cathedral, courthouse, and central fountain make it a picture spot. To write the past history of this plaza one would have to write at the same time, the history of the city or even of all Texas. So many

113

colorful and portentous characters have appeared here, to play some part of their role. So many tumults have been spawned. So much blood has been spilled. The barest chronological notes, or a mere list of the famous and the notorious, would fill a small book.

On this plot of ground, the royal pavilion of Spain was set out for the annunciation of each new king, and Te Deums were sung, amidst fireworks and the rodeos with bulls and the clatter of "skirmishes" with wooden swords.

Here, in 1749, the Spaniards celebrated their peace with the Apaches: four chiefs, in full paint and feathers, danced around a hole dug in the center of the plaza; in it were a live horse, a tomahawk, a lance, and six arrows; the chiefs danced, holding hands, with the officers of Spain and with the padres of the missions; then the horse was buried alive with the tomahawk and lance and arrows.

Here, in 1789, six Apache braves, determined to assassinate the governor of Texas, who had made peace with the hated Comanches, forced their way into the Royal Houses and were cut down by the guard.

Into the same offices, in 1813, rushed Bernardo Gutiérrez, to announce the murder of the Spanish governors Salcedo and Herrera by his men.

To these same offices, in 1820, came Moses Austin (and not to the Spanish Governor's Palace on Military Plaza, which his statue faces), seeking permission to settle Anglo-American colonists in Texas.

On this plaza and north of it, in 1835, was fought the bloodiest battle of the siege of Béxar. In the middle of the plaza, in 1836, Davy Crockett stood on a box and made a speech, asking to be a private in "our common cause." At the west corner on the north side, Santa Anna, president and dictator of Mexico, had his quarters.

In and around the old Spanish council hall, in 1840, thirty-three Comanches, who had come to parley over captives, screamed betrayal when the whites tried to hold them as hostages, drew their bows and arrows, and, before they were shot to pieces, took with them seven Texans. A few weeks later the young chief Isimanica rode into the square, circled it, rose in his stirrups, shook his fist, raved, and foamed at the mouth, offering fight.

In 1842, Texans on the roof of Samuel Maverick's house, then in the northeast angle, fired on Mexican soldiers marching into the plaza with their band playing; these Texans became prisoners in Perote Castle, far down in Mexico.

San Antonio's first real hotel, the Plaza House, was erected in 1847 on the north side, and ten years later the first stagecoaches for San Diego, California, started from in front of it.

From the Plaza House, in 1860, Governor Sam Houston, crusading to keep the state in the Union, was called to the balcony by a cheering crowd.

In this plaza, in 1861, General

D. E. Twiggs surrendered the United States troops in Texas to the Confederacy. And in a hotel then on the south side, a little later that day, Robert E. Lee paced the floor all night, making a historic decision.

In the heyday of the cattleman his chosen stomping ground was the Southern Hotel, then between the two plazas, on the north of Dolorosa Street, near the stockyards on South Flores Street and also near the better saloons, which were around Main Plaza. Until 1887 there was the plushy White Elephant on the north side (its skeleton is still there) and the Revolving Light (long extinquished), gambling dens rather than saloons.

Near the northeast corner, at the Jack Harris Vaudeville, the killing of Harris in 1882 and of Ben Thompson and King Fisher in 1884 stirred excitement that boiled up for decades wherever drunks met to argue.

A bloodless duel, in 1887, between a Montana judge and a Kentucky colonel added, according to

San Fernando Cathedral

the *Express*, a note of comedy to the turbulent history of the plaza: "They fought hard, using their canes and fists alternately, and rolling in the mud, until they looked like hod-carriers."

San Fernando Cathedral

San Fernando Cathedral (west side of Main Plaza), a simplified French Gothic structure, was built along the walls of the old Spanish parish church that dominated the life of San Antonio and figured in every dramatic event.

The parish church was begun in 1738 by the Canary Islanders, who arrived in 1731. At first they attended the church at Mission San Antonio de Valero (the Alamo), across the river. But when the padre there refused to admit them (see Chapter 4), they were forced to use the chapel in the military barracks, a room so shakily built, they com-

plained, that "only a strong Christian feeling" could persuade them to risk their lives in it. Although the corner-stone was laid in 1738, the people could not scrape up enough money to make a good start and had to appeal to the viceroy in Mexico. The king of Spain footed the bill, and the church was finished by 1758, in time for the visit, the next year, of the bishop of Guadalajara, who confirmed the first communion class.

The life of the town and the emotions of the people, who had their weddings, baptisms, and funerals there to the sound of the bell and heard the announcements of the great unseen lords of the realm trumpeted from the steps—everything centered about the church. In troubled times the tower was used as a lookout and gun emplacement. The glittering cross on its dome was a sign of hope to the traveler hedged in by the hostile wilderness, weary and athirst.

The cornerstone of the present cathedral was laid in 1868. The new

structure so enclosed the old that it was possible to hold services while the work was going on. In 1872 the original dome was demolished; the church was formally re-opened on October 6, 1873.

The Cathedral: Interior

A plaque on the front of the cathedral states that the heroes of the Alamo were buried there. That, unfortunately, is an error. Not only does a preponderance of the testimony rule out the possibility of their burial in the parish church (as it was then), but it is extremely unlikely that non-Catholics (as most of the heroes were) would have been buried in a Catholic church. What is final: the bodies disinterred here and assumed to be the heroes were evidently uniformed, and the men in the Alamo had no uniforms.

The interior of the church is plain. Until fairly recent years this was the church of the Mexican parish and therefore a poor church. It is best seen on some festive occasion like High Mass on Christmas Eve, when it glows with color.

Military Plaza

On Main Plaza, with all its dramatic history, there is little to see but the cathedral. And on Military Plaza, the first permanently settled spot in Texas and, for half a century, the liveliest, there is little to see nowadays but the Spanish Governor's Palace.

The presidio, or fort, of Béxar was moved here in 1722 by the great Marqués de Aguayo from a site farther north; a grove was cut down; fortifications were made of adobe brick, and the soldiers built huts of mesquite stakes daubed with mud for their families.

The chronicle of Military Plaza is not so bloodstained as that of Main, but it was always considered an appropriate place for executions, whether official or impromptu. A pike on Military Plaza was adorned with the head of the traitor Casas, in 1811. Some of the mass executions of rebels were carried out here in 1813.

In the era of the Civil War, when the vigilance committees were busy, they had their lynching bees here, at an oak on the southeast corner, at Flores Street, or at the row of chinaberry trees in front of the priest's house, on the northwest corner. The priest finally chopped the trees down. A little later, the Silver King Saloon contributed more than its quota of gamblers and would-be gamblers, plugged with lead.

But until the advent of the Republic of Texas (1836) this was not really a plaza for the people, but a military post with streets around it and a drill ground in the center. Not until the 1840's was it finally cleared of the buildings and corrals that cluttered it. In the 1850's the courthouse, which had been in the ancient *casas reales* east of Main Plaza, was built by the architect John Fries on the ruins of another Spanish structure, and the old guardhouse of the presidio was revamped for a jail. This courthouse became known as the "Bat Cave."

Then for half a century Military Plaza was the liveliest spot in Texas. It was the municipal market, the open-air restaurant. And it naturally became the stomping ground of many questionable characters: quacks and charlatans, like the "Diamond King," who had a confederate beat a drum to drown out his victims' cries while he practiced "painless dentistry"; there were panderers, pickpockets, newspapermen, strolling musicians.

It was not only the color of the place that attracted people but also, quite literally, the flavor. The first rickety chili stands were set up on this plaza. And the legendary chili queens, beautiful, bantering, but virtuous, made their first appearance here. All night long they cooked, served, and flirted in the picturesque flare from hand-hammered tin lanterns, in the savory haze rising from clay vessels on charcoal braziers.

The chili stands were on the south side of the plaza; on the east were the fresh vegetables; eggs, poultry, and butter were sold on the north. And on the west, serried ranks of wagons stood, bulging with hay piled high, with wool or hides. Here, on the ground, sat the Mexican vendors of chili peppers and the women who sold songbirds—canaries, mockingbirds, cardinals—in wicker cages.

On the west side of the square, from 1885 to about 1890, the Fashion Theatre flourished. Built by Billy Simms after the killing of Ben Thompson and King Fisher in 1884 had put a damper on the old Jack Harris Vaudeville on Main Plaza, the Fashion was, it seems, much fancier, even though admission cost only ten cents, with a "superb orchestra, complete change of program three times a week, and perfect order maintained at all times." But

boys in knee pants were not admitted after the dancing started.

With the building of the new City Hall right in the middle of Military Plaza, the market was doomed, and an *Express* reporter in 1891 mourned the imminent eviction of the "pretty *señoritas*, huffy old mamas, lady marketeers on foot or in carriages," the donkeys, the new hay, the piles of pecans, and the stacks of honey.

But as late as 1897, although the chili queens had been banished to Alamo Plaza, the reporter tells us, the market was still lively all around the huge white stones of the new City Hall.

Activity began about 3:30 A.M., at an hour when there was no sound on the plaza but the yawns of the policemen in City Hall and the faltering steps of an occasional reveler weaving his way home after an evening of frolic on the West Side.

The wagons of the vendors converged on the plaza. Most were Mexicans, but there was a sprinkling of Belgians, Germans, French, Italians,

and even a few Anglo-Americans. There were wrinkled old ladies, and little boys in nothing but a shirt; everyone lent a hand in the struggle to find a good place and set up shop. Arguments arose, horses and wagons got snarled, curses were bawled in half a dozen tongues.

The earliest customers were caterers in white aprons from the high-toned hotels. They chose the best of everything, majestically, without stooping to haggle. Then came the cooks from the boardinghouses, anxious for bargains. At dawn the peddlers replenished their carts. About eight o'clock the housewife made her rounds. By ten it was all over.

The market was finally moved to the vicinity of Milam Square, where it is at this writing (see Chapter 9).

Military Plaza market and Fashion Theatre

Spanish Governor's Palace

Spanish Governor's Palace (west side of Military Plaza) is the only remaining example in Texas of an aristocratic early Spanish home. It is owned and operated by the city of San Antonio.

When you step into the palace you find yourself in the eighteenth century, with all the elegance of Old Spain around you. But it is the simple and subdued elegance you would expect in the provincial capital that was also a precarious outpost on the farthest rim of civilization.

When the building was restored in 1929/30, every effort was made to keep as close as possible to the original design. The furnishings also have been chosen with a proper regard for the spirit of the time and place.

The Palace: Interior

Over the entrance is the original keystone on which is carved the imperial double-headed eagle of the Hapsburg coat of arms, and the inscription "Se acabó 1749" (finished in 1749). There is also the monogram "Viva Jesus." On the wall beside the door is an ancient hitching ring.

From the entrance hall can be seen through the stone architrave of a doorway the graceful winding stairway in the rear, with its barred window framing the luxuriant foliage of the patio.

The floors of the palace are native flagstone or tile. Most of the walls are nearly three feet thick.

To the right, from the entrance hall, is the restoration of a Spanish family chapel, with rare devotional relics—saints painted on wood, images, elaborate candelabra, a carved Virgin of great age and beauty, straight-backed pine benches, and a *prie-dieu*.

The visitor steps down to the

dining room, lit by antique chandeliers and candles in sconces. The long, narrow room, its walls painted a severe white, as are all the walls in the palace, is furnished with a refectory table and benches. On one wall is a wine chest. On another is the lavabo for washing hands. Copper kettles gleam on the hearth of the high, wide-throated fireplace, and in chilly weather a wood fire burns.

The kitchen is delightfully primitive, with an open stone brazier for cooking with charcoal, and brass and copper and wooden utensils for preparing food. The graceful stair-

Spanish Governor's Palace: keystone and patio

way, seen from the front entrance, invites the visitor upstairs to the *dispensa* (pantry).

The oven is outside the kitchen door, near a small herb garden. The imagination of visitors has transmogrified a service well into a wishing well.

The patio is enticing. Pebbled walks, bordered by native flowers, shrubs, and trees, lead to a water-lily fountain. On the south is an arcade (*portales*) covered with wild Texas mustang grape. Throughout most of the year the patio is a place of light and color and welcome shade.

Entering the palace from the patio, to the right are the bedrooms and family room, which reflect the manner of living among the aristocrats of Spanish Texas. In one bedroom is a high tester bed, elaborately carved, covered in antique-gold damask cloth; the only heat here is provided by a charcoal brazier, a copper pan framed in walnut. A water pitcher and bowl are the accommodations for washing. The family room,

though, is comfortably warmed by a fireplace.

The *sala*, where social affairs were held, is a long, beautifully proportioned room with a raised corner fireplace at each end. The authentic Spanish tables, cabinets, and tooled-leather chairs will delight the connoisseur of that period. A portrait of the Marquis of Valero, viceroy of Mexico when San Antonio was founded in 1718, hangs on the wall. This, a copy of the original in Béjar, Spain, where the marquis was born, was a gift of that city to the city of San Antonio.

The whole palace has been furnished by members of the San Antonio Conservation Society with understanding not only of the elegance of eighteenth-century Spanish style but also of the rude conditions of life in Texas at that time.

Background of the Palace

There seems to be an impression that the Spanish government built the palace as an official residence for the governors of the province of Texas. This is not so. The governors were also captains, until 1773, of a dismal post on the frontier of Louisiana (Los Adaes, now actually inside Louisiana). Although the governors spent as little time at Los Adaes as they could, there was no residence for them in San Antonio, and the Barón de Ripperdá, who was officially stationed here, in 1778, had to live in the calaboose, on the east side of Main Plaza, where the Royal Houses were.

The palace was the residence of the presidial captain, who was, in the absence of the governor, the ranking representative of the king of Spain. An early reference to it is in the report of an inspection by Governor Navarrete, in 1762, which describes the house of the captain, with his office, on the west side of Military Plaza, as "built of stone or rubble and mortar, and a very strong edifice."

Next, we have the complaint of the learned Father Agustín Morfi, one of the distinguished early writers of Texas history, who was lodged in the palace when he accompanied the great Caballero de Croix, commandant general of the Interior Provinces, on a tour in 1778. The father, who did not like anything about San Antonio except the Mission San José complained that his quarters in the palace were cramped and that the sentinel in the guardhouse on the plaza kept him awake all night by blowing the bugle.

Two Spanish families have had private ownership of the palace: the Menchacas and the Pérez. Both ranked high; among them were governors, acting governors, captains of the garrison, and civil alcaldes. Enough jingling spurs and clanking swords and rustling silks have been heard in these old rooms to satisfy the most avid romantic fancy.

The property somehow came into the possession of Luís Antonio Menchaca, captain of the garrison, or presidio, in 1763, and son of an original settler (1718) of San Antonio. His own son José was acting governor for a time. The palace was inherited by another son, but he deeded it to brother José in 1803. The next year José sold it to Ignacio Pérez, whose heirs retained title until the city of San Antonio bought it in 1928. Ignacio Pérez had a daughter, Gertrudis, who married Antonio Cordero, governor of Texas from 1805 to 1807.

"As Ignacio Pérez purchased the property [writes Frederick Chabot, historian], it is very likely that the palace was occupied by his relative, the governor, and hence was called the Governor's Palace."

But Cordero was still a bachelor in the summer of 1807, says Zebulon Pike, who was royally entertained by him. It seems much more reasonable to conclude that the Governor's Palace got its name from old Ignacio's own tenure of office: he was himself governor of Texas, in the absence of an appointee who never did arrive, from mid-1815 to March, 1817. He was the absolute boss of the province, according to the bitter complaints of Antonio Martínez, last Spanish governor. In the turbulence of revolution against Spain, Ignacio Pérez was fanatically loyal to the king. He captured James Long, American filibuster who invaded Texas, in 1821 and wanted to have him shot. His rank was that of lieutenant colonel, a high one for the time and place.

In the will of the junior Pérez (his son bore the same name), drawn up in 1849, the palace is described as a dwelling. And yet, J. M. Rodríguez tells us in his memoirs, during the siege of San Antonio, in 1835, the palace was headquarters of the military commandant, which is exactly what it was to begin with.

In the 1860's the building was a public school. In later days it was a bar—some say a barrel house.

From such sordid uses, and from the danger of total demolition, it was finally rescued by the nearly simultaneous efforts of San Antonio citizens too numerous to mention. But the Conservation Society and the Historic Landmarks and Buildings Association deserve special honor.

The palace, as restored, is a fitting commemoration of the Spanish-speaking pioneers who brought the first European culture to Texas. It is also a monument to those patriotic citizens who have had the good sense to appreciate the treasures of the past and the good taste to restore them faithfully.

Around the Plaza

Plaza de las Islas (Main Plaza) was the center of the town of San Fernando. On the west side is San Fernando Cathedral. In the middle is a variable water fountain and activity center that compares with those in Paris and Madrid. The plaza and the north side were at the center of the Battle of Béxar in 1835.

On the south side of the Plaza at Commerce Street was the location of the Músquiz house. The survivors of the 1836 Alamo battle were brought here to meet General Santa Anna and receive his munificent gift of a blanket and two dollars. On the same block and near Market Street was the site of the Council House Fight. In 1840 twelve Comanche chiefs were invited to meet, bring their captives, and arrange an exchange. The chiefs brought only one little girl, and in the ensuing melee all the chiefs were slain.

Old Ursuline Convent

The architecture of the old Ursuline Academy and Convent (300 Augusta) has been carefully preserved, making it virtually the only remaining example of French design in the city. The deed for the Ursuline property was granted to Bishop Jean Mary Odin in 1848 to establish the first girls' school in San Antonio. After making the harrowing jour-

Old Ursuline Convent

ney from Galveston, the small but brave group of nuns opened their school within six weeks of arrival. When the school moved to the north side of town in 1965, the property was bought by the Conservation Society and then sold to the Southwest Craft Center. Today the center runs a nationally recognized school offering courses and workshops in many areas of the arts.

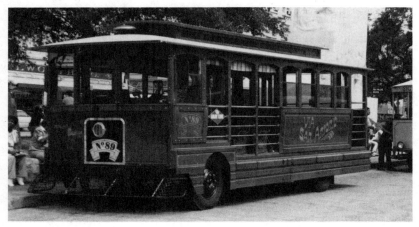

Trolley buses by the Alamo Cenotaph

First National Bank

On Commerce Street between Main Plaza and Alamo Street, there are many interesting old buildings. On the north side is the old First National Bank site (No. 239), built in 1886 by George W. Brackenridge. Its character has been carefully preserved, with the decorations in the style of the 1880's. It is now private offices.

In 1908 the old, large buildings on the south side were moved back or the building fronts were sliced off to make the street 65 feet wide.

Getting Around in San Antonio

Any city with a lot of tourist attractions has transportation problems. The places are too far apart to walk to, waiting for regular bus transportation is too time consuming, and taxis can be expensive. As a solution, San Antonio presents these picturesque trolley buses. They travel in several circular routes between different attractions. One of the most popular is from the Alamo to El Mercado and back.

South of the Plazas

Flores, Main, and Dwyer streets lead south from the plazas to an area where historic structures have gone down the drain.

This section of San Antonio is on the opposite side of the river from the King William area but has been touched by the "progress" of industry and bureaucracy.

Some of the missing history includes:

The *Vance House*, a large white house with columns where every historic figure of the time seemed to have stopped and slept.

The old *Barrera House*, the home of a leading San Antonio family from the arrival of the Canary Islanders to the present.

The *Thomas Jefferson Devine House*, a gothic U-shaped building with a porch that ran around the outside. It was famous for its tropical gardens.

The *François Guilbeau House*, built in 1847 and destroyed in 1949.

Guilbeau received a medal from the French government because, when the grapevines in France were suffering from a disease, he sent over some wild Texas mustang grape roots. They were grafted to the delicate French grape stock and the wine industry was saved. According to reports, the wine was never the same again.

The *United States Arsenal*, established in 1858. Until that time all the army supplies, ammunition, and weapons were stored in the Alamo. Upon completion of the Arsenal all the firearms and ammunition were transferred to the new facility.

The Arsenal was taken over and used by the Confederates and later served its part in the winning of the West. In 1949 its use as an arsenal was discontinued, but it housed government offices for a time.

The Commander's House has been restored and the area around it turned into a park. The San Antonio Junior Forum has taken it over and operates a senior citizens' craft center and hot-meal service.

7

Tour of the Missions

On November 10, 1978, the Congress and president of the United States authorized San Antonio Missions National Historical Park, which will encompass the four missions and the area in between. The churches and their members are not controlled or aided by the park contracts.

Even though not in charge of it, the National Park Service has outlined and recommends a tour of the missions starting from the Alamo. By following the map (p. xix), one eventually reaches the parkway and the four missions and the dam.

The first mission in San Antonio later became the Alamo, and still later it was sold by the Church in 1883. In 1905 the remaining historic property became the property of the State of Texas but was turned over to the Daughters of the Republic of Texas to operate and maintain without charge.

This simplified, but confused, explanation gives some idea why the federal government avoided including the Alamo when it set up the Missions National Historical Park.

The four remaining missions are approximately a progressive two miles apart. The National Park Service is performing a miracle connecting these buildings and sites together. It is bringing the history up to date from every available source and doing everything possible to display the missions graphically.

Open: daily, 9:00 A.M. to 6:00 P.M., DST; 8:00 A.M. to 5:00 P.M., CST. Admission: free.

Mission Concepción

Mission Concepción (*Nuestra Señora de la Purísima Concepción de Acuña*) is the oldest unrestored church in the United States that has remained intact and is still in use as a church. It is the most beautifully proportioned of the mission churches. But nothing is left of the defensive wall and outer buildings.

The twin towers, handsome dome, and exquisitely carved doorway still satisfy the beholder, although the glowing color that once dazzled the Indians has faded away since 1890, when Corner described it as quite distinct.

Above the door, in delicate lettering, is this quatrain:

A Su Patrona Y Princessa
Con Estas Armas Atiende
Esta Mission, Y Defiende
El Punto De Su Pureza

Which means, translated, "This Mission serves with these arms its Patroness and Princess and defends the doctrine of her purity." The doctrine is, of course, that of the Immaculate Conception. The "arms" are three seals above the door: Franciscan emblems. Above these is the knotted scourge of the Franciscan Order and the date 1754.

On entering the church, to the right is the baptistry; carved on the original stone font is a figure with outstretched arms. Above it is a faded fresco of the Crucifixion. On the opposite side, the belfry, once a chapel to St. Michael, shows origi-

Mission Concepción

nal designs, and many, many carved initials of visitors.

The nave of the church is famous for its acoustics, which are inevitably compared with those of the Mormon Tabernacle in Salt Lake City.

In the sacristy, to the right, is the original stone lavatory. Next is a hall, from which a graceful stone stairway rises to the "infirmary." The doubt in this case, and in the other cases where the names given to rooms in this mission are set in quotation marks, is raised because the names seem to have been given by someone long on fancy and short on fact. Spanish documents describing this mission say nothing about an infirmary. And yet, this charming upstairs room has an aperture connecting it with the sanctuary, for the purpose, it is said, of enabling the sick to hear services. A window of lovely design looks out to the east.

On the ground floor again, an arched doorway leads to a court. A modern stairway connects with the original stone steps to the tower.

To the west of this court are vestiges of a hall with a vaulted roof. This, it is claimed, was the "refectory," or dining hall of the friars. The theory is probably derived from the proximity of the "kitchen," a small room to the right, where a remnant of chimney and an old floor have been preserved. It should be pointed out, before we go farther, that the convent of Concepción was used as a dwelling for many years after the church was reopened in 1887, and perhaps for many years earlier. No careful study has been made, it seems, to determine just which features of the convent were original and which were added by generations of tenants.

An obvious error is the statement that the roof of the "refectory" was destroyed during the Battle of Concepción, October 27, 1835. The fight was a good quarter of a mile away, in a bend of the river now almost obliterated, between Hicks Avenue, Mission Road, and East Mitchell Street, and there was no reason why a cannon should have been aimed in this direction.

From the ruined hall a door opens into the library, another charming room, aptly named, as there are flagstone slabs in the wall for shelves. The arched ceiling is limned about with colored lines of decoration still plain, and looking down from its center is the All-Seeing Eye of God, designed, no doubt, to keep the friars' minds on their sacred studies.

To the right is the "living room"; two apertures here are puzzling. The hole in the ceiling is said to be for the purpose of letting in light (and rain?); the other is explained as a vent for smoke.

To the right again is the "store room," where "original timbers on which meat was hung to dry" are pointed out. Meat was hung to dry outdoors. If any meat was hung here, it was probably hung by the

United States Army, which occupied the mission in 1849. The timber seems to be solidly set in the walls.

On the west, the three remaining arches of the convent's cloister open on a patio with a well. Early drawings show fragmentary walls and arches on the southwest, where a room was restored in 1957. Here, perhaps, were the cells of the friars; some were described in 1756 as already in ruins.

Background of Concepción

For several years during the 1720's a tribe of Indians belonging to the Tonkawan group camped on the exact site of Concepción. They had asked for a mission. The Spaniards, who considered them already in the bag, gave them a name, Mission San Francisco Xavier de Nájera (for a saint and a viceroy), and nothing else. Discouraged, the Indians joined their kinsmen at San Antonio de Valero (the Alamo).

In 1731 the Mission of Our Lady of the Immaculate Conception was moved to this spot (the tag "of Acuña" being added in honor of the viceroy) from East Texas, where it had been founded in 1716. It was moved because nearly all the Indians there had died of the white man's diseases. After it was moved, and fresh tribes of Indians were converted, they, too, nearly all died of the same diseases. They also suffered "almost daily" attacks from the hostile Apaches, who were especially fond of taking them by surprise while they worked in the fields and pastures. Of 792 Indians that had been baptized in 1762, 588 had been buried; there were then 207 living at the mission. In 1783 there were 77; in 1792, 53; in 1805, 41. In 1819 there were not any.

The church took about twenty years to build. It has stood intact since December 8, 1755, when it was dedicated with great ceremony, on the Day of the Immaculate Conception. Everybody who was anybody was there.

The light porous limestone used in building this church (and also, we are told, San José and the Alamo Church) was quarried a few yards from it, just across Mission Road, where shallow pits only recently filled in are barely discernible in the yard of the orphanage. The façade was originally covered with brilliant quatrefoils and squares of red, blue, orange, and yellow. The colors—except the blue, which was taken from the native wild indigo—were made by pulverizing field stones. Goat's milk was added to make the paint adhere.

It was entirely abandoned as a church for three-quarters of a century, and as early as 1819. In the late 1840's, United States troops were stationed there. It was later used as a cattle pen. Not until 1887 was it reopened and dedicated to Our Lady of Lourdes.

Mission San José

Mission San José (*San José de San Miguel de Aguayo*), a National Historic Site, is one of those rare triumphs of the human spirit which inspire awe in even the dullest observer.

It is not merely the magnificence of the architecture that imposes: you feel the grandeur of spirit in the whole plan.

San José Compound

The present entrance to San José, near the southwest corner of the compound, is on the site of an old one. In 1778, said Father Morfi, there was an entrance at each corner, although the one on the west, near the granary, was "the only one that was open every day." It is also the one that, elaborately restored in the 1930's, was used as the entrance until 1955.

The entire outer wall of the compound, including the Indian houses along it, was restored on the original foundations. Most of the stone had been carted off about 1824.

Other foundations, unrestored, are visible in the great open plaza of the mission, especially toward the northeast. These are vestiges of buildings that existed in the earlier phases of the compound, which was, apparently, once smaller and more compact than it is today. It seems there was a radical revision of the ground plan between 1758, when Governor Jacinto Barrios described it in a report, and 1768, when Father Gaspar Solís and Governor Hugo Oconor laid the cornerstone of the present church.

In 1758, Governor Barrios found 281 Indians living in eighty-four stone houses in the form of "barracks" (the governor was a military man), with flat roofs, battlements, and merlons, arranged in four squares, having interior patios with ovens and water ditches in them,

San José: adobe and stone oven

133

San José: granary, flying buttresses

and closed in "for the convenience of the Indian women." Four small plazas were formed by the "barracks" (he meant the Indian apartments, as there were no soldiers at San José), carpenter shop, granary, and workshop—all of these, it seems, in buildings that were razed before 1768. There was a mill, where sugar loaf and molasses were made, and the convent and church, "all arranged with such beautiful symmetry that it seemed a miracle of Providence, for the total cost was only 150 pesos, the stipend of a single minister."

The governor describes a large plaza between the "Royal Houses" (he meant the offices of the mission) and the church, which he said had a "nave and transept" spacious enough for two hundred persons, and a "well-proportioned tower with a set of bells." This was not the present church. Where was it, then? There can be no doubt: it was the building later made into a granary, and it still stands. As early as 1749, Father Ciprián mentions the church with a capacity of "two thousand." We have, then, at the northwest corner of the compound, past the gate on the west, the oldest building to remain intact in all Texas, older than the Concepción church, finished in 1755, and older than the Spanish Governor's Palace, which was finished in 1749, when the granary (then the church) was evidently not new.

The large plaza described by the governor was the space we see now between the granary and the present church, which was built on the site of the old offices, the "Royal Houses," after 1768, when its cornerstone was laid.

The Granary, San José

The first thing you notice about the granary is the array of flying buttresses. These were added when the function of the building was changed, to offset the stress of the great stacks of corn.

San José: arches of the convent

San José: granary interior

The second thing you notice is the churchlike aspect of the structure. The walls of the south nave are higher; the tower was undoubtedly at this end; perhaps it rose from the ground. An expert says the roof was at first flat. That there was a transept, completing the form of the cross, is clear to any eye. An inventory of San José made in 1823, with a view to selling the rock of the walls and vacant buildings, refers, even at that late date, to the granary as "the room known as a church."

The buildings along the north wall between the granary and the exit to the mill were (it appears from the inventory made in 1794 and from other descriptions) the weaving shop and the carpenter shop of the Indians. Farther east were Indian houses against the wall, as on the other sides of the great square.

San José Mill

Through a narrow gap in the north wall, you can reach the exterior yard of the mission. The irrigation ditch, once the conduit of water for many miles from a dam then on the river just south of Mission Concepción, can be seen here, dry and partly filled in. Note the ancient steps.

The old mill, elaborately restored on its foundations, conserves the vaulted chamber, the flagstone floor, and four steps leading up. It also displays a modern reconstruction, built according to indications in the ruins, of a primitive device known as a "Norse" mill, although the prototype was found also, experts say, among the Romans of antiquity.

Ingenious though the reconstruction is, probably the mission never had any use for a gristmill. The grinding of corn was done by the female hand in a metate. It seems likely that this was the sugar mill referred to by Governor Barrios (above).

The fall of the ditch to the fields below can be clearly seen here. There are also vats, which were evidently used in tanning.

Theater at San José

San José Mission has carried on the association of the Catholic church and the theater from medieval times. An amphitheater was laid out in the 1930's. In 1958 it was rebuilt and turned into a Texas State Historical Theatre, but very little activity followed. Plans have been put forth several times for other uses of the area.

Meanwhile, San José Church continues the theatrical tradition. It has become famous for its outstanding Mariachi masses. *Las Posadas*, described in Chapter 15, is performed in December and is a moving, unusual experience. From time to time special events are scheduled in the mission's awesome patio.

San José Church

Father Morfi, in 1778, thought the ornamentation on the famous façade of San José Church was "trifling." No one has thought so since. But even he admired the artistry of the stone carving and was amazed to find work of this quality in a place so remote, done by a resident of the mission. The workman is supposed to have been one Pedro Huizar, who is likewise given credit for the famous "Rose Window," mentioned below.

At a short distance, the doorway gives the viewer a sense of perfect symmetry, though there is but slight formal symmetry of pattern. Instead, there is the most delicate and subtle balance of forms.

There have been differences of opinion between ecclesiastical authorities regarding the identity of the sculptured saints. Certainly the figure above the window is St. Joseph (San José), patron of the

San José: rose window

mission; once mutilated, it has been restored. Below it is the Virgin of Guadalupe, patroness of Mexico, unharmed. The statues to the right and left of St. Joseph are identified as St. Dominic and St. Francis of Assisi (holding a skull); these are the originals. The statues below, beside the door, are St. Joachim and St. Anne (holding a child); these were both mutilated and have been restored.

The carved cedar doors are copies (made from photographs) of the originals, which were stolen between 1880 and 1890, some say by a railroad magnate, others say by a noted architect.

The interior of the church is plain.

The sacristy (also called the baptistry), to the right, is an exquisite piece of architecture. It was described by Father López in 1785 as "the most beautiful room this side of Saltillo." The ornamentation here, the capitals of the pillars and the conch shells of the recesses, is restrained and particularly graceful. It "invited devotion," said Father Morfi.

The original carved doors open on to the convent walk. The original design around the doorway has been reinforced. Around the corner to the right is the celebrated Rose Window, opening from the sacristy.

The Rose Window, which architects insist is not a real "rose" window at all, has been celebrated often and in many more or less literary styles. It is better simply to look at it than to read about it. Here again, a little way off, we have the illusion of perfect symmetry. But a closer view brings out an exuberance of detail even more delicately varied than that on the portal of the church.

There is no reason to doubt that the window is the creation of Pedro Huizar. But the well-worn legend—that he was a Spaniard who did not chase the available nymphs but pined for his loved one across the seas, and, when he learned that she had broken her troth and wed another, took vows of celibacy, and kept right on pining and sculpturing until released by a merciful death—does not jibe with the known facts. Pedro Huizar was born in Aguascalientes, Mexico, in 1740. In 1778 he was married to a woman named María and living at San José, for he had a child baptized there. He was known as a carpenter and then as a surveyor, married a second time, and his children were granted a part of the San José property as reward for his services. There were, at last count, at least eighteen heads of families in San Antonio named Huizar, all, apparently, direct descendants of Pedro. So much for the vows of celibacy.

The stairway to the seventy-five-foot tower of the church is notable for its ancient steps of solid hewn oak. The story in a romantic novel that a cannon was once hauled up these stairs is ridiculous, of course. The Apaches seem to have made an unsuccessful attack on San José in 1749; there never was a siege.

San José Convent

Returning to the convent walk, and following it east, we find ourselves in the arabesque half-shadows of the cloisters. The original arches are on two stories. Apparently this part of the mission is, along with the granary, the oldest. It is described as two-storied and extensive in Father Ciprián's report of 1749.

The occasional Gothic arches formed with red brick were made by the Benedictines from Pennsylvania who lived in the mission for eight years after 1859. The oven on the east is also attributed to them. The gate can be reached by way of the east walk.

Background of San José

San José was an oasis of civilization in a barbarous wilderness. It was an outpost of urbanity set down in the midst of a land inhabited by the blood-thirsty Apaches, who ate human flesh, and a number of other tribes less ferocious but nonetheless half-starved and in constant fear for their lives.

To these wretches the fathers from Zacatecas brought security, peace, the comfort of a full stomach, the consolation of religion, and no little knowledge of the arts.

San José was founded by Fray Antonio Margil de Jesús, saintliest of all the Franciscan missionaries, in February, 1720.

That the Indians at San José were treated with charity is shown by the report made by the governor of Texas in 1758: "The best proof of their contentment is that there have been no fugitives, nor are there any chains or stocks in this Mission." The Indians elected their own officers, in democratic style. They had their own guards who made the rounds at night and their own judges who administered justice "without bloodshed."

That the Indians were secure in their mission is shown by an earlier report. In 1749, San José was described by Father Ciprián as "a veritable fortress. Although greatly exposed because of its location to attack by the Apaches, who have become so daring that they threaten the Presidio of San Antonio even in the daytime, they have never bothered the Mission. Whenever they have attacked the Mission Indians it has been out in the open country."

That the friars did a thorough job of civilizing is shown by all reports.

The Indians owned a considerable stock of cattle for beef, had large herds of sheep and goats for wool, and raised cotton, corn, sugar cane, and all kinds of vegetables and fruits, including peaches that weighed "about a pound."

They wove their own cloth and blankets; they even had a tailor shop.

But their life was not all work. They had a fine choir, which sang so beautifully it was "a delight to hear it." Nor were they forced to lead a puritanical life. Most of them, we are told, could play some musical instrument—the guitar, the violin, or the harp. "Both men and women," wrote Father Solís in 1768, "can sing and dance just like the Spaniards, and they do so, perhaps, with even more beauty and grace."

He sums up: "This Mission is so pretty and in such a flourishing condition, both materially and spiritually, I cannot find words with which to express its beauty. These Indians are so polite, so well mannered, and so refined, one might imagine that they had been civilized and living at the Mission a long time."

The present church was begun in 1768 and finished in 1777. After that, its history, until recent years, became simply a matter of continuous destruction and decay.

The missions at San Antonio were partly secularized in 1793, but not until 1824 was the process completed—the lands parceled out to individuals and the padre sent home to his college in Zacatecas.

A terrific storm in 1868 crashed in the church dome and roof. For more than sixty years after, only the adjoining sacristy could be used for services.

Research Library

The Old Spanish Missions Historical Research Library was located at San José Mission for years. It is now in the Library at Our Lady of the Lake University.

The purpose of the Missions Research Library is to promote interest in and appreciation of the Spanish Colonial period of Texas history in general and the history of the Fran-

ciscan missions in particular. In 1968, copies of the original documents concerning Fray Antonio Margil, other Franciscan missionaries, and the Texas missions began to be acquired for use by administrators of the mission sites. Since the expanding of the collection, and the incorporation of the library in 1974, historical information has also been supplied to professors, students, and various institutions.

Additions to the extensive collection of microfilms, photographs of maps, and other materials are continually being made from sources in Mexico as well as major archives of Spain and other European countries. Numerous private collections have also been copied. Library personnel are available for contract research. Because nearly all of the materials are in the Spanish language, the research library in its translation center constantly transcribes and translates documents so as to disseminate accurate information to the public.

Restoration of San José

A postcard sold to tourists about 1890 showed the hollow shell of San José: roofless, tumbled walls, with brush growing in the nave of the church and cactus on the tower. Printed on the reverse was this lugubrious comment: "The Mission, between the elements and the festive vandal, will soon be no more."

By that time the great doors of the front entrance had already disappeared. The statuary of the façade was mutilated—some of the figures had been used for target practice, it seems, or lassoed from their pedestals by roistering cowboys.

Only a short time ago, well within the memory of many who are living today, this process of destruction was still going on, and any tourist could buy a "souvenir" of the mission—some trifling piece of the original structure—for a very moderate price.

What a fate for a place which, two hundred years ago, was de-

Mission San Francisco de la Espada

scribed as an ideal community, buzzing with cheerful life!

Anyone who sees San José for the first time as it looks today will find it hard to believe that only a few years ago it was a dismal ruin, covered with brush. The saving of San José, the slow, painstaking task of bringing it back to life, has been achieved through the tireless efforts of a good many people, working together and separately, but all devoted to the same ideal.

In the 1920's the steps of the spiral stairway were found scattered about and replaced. Cracks in the façade and chapel (or sacristy) were repaired.

An important date in the history of the mission is 1924, when the San Antonio Conservation Society was founded—a group of people "drawn and held together and inspired by an interest in the preservation of the Missions," to quote their historian. From the beginning they had plans for San José.

In 1930 the society bought the

granary, with its curious flying buttresses, guarding the gateway to the mission.

By 1933 the society had acquired six acres of land and had invested in this and in the granary about $12,000. "Further reconstruction required more money, but the depression prowled."

The society found, however, that, if it would furnish materials for the restoration of the granary, the federal government would supply the unemployed labor that was "on relief" at the time.

"The complete restoration of the granary and the landscaping of the ground around it for some years occupied the entire attention of the Conservation Society."

In 1930 the tower of the church fell and was immediately rebuilt by the Catholic diocese of San Antonio.

In 1934 the restoration of the whole church, which had neither roof nor dome, was undertaken, and in April, 1937, it was opened with jubilant ceremony. Now, for the first time in nearly one hundred years, it became again a living, functioning church, where people came to pray and to get married. Still, many things, such as an altar, were lacking.

Another important date in the history of San José is 1941. In that year it was officially named a National Historic Site and so came under the supervision of the National Park Service. Not the slightest change can be made in any part of the area without the permission of the experts attached to this branch of the government.

In 1949 the statues on the façade, which had been cruelly mutilated by vandals many years ago, were restored. A liturgical altar of hand-carved stone was installed, as were a hand-carved walnut tabernacle, a crucifix, and candlesticks.

The entire structure of the church was found to be in danger. It has been strengthened in every part, including the famous Rose Window, which was rejointed and made waterproof.

All the San José Mission property, except the church, came under the supervision of the State Parks Board in 1950. With the congressional act in 1978 setting up the San Antonio Missions National Historical Park, the property (except the church) was transferred to the federal government.

The Espada Dam

The Espada Dam is a mile north of Mission San Francisco de la Espada and was built by the early Spaniards as the start of the irrigation ditch for the mission.

The San Antonio Conservation Society, in one of its munificent public gestures, acquired a grove of pecan trees on the east side of the dam. This area has become part of the Missions National Historical Park.

The dam across the river was

Espada Aqueduct

built some time between 1731, when Mission San Francisco de la Espada was founded, and 1745, when the irrigation ditch had already reached the compound. It has stood against the floods all these years, with only a bit of patching to bolster it now and then. It is said by experts to be a remarkable engineering feat, as it is "curved the wrong way." There is a tradition that the mortar was mixed with goat's milk (the casein of those days), to make it waterproof, and then allowed to dry slowly, stone by stone.

Immediately below the dam, on the west bank, issues the Mission Espada ditch, running through a corner of Mission Burial Park. It has never ceased to flow, so far as it is known, for any length of time.

The Espada Aqueduct

The Espada Aqueduct (Espada Road) is about a mile south of the dam.

A short distance past the beginning of Espada Road, and visible to the left, is the only Spanish aqueduct in the United States. Its two spans over Piedras Creek are lovely and well worth stopping to see. It is the property of the San Antonio Conservation Society. The aqueduct, like the dam, dates from 1731 to 1745.

Mission San Francisco de la Espada

Mission San Francisco de la Espada (end of Espada Road) was "moved" from East Texas and founded here on March 5, 1731. It changed its name in the process of moving. Why it is called "St. Francis of the Sword" here, when it was established as plain "San Francisco" in East Texas is a mystery. While the tag end of all the other missions' names has been dropped, in this case the principal name was dropped a century and more ago, and the mission has long been known simply as "Espada."

The tag "of the Sword" is in the Spanish title to the grant, written on the day (March 5, 1731) the mission was founded here, and so it cannot refer to any architectural feature. One explanation, that it refers to a vision St. Francis had of a sword in the sky, seems far-fetched. The very idea of associating an instrument of warfare with the meekest and gentlest of saints continues to baffle and to horrify those who know his story. But is it not possible that the mission was named for an image, the image that still is found in the chapel? It can hold a cross in one hand, a sword in the other. Perhaps the Indians wanted a saint with a sword! Compare the belligerent image at the sister mission, San Juan Capistrano.

The church at Espada was not a "chapel for monks," as it has been

Espada Aqueduct

Espada: interior of chapel

146

called, but a church for Indians. We will call it a chapel, however, because it is small and to distinguish it from the larger, later church, which is now nothing more than an outline of foundations, to the southeast of the chapel. Like most of the ruined walls of the compound, it has been reinforced.

The chapel was one of the first in the five San Antonio missions to be built of stone, and it was one of the first to collapse. It was under construction in 1745, and in 1756 it was in use and had a roof of carved wood. By 1758, apparently, the roof had fallen in. By 1778, said Father Morfi, the chapel was in ruins; a new church was going up, which, in 1785, was described as "superior." It was probably demolished in the nineteenth century to get building materials.

The old chapel was not rebuilt until about 1868. Only the front and back walls remained. It has been noted that the two lower stones of the Moresque door, which give it character, are upside down. This inspired mistake was, no doubt, the fault, or whim, of the Indians. The restoration was done by Father François Bouchu, resident priest for forty years, with his own hands. He made the walls only half as thick as the original foundations.

The plain wooden cross beside the chapel door has stood there a long time, perhaps since about 1870. It was placed there by order of Father Bouchu. The congregation had carried it about the plaza, praying for rain, and suddenly rain fell in torrents. The cross was placed to remind the faithful of the power of prayer.

The interior of the chapel glows with the presence of three fine old images. Most remarkable is the figure of St. Francis, above the altar. He has a cross in his hand, one foot on a globe. Tradition says he once had a sword in the other hand. This is surely the same image that was owned by Espada in 1745. There was also an image of La Dolorosa; whether it was the same Mary that is seen here now is a question. There is now also a Christ. All three are of wood, excellently carved, with the patina of age.

A two-story residence for priests was south of the chapel. This was the stone building described in 1745 by an inspecting friar: "The ministers live in two upstairs cells and have two offices downstairs." In 1958 the two upper cells were demolished, the lower ones were restored, and an arcade was built between the residence and the chapel.

The original (?) entrance to the compound, in the center of the north wall, was hideously restored in the 1930's. A corresponding gateway is in the south wall.

Stephen F. Austin, camped here with his buckskin army in October, 1835, impatiently awaited news from James Bowie, who (as Austin did not know) was fighting the Battle of Concepción.

Perhaps the most interesting feature of the Espada is the bastion, or

Espada bell tower

fortified tower, on the southeast corner, the only one left intact in all the missions. It has a vaulted roof; its walls of curiously assorted rocks are one yard thick. There are large holes for the muzzles of cannon down below and small holes for the muskets up above. At times the southeast corner, with the bastion and adjoining rooms made into a small museum, has been open to the public. At times it has been closed. Better inquire.

There are connoisseurs of the Spanish period in Texas who prefer the smallest and most remote of the missions, Espada and San Juan Capistrano, to any of the others. Concepción is justly celebrated as the best preserved of the churches. But where are its Indian houses, granaries, outlying walls? San José is by far the most magnificent, and it has been lavishly restored. San Juan and Espada are in ruins. But people live here. And, what is more, with all the inevitable mutations and admixtures, they are descendants of the same people, Indians and Spaniards, who lived here more than two centuries ago. There has been continuous flow of life all that time, as there has been continuous flow of water, from the dams on the river, down the ditches, to the gardens, giving life to the green patches strung like emeralds through the gray brush, giving life to the people whose forebears were nourished by that same flow.

The two missions were moved together from East Texas in 1731, and they have remained sister missions ever since. Being farthest from the town, they were the most exposed to hostile Indians, who dared to attack them even when they were behind walls.

In 1760, Father Bartolomé García, at Espada, produced a guide, printed in Mexico, to aid priests in confessing Indians who spoke the Coahuiltecan tongue. It affords knowledge of that tongue and, what is more intriguing, data on the habits of the Indians, who ate the narcotic buds of the cactus peyotl, drank liquor made of the intoxicant Texas mountain-laurel bean, and did a number of things that would interest the Kinsey Institute.

Mission San Juan Capistrano

Mission San Juan Capistrano has a chapel that is larger than the one at Espada. But it shows a kinship of design (each has a pierced belfry for three bells); they are of the same age. At both missions the chapel in use is older than the church in ruins. In 1745 there was no stone church at San Juan; but in 1756 there was one, and this present chapel was it. In 1785 the large new church opposite, across the plaza, had not been finished. The missions were already in full decadence; it was never finished and is now a mass of ruins. The present chapel was praised for its graceful proportions by Father Morfi in 1778. It was in use all dur-

Espada gate decoration

149

Mission San Juan Capistrano

ing the nineteenth century, as old paintings attest. In 1890, according to William Corner's *San Antonio de Bexar*, there was no roof, but there were still murals showing musicians playing various instruments. Nothing, alas, remains of these. A new roof was put on the chapel in 1910.

The images, as at Espada, are fascinating. There is a badly damaged Christ, a Virgin, and, on the altar, a most curious rococo St. John of Capistrano in a suit of armor, his foot on the neck of a turbaned Turk. St. John led a crusade that hurled the Mussulman back from the gates of Belgrade in 1456. The Virgin has movable arms, like the image described as being at Concepción in 1745. It is not surprising that an image should migrate from an abandoned church to one in use.

The Christ and the Virgin are extremely ancient, for they are made of cornstalk pith, a process perfected by the Indians of central Mexico before the Conquest and lost soon thereafter.

The noble arches at the southwest corner of the compound are the remains of the convent. The long building between it and the chapel was once the granary.

The people of Berg's Mill, the village near San Juan, have kept up the beautiful tradition of the cockfight, even though the sport has long been outlawed. No one is going to see any of it uninvited.

Two Spanish Ranch Houses

Quite apart from the tour of the missions, but in the general area, are two historic houses.

At 407 East Glenn, near Probandt, is a private fenced-off home built before 1810. It originally was a ranch house centered between San Pedro and Concepción creeks and between the town tract on the north and the lands of Mission San José on the south. In the 1870's, Roy Bean, later Judge Bean, "Law West of the Pecos,"

had a dairy here. When the customers found minnows in the milk, he complained that his cows kept lapping them up from the river.

On Mission Trail at Yellowstone (No. 257) is the Yturri-Edmunds home and mill. It was built by the Yturri family in the 1820's, on land formerly belonging to Mission Concepción. The property now belongs to the San Antonio Conservation Society. The mill has been restored, the house and its furnishings are interesting, and light meals are sometimes served. Check with the Conservation Society as to availability.

8

The German Town

Along King William and Washington Streets

Old houses keep the atmosphere of the 1870's and 1880's.

Steves Homestead

(509 King William Street)
A small but select museum of Victorian antiques.
Open: daily, 10:00 A.M. to 12:00 M., 1:00 P.M. to 5:00 P.M.
Admission: adults, $2.00, children under twelve, free.

Droves of Germans came to Texas toward the end of the Republic (1845). Still more came later. They settled in colonies, mainly to the north of San Antonio. Many were intellectuals, fugitives from the petty tyrants of the Fatherland, and they did not find the privations of backwoods life appealing. They preferred to hear their Beethoven and Mozart in more civilized surroundings. They gravitated, as a matter of course, to San Antonio and here became powerful enough to give their firm impress to the city, and especially to that part east of the San Antonio River.

The Germans built their homes along the Alamo Ditch, the Acequia Madre, all the way from the point where it issued, near the head of the river, to the point below King William Street where it flowed back in. They surrounded entirely the Irish Flat, which was there first.

The always perceptive Frederick Law Olmsted, who rode into San

Steves Homestead

153

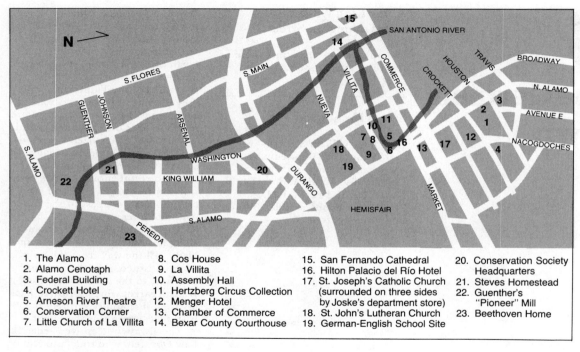

N →

SAN ANTONIO RIVER

S. FLORES
JOHNSON
GUENTHER
S. MAIN
ARSENAL
NUEVA
VILLITA
COMMERCE
CROCKETT
HOUSTON
TRAVIS
BROADWAY
N. ALAMO
AVENUE E
NACOGDOCHES
MARKET
WASHINGTON
KING WILLIAM
S. ALAMO
DURANGO
S. ALAMO
PEREIDA
HEMISFAIR

15
14
10 11
7 8 5
18 9 6 16 13 17 12 4
19
20
21
22
23
3
2 1

1. The Alamo
2. Alamo Cenotaph
3. Federal Building
4. Crockett Hotel
5. Arneson River Theatre
6. Conservation Corner
7. Little Church of La Villita
8. Cos House
9. La Villita
10. Assembly Hall
11. Hertzberg Circus Collection
12. Menger Hotel
13. Chamber of Commerce
14. Bexar County Courthouse
15. San Fernando Cathedral
16. Hilton Palacio del Río Hotel
17. St. Joseph's Catholic Church
    (surrounded on three sides
    by Joske's department store)
18. St. John's Lutheran Church
19. German-English School Site
20. Conservation Society
    Headquarters
21. Steves Homestead
22. Guenther's
    "Pioneer" Mill
23. Beethoven Home

Map 7. *The German Town*

Turner-Halle (now part of Menger Hotel), about 1872

Antonio from Austin on horseback in 1854, remarked (in *A Journey through Texas*): "The singularly composite character of the town is palpable at the entrance. For five minutes the houses were evidently German, of fresh square-cut blocks of creamy white limestone, mostly of a single story and humble proportions, but neat, and thoroughly roofed and finished. Some were furnished with the luxury of little bow-windows or balconies."

The Irish Flat

The Irish came first, as sutlers and teamsters with the United States Army about 1846, and settled on the vacant land nearest the Alamo, which became the quartermaster's depot. They were just a few families. The Irish Flat was small: from Alamo Plaza north to Sixth Street, and from Broadway east to the Alamo Ditch. This abundant stream nourished the tall pecan trees and other growing things and gave the Flat the look of a somewhat neglected garden village of old Europe.

But now the cottages of soft chalkstone, with green shutters nearly to the ground and broad, stacked chimneys, the shady big pecan trees, the huisaches, the bright-blooming cosmos and crape myrtle have disappeared almost entirely.

The people who lived in those houses have gone elsewhere.

If you want to see how the Irish Flat looked as late as 1914, there is the fine painting with that name by José Arpa in the Witte Museum.

Alamo Plaza

For many years after the massacre at the Alamo a miasma of death and decay seemed to hang over the ruins. The only buildings in the neighborhood were flat-roofed adobes with prickly pear growing on top of them in a long row following the west line of the old mission. No effort was made to clean up the debris in the church until 1849, after the United States Army had moved in, and then a number of skeletons were found in the rubble.

It was the Germans who gave the plaza a more respectable appearance, with the opening of the Menger Hotel in 1859.

Just north of the Menger, on the plaza, the Germans built their first Turner-Halle (athletic club). When the Menger expanded, in 1875, and incorporated the club building, a larger one was built on the southeast corner of Houston Street and St. Mary's. It was the principal theater of the city, and in 1901 the large, imposing Turner Hall which still stands on the corner of East Houston Street and Nacogdoches was built. But this extremely popular and active club went to pot during the hysteria of the First World War and is no more. The *Turnverein* furnished the first volunteer firemen in San

Antonio, young men who worked hard, after hours, learning to form pyramids (standing on shoulders) and other gymnastic feats, and it never occurred to them to ask pay for their services.

In 1876, Alamo Plaza, a mudhole at the time, was the scene of a demonstration by a pair of barbed-wire salesmen for the benefit of some cattlemen. Posts were put up and wire strung to make a good-sized corral. The skeptical cowboys joshed the salesmen as they went about their preparations. Then a bunch of steers were driven into the corral. To the astonishment of the onlookers, who expected to see them tear the fence down, or jump it, the wire held; the steers stayed put.

A little later this dismal picture of the plaza appeared in the *Express*: "In the evening a few Mexican lunch tables assemble around the dry fountain that keeps the lone telegraph pole company near the centre of the plaza."

But in 1882 the modern business building known as the "Crockett Block" enhanced the plaza; in 1886 the Grand Opera House was built on the north corner of Crockett Street, and its upper rooms were occupied by the ultrasmart San Antonio Club; about 1890 the really beautiful planting of a park, with roses and palms, by Anton Friedrich Wulff, was completed.

Thus, it seemed the natural thing, when the Battle of Flowers was inaugurated in 1891, for the town's elite to hold their first festival on Alamo Plaza.

The Menger Hotel

The Menger Hotel, opened in 1859, continued to be San Antonio's fashionable hostelry for many a decade. Built on the site of the Menger Brewery, the hotel made its own beer, reputed to be the best in the entire United States. The house was famous also for its wild-game dinners, which included turtle fresh from the San Antonio River.

The Menger's history is a procession of celebrated names, beginning with Robert E. Lee, of course. Sidney Lanier, the poet, was here in 1872, although he soon found it necessary to seek cheaper lodgings; a suite in the hotel is named after him, nevertheless. O. Henry (William Sydney Porter then) was also too poor to stand the tariff, but he no doubt patronized the bar.

When the Menger was remodeled, after a long period of decadence, the bar, which is supposed to be an exact replica of the one in the English House of Lords, was moved from its historic position (opening onto the patio) to the Crockett Street side of the new building. Much of the old building, on the south side, retains its antique charm. The lobby has been cut in half, but the stately rotunda remains. And the dining room, where so many distinguished guests and honeymooning couples have been catered to, keeps its atmosphere. You will find the famous Menger patio as beautiful as ever.

Menger Hotel

158

The "Alameda"

East Commerce Street was the center of the German colony. The Alamo Ditch was crossed on a viaduct just east of St. Joseph's Church, and a broad avenue, lined with great cottonwoods, stretched for a space eastward. This had been laid out in Spanish times, and was called the "Alameda," after *alamo* ("cottonwood"). Some prominent German families built their homes along there.

St. Joseph's Catholic Church

St. Joseph's Catholic Church, on Commerce Street, now surrounded on three sides by Joske's of Texas, is, like St. Mark's Episcopal Church, unique, in that both possess a personality all their own. In this case, the personality is distinctly German. The color scheme could have come straight out of a Bavarian church. The stained-glass windows are, in fact, from Munich. Like St. Mark's, the church owes much to one man. The cornerstone was laid in 1868, after the German congregation had failed to obtain the use of the Alamo for services; in 1874, Father Henry Pefferkorn was made pastor. This remarkable man painted the murals (the Annunciation and the Assumption) over the side altars. He founded the St. Joseph Society, a benevolent organization, and the *Liederkranz*, a singing society, which flourish to this day. In 1896 he became chaplain at Our Lady of the Lake College.

St. Joseph's Church

159

"The Little Rhein"

The German colony spread down South Alamo Street to La Villita and on beyond.

"That neighborhood south of Commerce Street bridge," wrote Frank Bushick (*Glamorous Days in San Antonio*), "was called the Little Rhein."

The Alamo Street saloons were very different from the mirrored and frescoed liquor saloons in other parts of the city. Patrons dropping in would be waited on by a barmaid, possibly the "mama," a large, round-waisted house frau in a comfortable house wrapper, knitting or sewing in the family quarters where she could watch the bar and attend to the business.

There were no six-shooter brawls or glass throwing, no vulgarity or vice, in the German saloons of this type. Instead, one's ears would most likely catch the blasts and tremolos of brass horns and flutes of an itinerant little German band, with volunteered singing by a few husky bass and tenor voices of lung-splitting power.

Old Beethoven Hall

Old Beethoven Hall, 418 South Alamo, fell to unesthetic uses after the debacle of German prestige in the First World War. It even literally "lost face," in the widening of South Alamo Street. It was once considered the best concert hall in the Southwest. Built in 1895, it burned in 1913 and was immediately rebuilt. Operas were heard here; so were the efforts of the first two symphony orchestras organized in San Antonio (in 1906, and again in 1916) with local talent. Momentous political rallies were held here. Fiesta Queens were crowned. From these lofty functions, it indeed sank low, becoming, among other things, a warehouse. The nadir was reached in 1924, when it was a meeting place of the Ku Klux Klan.

The building was rescued by the HemisFair in 1968 and fittingly restored as a theater. It is city property and is used from time to time for special events.

Beethoven Hall was built by the Beethoven *Männerchor* in its heyday, when it had some 250 members. Founded in 1867, this remarkable singing society is still going strong.

Old German-English School

The German-English school, 419 South Alamo, across the street from Beethoven Hall, was founded in 1858 by a group of German intellectuals. The first buildings were dedicated to the poet Schiller in 1859; the second group was dedicated to Alexander Baron von Humboldt, on the centenary of his birth, 1869. Says one alumnus:

During the early years the extremely high calibre of the teaching staff and the dedication of the leading German-American family heads gave all the first German-born a really outstanding educational opportunity, which, in the case of the more prosperous families, was augmented by sending the male members for a year or two to Germany. There were a number of genteel ladies' seminaries in the city where the girls could be "finished."

The German-English school fell a victim to the rise of the public school system and eventually succumbed in 1903, when the buildings were bought by George W. Brackenridge and presented to the city of San Antonio. They are now used as offices.

The King William Area

By 1870 the Germans dominated the town. In 1876 there were, according to the city assessor, in a total population of 17,314—to give only the three most numerous elements—5,630 Germans and Alsatians; 5,475 Americans, English, and Irish; 3,750 Mexicans.

Some Germans had acquired considerable wealth. It was for these prospering sons of the Fatherland, who were beginning to find the older parts of town too cramped for their exuberance, that Ernst Altgelt, who was a founder of the Texas town of Comfort (northwest of San Antonio) and an ardent admirer of the King of Prussia, Wilhelm I, planned to lay out a magnificent avenue, an exclusive residential development, in the modern manner. He actually planned a street that would be miles long, a sort of monument to the glory of the race, to be named, of course, after the great king. But, unfortunately for this grandiose project, a young German miller, C. H. Guenther, purchased in 1859 a tract of land at what became then and forever the end of King William Street. This was the beginning of a highly successful enterprise, the Pioneer Flour Mills. The Guenther house, occupied until recently by members of the family, still stands, although "done over," at the end of King William Street (at 205 Guenther Street).

Along King William and Washington Streets

For several generations the King William area ruled the town, in more ways than one. Not all the wealthy families were German. Now but few of the old aristocrats remain. The area has preserved its cachet, however, on the whole. Lovers of early Victorian architecture (the styles are *not* German, as they have been carelessly described, but European types that were fashionable in the eastern part of the

107 King William

120 King William

United States many years before the seventies) will find the neighborhood appealing.

Beginning with the entrance to King William Street on South St. Mary's, a few of the most interesting houses are listed below. Many of these have fine interiors, furnished with antiques, but all are private homes except the Steves Homestead, described below. However, selected houses are open to the public for a tour during Fiesta Week.

Number 107

This charming Italian villa near the corner of South St. Mary's was built in 1878 by Anton Friedrich Wulff, who performed the miracle, in the early nineties, of converting the dustbins and mudholes that were San Antonio's plazas into rose gardens. The bust under the eaves is of his daughter, done by his son. The restoration of the house and gardens has provided a beautiful gateway to the King William area. This is the headquarters of the San Antonio Conservation Society in its efforts to preserve San Antonio history. It has an outstanding local-history library.

Number 120

The oldest house on the street, this is an adobe, "done over."

Number 226

The simple, gracious house, the second one built by Ernst Altgelt on his street (the first no longer stands, except the outdoor kitchen at the rear of No. 228), dates from 1878 but looks older. The walls are of quarried, dressed limestone—note the chisel marks. Splayed windows and balconies give an effect of modified colonial architecture, sometimes called Monterrey Colonial.

Number 335

One of the outstanding Gothic Revival houses in Texas, it was built about 1880 for Carl Groos. Walls are of cut native limestone with beveled quoins. Note the brick chimneys, iron pipe columns on the two-story porch, and hipped roof with a flat central deck and watch tower. Inside, floors are of pecan and walnut, ceilings are molded.

Number 401

This lovely two-story house of cut limestone was built by Russel C. Norton, a hardware merchant, a few years after 1873. The second owner, Edward Polk, a stockman, acquired the property in 1881 and proceeded to enlarge it by a brick wing of two stories and a porch. The third-story tower was added after that. Mr. Polk sold the house in 1895 to renowned trail boss and cattleman Ike T. Pryor. Through the following years there was a succession of owners. In 1967 Walter N. Mathis bought the property and has painstakingly restored it throughout. In 1971 it was recorded as a Texas Historical Landmark.

From the street one can see such details as the wide entranceway of oak framing the front door with an intricately carved arch over the top, the formal garden on one side of the grounds, the front fence of stone and lacy ironwork, and the Texas red oak trees and liriope beside the front sidewalk.

Number 419

Built in 1867 by Colonel Elias Edmonds. All material was brought by oxcart from Indianola, on the Texas coast. In that year it was listed as "Ladies Boarding School—Mrs. L. N. Edmonds, Teacher." One diploma read, ". . . for literary, classical and scientific knowledge and her polite and dignified deportment."

419 King William

209 Washington

Washington Street may be entered from King William at the small triangular park, which has at its center the old kiosk, or pavilion, from the arsenal grounds.

Number 209

Perhaps the most imposing antebellum house remaining in San Antonio today, it is known as the "Oge House," after George Oge, an old-time ranchman, whose family occupied it until recently. It was built in 1860 by the United States government for the resident general.

Number 213

The age and builder of this house are unknown. It stood unoccupied for several years before the Gus Groos family made it their home until their own house could be built next door. This was in 1865. It is now occupied by descendants of the Groos family.

213 Washington

231 Washington

Number 231

This house was built by Gus Groos in 1875. It is one of the best examples of the ornate and careful craftsmanship of the German workers of that period.

Steves Homestead

The Steves Homestead, 509 King William Street, owned and operated by the San Antonio Conservation Society as a museum of antiques, is one of the finest examples of the fashionable old German residences. Built in 1876 by Eduard Steves, who also planted the grove of pecan trees on this property and on the neighboring streets, it typifies in both exterior and interior the elegant Victorian décor of the period. It has a mansard roof and an unusual rope design around doors and windows.

Those interested in antiques will find the house a treasure-trove of Victoriana. Its furnishings include a hundred-year-old rosewood Chickering piano—a rare cocked-hat model, the gift of Yale University—and a canopied bed on which Robert E. Lee once slept during his sojourn in Texas (but not in this house). One of the tables in the house is an elaborate Belter.

The great windows are hung with lace curtains of rare design, and the floors are covered with fine Oriental rugs.

The Venetian mirrors and the very old Crown Derby and Bristol ware, the antique music box, the melodion, the handsome *étagères*—all contribute to the genteel atmosphere.

Many visitors are fascinated by the furniture and accessories in the remarkably complete old-fashioned kitchen, which gives the homestead a used and lived-in look. There are a zinc-topped walnut table, a red-iron coffee grinder, a pepper grinder, a brass bell for calling the servants,

226 and 401 King William

and a wooden butter mold and milk pans.

The grounds of the Steves Homestead are enclosed by a picket fence constructed without nails, being joined by wooden pegs. The old-fashioned garden flourishes. An original fountain in the front yard is still in use.

River Haus

River Haus, in the rear of the homestead, and on the bank of the San Antonio River, was formerly called the Natatorium because it housed the first private indoor swimming pool in the city. The pool has been floored. The house is now used as a hall for meetings and gatherings.

Beethoven Home

Beethoven Home, 422 Pereida Street, the modest heir of the abandoned Beethoven Hall, is located several blocks east of King William Street in a remodeled German residence of the 1850's. Here the Beethoven *Männerchor* still meets and sings. It is open to the public for special events.

The Old Casino Hall

The Old Casino Hall (West Market Street), unlike the other remains of German culture, was on the west side of the San Antonio River, where, indeed, the German businessmen had their offices. It is like the other remains in that it has ceased to function as a living organism.

In 1959 the City Water Board, which under one name or another had occupied it since 1923, moved out, and the Public Library, then next door, was planning to appropriate it, but, instead, it was demolished and the library was moved.

And yet, Robert E. Lee danced here, as did Ulysses S. Grant and his wife. This was once the most glamorous place in San Antonio: the first good theater, the first respectable social club.

The Casino Association was founded in 1854 but had no building of its own until 1857, when the hall on Market Street was finished and inaugurated with a grand cotillion. The founders were all of German origin, and for nearly half a century membership was pretty well restricted to people who spoke the "mother tongue," which was the official language of the Casino.

There was an exception to this rule: officers of the United States Army were admitted to club privileges. And even the German-speaking members became more and more a mixed lot as the inevitable marriages took place between young folks whose fathers had lived on the Rhine and young folks whose fathers came from the Canary Islands or the banks of the Thames or the Seine.

The German members themselves were not all of one class. From the

Old Casino Hall, about 1872

beginning, the association was dominated by people with a lively interest in the arts. There were also some well-educated, down-at-the-heel aristocrats who would have been counts or barons if they had stayed in the old country. Then, there were wealthy merchants with scarcely any education, who were rather looked down on by the rest. Two of these, brothers, once approached the official in charge of the masquerade ball, the big affair of the year.

"We would like to come as peasants," they said. "What shall we wear?"

"Just come as you are," was the caustic answer.

But the wealthy German families, in those days, had a great deal of respect for the artist and the savant. They felt it was a privilege to entertain such luminaries.

The most vigorous effort to bring good music and good drama to San Antonio was made by Casino members. They not only sponsored celebrities from out of town; they also formed a theatrical group among themselves. They even gave a series of full-dress operas. There was nothing cheap about these shows. The costumes for a single opera cost more than seven hundred dollars. A gala performance of Weber's *Der Freischütz* was the grand climax of the season.

The Casino was not merely a temple of culture: it was dedicated, above all, to joyous living. The club —and its commodious bar—was open daily to male members and their guests. Among the latter, a decade apart, were Robert E. Lee and Ulysses S. Grant. There was a monthly entertainment for families, a concert or amateur play, followed by a dance, or "hop." There was a masked ball every Christmas for children, and another ball was held on Shrove Tuesday. Fathers reserved memberships for their sons and formally introduced their daughters on New Year's Eve. Everything was always perfectly proper. No breach of decorum was ever heard of. Troupers that wanted to rent the theater—minstrel shows were especially popular in that era— had to give a detailed account of their act before they were allowed to go on.

But there was a good deal of friendly gambling among the members. The favorite game was skat.

The Noble Experiment of Prohibition hit the Casino a blow from which it never recovered. The water company (now the City Water Board) had already built its offices so close that one of its executives could sit in the club by the window, sipping his beer or highball, and still keep a watchful eye on his underlings next door. In 1923 the Casino sold its building to the water company. There is still a Casino Club, at another address—quite a different outfit.

The stones and rafters of the old Casino have ceased to vibrate to the lilt of voices in song, the laughter of children, the banter of the adult and the aging, the tap and shuffle of dancing feet, the cadence of the waltz or polka. The glamor is gone forever.

9
The Mexican Town

José Antonio Navarro State Historic Site

(South Laredo and West Nueva streets)
Open: Tuesday through Saturday, 10:00 A.M. to 4:00 P.M.
Admission: adults, $1.00; children six to twelve, 25¢.

Chapel of the Miracles

(1127 North Laredo)
Open: daily, 9:00 A.M. to 5:00 P.M.
Tiny, unsanctified, privately owned remnant of eighteenth-century San Antonio's traditions, with a miraculous image.

El Mercado

(West Commerce and Santa Rosa streets)
This large market area is the result of an urban renewal project of 1976. Previously it was a composite of dirty, colorful, makeshift farmer's markets, stores that sold tourist nicknacks, and old-fashioned Mexican shops. Known as Haymarket Plaza, it was a common meeting ground with picturesque Mexican atmosphere and visitors from everywhere. San Antonians made regular treks to the area because, for years, it was *the* farmer's market.

The Mexican town, per se, is hard to find because it has been integrated into San Antonio. About the same time that it ceased to have a living, throbbing center, the town was spreading into new suburbs, far to the west and south, where nothing had stood a few years past, where families of small means could have a garden and a house of their own, far from the crowded *corrales* of the old West Side. About the same time it was noticed, with some shock, that candidates with Spanish names almost invariably got elected when they ran for office. The Latin Americans not only numbered more than half of the city's total population: they had now decided to take a hand in civic affairs. This was a surprising turn for in earlier times Mexicans seldom had voted. But the great government installations here since the Second World War gave the poorest of them a chance to earn a decent wage. A large family, with all the adults working, can earn quite a fair income.

There are many Mexican towns. And, for even the casual visitor, there is still something to see on the West Side. There are still lots of quaint, picturesque houses, little and old, though how long they will be allowed to remain there—*¿quién sabe?*

Statue of Ben Milam

Milam Square

On the opposite side of Commerce Street, across from El Mercado, is Milam Square, originally a cemetery from 1808 until 1860. Many heroes were buried here, including Ben Milam, Gregorio Esparza (the only one of the Alamo defenders here), and Lieutenant José Torres (a hero on the Mexican side of the Alamo battle).

There is a statue of Ben Milam, who was killed in the Battle of Béxar, December 7, 1835, about three months before the Alamo battle.

Santa Rosa Hospital

Santa Rosa Hospital, on the north, is built over the old Catholic cemetery, which succeeded the churchyard (at San Fernando Cathedral).

In the general area of Santa Rosa Hospital and El Mercado, one may find quaint little shops and restaurants. Musicians sometimes play and sing for a price here, especially at night.

The shops have for sale, among other things, religious medallions, statuettes of Cantinflas (the great Mexican comedian), and medicinal herbs with such names as Deer Eye, Rattlesnake, Bad Woman, Giant's Bones, Spider Web.

José Antonio Navarro House

José Antonio Navarro House (228 South Laredo Street) is attached to a perfectly square store of two rooms, one upstairs, one down. With its overhanging eaves and gently broken roof line, the residence is typical of homes built here in the 1850's. It was once the homestead of José Antonio Navarro, one of the two native Texans who signed the Texas Declaration of Independence, March 2, 1836 (the other was Francisco Ruiz, his uncle). A member of the ill-fated Santa Fe Expedition of 1841, Navarro was sentenced to life imprisonment by Santa Anna but es-

José Antonio Navarro House

caped and made his way home in 1845. He died in this house in 1877. The home has been restored and is now open to the public.

About a quarter of a mile north and south of Navarro's house, Laredo and Santa Rosa streets cross. The southern juncture was known as "Laredito" (Little Laredo). The northern point was known as "Chihuahua" because wagons bound for Chihuahua used to gather there.

Guadalupe Church

Guadalupe Church (1321 El Paso Street). This Catholic church, rather ugly and of red brick, has, nevertheless, a personality all its own. It is the mainstay of the very Mexican (or very Indian) Catholic, who clings to the old customs like the oyster to his shell. The church should be visited on some special occasion, such as December 12 (Guadalupe Day), or for the *Pastores*, or for the *Pésame* on Good Friday (see Chapter 15).

Fr. Carmelo Antonio Tranchese, S.J. (1880–1956)

Carmelo Tranchese, born in Italy, studied for the priesthood there. He was ordained after completing his studies in northern Wales. His first missionary assignment was in Albuquerque in 1911. In 1932 he was assigned to Our Lady of Guadalupe Church in San Antonio.

He found, within a square mile, 12,000 people living in flimsy shacks, with disease, poverty, unemployment, and a complete lack of sanitation. Fr. Tranchese wrote to President and Mrs. Roosevelt and worked closely with his friend Maury Maverick to alleviate the conditions. In May, 1939, approval was obtained for Alazan Courts for 932 low-income families. Fr. Tranchese served on the local housing authority and saw the completion of Apache Courts, Victoria Courts, Wheatley Courts, and Lincoln Courts.

He founded a small parish paper, which has grown into the diocesan

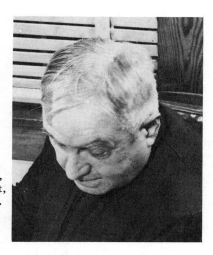

Father Carmelo Tranchese

Spanish weekly, *La Voz*. He encouraged the production of *Los Pastores*, now performed every Christmas season. All this was done while he served as pastor of the Guadalupe Church.

173

Chapel of the Miracles

Martin Street is one of San Antonio's main east-west arteries. If, despite the frustration of the one-way streets, you can locate the beginning of West Martin on North Main, drive west a few blocks to Frio Street, go north on Frio to North Salado, and turn right; at the end of the block at the corner with Laredo is the Chapel of the Miracles.

This is the shrine of El Señor de los Milagros ("Our Lord of Miracles"), a shrine not sanctioned by the Catholic church. It was built to house a crucifix, an ancient, life-sized Christ carved of wood. Countless wonders have been attributed to the image, and until recent years the walls of the chapel were covered with *retablos*, mostly crude paintings on tin of "people being saved by miraculous intervention from death by overturning automobile, by onrushing train, by goring bull and striking serpent, by electric chair and grievous illness," wrote

the late Julia Waugh in *The Silver Cradle*. These have been packed away now because there was not room for them all, and none can be seen. But miracles are still in great demand. To quote again from *The Silver Cradle*:

The chapel is never more its own self, never more appealing, than on some clear Sunday morning when the altar is sweet with jasmine and roses, when points of candles gleam, and still figures kneel at prayer. . . . A soldier brings a rude cross in gratitude for some mercy granted. A country-looking boy and girl enter shyly to lay a wedding bouquet on the altar. . . . An old man kneels with head upraised and arms outstretched, himself a cross.

The chapel is entirely a family affair, the private property of the descendants of certain very early settlers named Ximenes and Rodríguez. One of their ancestors (the story goes) rescued the image from

Chapel of the Miracles

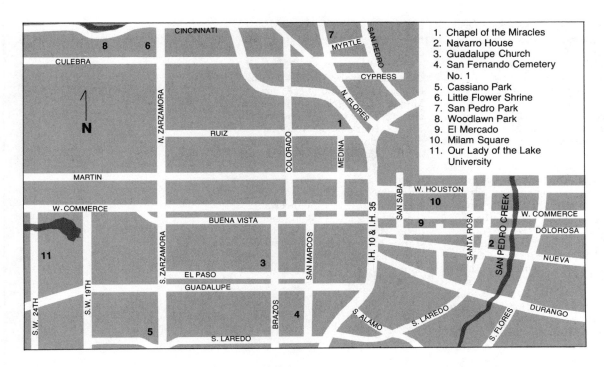

1. Chapel of the Miracles
2. Navarro House
3. Guadalupe Church
4. San Fernando Cemetery No. 1
5. Cassiano Park
6. Little Flower Shrine
7. San Pedro Park
8. Woodlawn Park
9. El Mercado
10. Milam Square
11. Our Lady of the Lake University

Map 8. *The Mexican Town*

175

the parish church (now San Fernando Cathedral) on the occasion of a destructive fire and was granted by the priest permission to keep it in his house until the church could be rebuilt. This fire occurred, they claim, in 1813, and that date is inscribed over the small, squat tower of the Chapel of the Miracles. It was a disastrous year: the town was nearly finished off by the Spanish army sent to punish the insurgents. And there is, indeed, a record of the church having been rebuilt immediately after the terrible month of August. As for the crucifix, a will dated in 1802 (writes Julia Waugh) directed that candles be lighted before the image of Our Lord of Miracles, which was then in the parish church of San Fernando.

Now, a crucifix two varas long (more than five feet) is mentioned in the early inventories of the church at Mission San Antonio de Valero, better known as the Alamo. In 1793 the mission was dismantled; some of the images may have been taken over to the parish church.

As we have noted in Chapter 2, the Chapel of the Miracles is situated near the original (1718) site of Mission San Antonio, and a similar chapel, where people came to "pray for the relief of their troubles," was on the second site, near the Alamo, in 1756. Among the confused oral traditions of the family now in possession is a persistent reference to an ancient "chapel for Indians" on the same spot. Is it inconceivable that the image was taken from the parish church with the idea of restoring it to the place where it was first venerated? There can be little doubt, anyway, that this crucifix is the one that was in the church of the Alamo: the size is extraordinary.

10
Parks and Museums

Brackenridge Park

(North of Mulberry Street; can be entered from Broadway or St. Mary's Street.)
Miniature train circles park with stations at Witte Museum, San Antonio Zoo, Golf Driving Range, and Japanese Tea Gardens.

San Antonio Zoo and Aquarium

(3903 North St. Mary's Street)
Open: daily, April through October, 9:30 A.M. to 6:30 P.M.; November through March, 9:30 A.M. to 5:00 P.M.
Admission: adults, $3.00; seniors, $1.50; children three to eleven, $1.00; children under three, free.

The San Antonio Museum Association operates three museums:

Witte Museum (Headquarters of the Museum Association)
(3801 Broadway)

San Antonio Museum of Art
(200 West Jones Avenue)

Museum of Transportation
(HemisFair Plaza)

The following applies to all three museums:
Open, Tuesday through Saturday, 10:00 A.M. to 5:00 P.M.; Sunday, 12:00 M. to 5:00 P.M. (June through August, 6:00 P.M.).
Closed: Christmas, New Year's Day, July 4, Labor Day, Thanksgiving Day, and Battle of Flowers Parade Day.
Admission: adults, $3.00; students, senior citizens, and military personnel with I.D., $1.50; children six to twelve, $1.00; children under five, free.

Pioneers, Trail Drivers, and Texas Rangers Memorial Building

(3805 Broadway)
Open: May through August, Tuesday through Sunday, 10:00 A.M. to 4:00 P.M.; September through April, Wednesday through Sunday, 11:00 A.M. to 4:00 P.M.
Admission: adults, $1.00; children six to twelve, 25¢; children under six, free.

McNay Art Museum

(6000 North New Braunfels Avenue)
Open: Tuesday through Saturday, 9:00 A.M. to 5:00 P.M.; Sunday, 2:00 P.M. to 5:00 P.M.
Closed: Monday, New Year's Day, July 4, Thanksgiving Day, and Christmas.
Admission: free.

Buckhorn Hall of Horns, Fins, Feathers, and Hall of Texas History

(Lone Star Brewing Company, 600 Lone Star Boulevard)
Open: daily, 9:30 A.M. to 5:00 P.M.
Admission: adults, $2.25; seniors, $2.00; children, $1.25; groups of 20 or more, $1.75 each.
Free parking and limited quantities of free beer and root beer available.

Hertzberg Circus Collection

(210 West Market Street)
Open: Monday through Saturday, 9:00 A.M. to 5:30 P.M.
Admission: free.

Institute of Texan Cultures

(HemisFair Plaza)
See Chapter 11

McNay Art Museum: patio

Here we have a variety, indeed: from merry-go-rounds for the braw four-year-old to the masterpieces of modern French painting for the nicely ripened esthete. In between we have polar bears, golf, Indian arrowheads, classes in Spanish dancing, and a miniature circus.

For the visitor with limited time and general interests, the San Antonio Zoo and Brackenridge Park and the Witte Museum, which are contiguous, and the Buckhorn Hall of Horns, which is on the way to the missions, may suffice. All of these will appeal to children. For the lover of art, the McNay Institute is a shrine worth a long pilgrimage. For the circus fan, the Hertzberg show is the big top. For the historian and antiquarian San Pedro Park may have charms. For the seeker of outdoor recreation, there are many varieties of clean fun at Woodlawn Park; the golfer will rejoice in the links at Brackenridge, at Riverside, at Willow Springs.

Brackenridge Park

Brackenridge Park (west side of Broadway) is really a conglomeration of parks and a patchwork of independent and varied attractions and concessions, spreading over about 370 acres. The largest area was deeded to the city in 1899 by the Water Works Company, under the presidency of George W. Brackenridge, and the deed prohibits the sale of beer or intoxicating liquors; if any should be sold, the land would be forfeited to the state of Texas for the benefit of the University of Texas. But another area, near the center of the park, was deeded by a local brewer, and the deed provides that permits be issued to sell malt liquors as long as the laws of Texas do not forbid.

The charm of Brackenridge Park, aside from the man-made amusements, is in its woods. Roads and bridle paths wind through thickets and under great oaks that have scarcely been disturbed since the

Spaniard's time. The riverbanks are enticing, too, although the river is no longer the pellucid stream that it was before artesian wells sapped the springs at the nearby head of the river. Artesian wells must now pump water into the riverbed. There are vestiges of a swimming pool in the river, but swimming has not been allowed since about 1950.

A conflict over the desirability of underbrush has been waged for many years between the authorities responsible for the maintenance of order, who want to discourage lovebirds, and the protectors of wildlife (strictly construed), who want to keep the natural cover as thick as possible.

There are speedboats and paddleboats on the river; there are riding stables, with good horses for hire; there is a splendid golf course (eighteen holes) at the south end of the park; at the opposite end is a miniature railway, strictly for children. Outstanding among the novelties is the Aerial Sky Ride.

Much too businesslike to be called a miniature train is the "Brackenridge Eagle," a one-fifth scale model of a diesel-type train. With three miles of track and four stations, it pretty well covers the park, crossing the San Antonio River twice and snaking its way through the lovely woods.

Japanese Tea Gardens

These gardens are in the northwest corner of Brackenridge Park near the North St. Mary's Street entrance. They have been called the Chinese and/or Oriental Sunken Gardens. On October 12, 1984, they were rededicated as the Japanese Tea Gardens.

Stones for the Alamo were quarried here. In 1880 the first cement plant west of the Mississippi was built adjacent to the pit. The chimney for the kiln and the houses for the workers still remain. There are many photo possibilities.

Walks and little rock bridges are

Japanese Tea Gardens

181

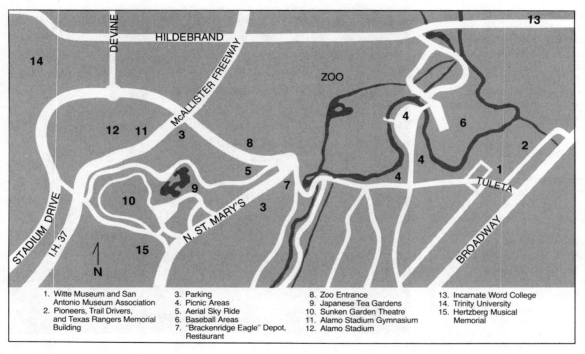

DEVINE

HILDEBRAND

McALLISTER FREEWAY

STADIUM DRIVE

I.H. 37

N. ST. MARY'S

N

ZOO

TULETA

BROADWAY

INCARNATE WORD COLLEGE

14

13

12 11

3

8

5

9

10

15

7

3

4

4

4

6

2

1

1. Witte Museum and San
   Antonio Museum Association
2. Pioneers, Trail Drivers,
   and Texas Rangers Memorial
   Building

3. Parking
4. Picnic Areas
5. Aerial Sky Ride
6. Baseball Areas
7. "Brackenridge Eagle" Depot,
   Restaurant

8. Zoo Entrance
9. Japanese Tea Gardens
10. Sunken Garden Theatre
11. Alamo Stadium Gymnasium
12. Alamo Stadium

13. Incarnate Word College
14. Trinity University
15. Hertzberg Musical
    Memorial

Map 9. *Brackenridge Park*

Steam Pumper

strung through lily ponds and beds of aquatic and semitropical flowers, artfully plotted to make a harmonious glow of assorted colors.

Sunken Garden Theatre

West of the Japanese Tea Gardens is this vast outdoor theater, also utilizing the old limestone quarries. It is used only for special events. The tradition is: to schedule an event causes it to rain.

San Antonio Zoo

One of the most delightful zoos in the country (3903 North St. Mary's Street), it is built on the ancient quarries from which the Spaniards hauled stone for their houses, and the water that runs through it is part of the ancient "labor" or "farm" ditch. The San Antonio Zoological Society was organized in 1929 and entered into an agreement with the city whereby all animals would be purchased by the society and maintained by the city. Today, the city makes an annual contribution, and the society operates and maintains the zoo and finances all construction and expansion.

The collection is comprised of birds, mammals, reptiles, amphibians, fish, and invertebrates. The bird collection is one of the largest in the United States. A walk-through flight cage, tropical birdhouses, and a pair of rare whooping cranes are some of the high points. Also of note are the fine antelope and exotic reptile collections. The animals are exhibited in areas simulating as closely as possible their native habitats. Many of them are displayed against the limestone cliffs of the abandoned quarry. A troop of baboons wanders freely on an island, which they share with a head of aoudad sheep. The bears are exhibited in moated enclosures against a backdrop of rocky ledges. The elephants take visitors for rides and perform for the amuse-ment and education of spectators. The aquarium is the home of colorful reef fishes, a nurse shark, an electric eel, and assorted fresh- and salt-water specimens. An innovative children's zoo provides a boat journey to the "continents around the world."

Witte Museum

The museum is at 3801 Broadway in the two blocks where Brackenridge Park touches that street. The building faces toward Broadway across a spacious lawn studded with oaks, magnolias, and pecan trees. Two mammoth cast-stone sculptures, *Mother and Child* and *Father and Child*, by the noted Texas sculptor Charles Umlauf, flank the dignified entranceway. A fountain, also by Umlauf, graces the walkway leading toward the museum.

Since it opened in 1926, the Witte has been a university of the people, where things are learned

San Antonio Museum of Art

that cannot be found in books. A group of enthusiasts headed by Ellen Quillin, long-time curator of the Witte and director of its growth, had already made plans for a museum when the city received a bequest of $65,000 from Alfred G. Witte, a broker, who made the condition that a museum be built within Brackenridge Park.

Since its humble beginning, the building and its collections have grown in size and escalated in importance until they now represent one of the major museums in the Southwest. Basically, the initial concept of the institution has been maintained and the displays reflect this trend. However, the wealth of its collections and the interest in changing exhibitions have engendered a flexibility that has resulted in displays of a more specialized character. The museum now, in addition to its permanent displays, offers a constantly changing program of exhibitions.

They Call Us Savages

One of the most impressive collections at the Witte Museum pertains to the native Americans, or Indians. Outstanding examples are on view in free-standing exhibits representing all the major tribes of the North American continent. There is a great deal of material that was gathered in the caves along the Rio Grande and the Pecos River back in the 1930's. Much of the work was done around Langry, where the legendary Judge Roy Bean held forth.

The Natural History Hall

This gallery houses one of the most popular permanent displays in the museum. Large lifelike habitat groups with animals indigenous to the state have been installed with meticulous care. Many creatures native to the area may be studied, from a group of majestic buffalo to the smallest of mammals or insects. Each

exhibit has a clear, explanatory label relating the story of the particular animal, bird, reptile, or insect. A large ecological map with regional divisions shows the areas where each species thrives. Outstanding, modern museum displays include "Sounds of South Texas," "Dinosaurs: Vanished Texans," and "Animal Senses," a participatory exhibit.

Texas Furniture and Paintings

This is a very important collection of paintings, prints, drawings, and artistic crafts, including furniture, by artists who worked in early Texas. These materials are used in the Witte Museum and the San Antonio Museum of Art as exhibits or to enhance other exhibits. They are as important historically as they are aesthetically, and they supply an insight into the

North American Indian collection, Witte Museum

past of simple activities, local scenes, and prominent people. Hermann Lungkwitz, a German, depicted the Texas hill country and views of early San Antonio; Théodore Gentilz, a Frenchman, made numerous, detailed paintings of daily life; and Carl G. von Iwonski recorded prominent citizens in competently painted portraits. Other artists include Luisa Wueste, Marie Gentilz, W. G. M. Samuels, Erhard Pentenrieder, Edward Grenet, Louis Hoppe, Seth Eastman, Thomas Allen, Louise Frétellièr, and Robert and Julian Onderdonk. As the most comprehensive collection of early Texas painting in the state, it assumes more importance as time goes on and is used as source material in many current publications.

Historic Houses at the Witte

In the rear of the museum are three houses of historic interest, which were moved here from their original locations to preserve the buildings. Each house, with the exception of the Ruiz house, is furnished primarily with hand-crafted furniture and accessories made by regional craftsmen. The resourcefulness of the frontiersmen is exemplified not only in the furniture they were often obliged to make, but also in the pottery churns, bowls, and jars thrown and fired at local kilns. The quilts, coverlets, hand-woven fabrics, and embroideries were made by the women, and the wrought-iron objects surrounding the fireplaces were often the creations of the local blacksmith.

The Francisco Ruiz House

The Ruiz house stood on the south side of Military Plaza until 1942. Believed to date from before 1765, it was the home of a signer of the Declaration of Texas Independence (1836). A great deal of other Texas history took place beneath the eaves of this house. In 1803 it became one of San Antonio's earliest schools; in 1828 Colonel Ruiz wrote a book on the Indians of Texas; during the 1836 Battle of the Alamo, Colonel Ruiz's son was the mayor and was responsible for disposing of the slain Texians.

The John Twohig House

The John Twohig House was the residence of a famous early character of San Antonio. Twohig, an Irishman, blew up his store on Main Plaza in March, 1842, to prevent his stock of gunpowder from falling into the hands of Mexican invaders. He had a bank on Commerce Street as late as the 1880's, with a footbridge across the river in the back of it to his house on St. Mary's. The house is said to date from 1841. In it he entertained all the notables of the period, among them, of course, Robert E. Lee. There is an outside stairway but none inside. The fireplace, mantels, doors, and walls—moved here stone by stone and set up in place—are original.

The Celso Navarro House

Celso Navarro was the son of José Antonio Navarro and lived in this house located, at that time, on Cameron Street where the athletic field of Fox Academic & Tech High School displaced it. To salvage the building the parts were marked, dismantled, moved to the Witte Museum grounds, and reassembled. Typical of restorations, even with all the care possible, fragile parts, such as the sawed caliche blocks, disintegrated and were replaced with hollow tile. Basically, the structure follows the shape and looks like the building as made in 1835. It is typical of the time and place.

Memorial Building

Pioneers, Trail Drivers, and Texas Rangers Memorial Building, an imposing edifice north of the Witte Museum, houses three museums, each dedicated to its particular organization.

The second floor serves as a meeting place and social hall for the three groups. The most active group seems to be the Old Time Texas Trail Drivers' Association, heirs of the old cattlemen but mostly, today, without a hide to their name. The Trail Drivers Museum displays photos of the cattlemen and their memorabilia.

The Former Texas Rangers Museum is pretty well organized in the limited space and shows photos, papers, and artifacts of this special breed of men. There is a state-supported Ranger Museum in Waco. This San Antonio museum is under the aegis of the Former Texas Rangers Association with the backing of the Former Texas Rangers Foundation.

San Antonio Museum of Art

The Museum of Art (200 West Jones Avenue) opened in 1981. Previously, it was housed on the second floor of the Witte Museum in limited space. This new museum complex is in the old Lone Star Brewery. The architects received a design award from *Progressive Architecture* magazine, and *Time* magazine recognized the project as one of the five best architectural designs of 1981.

Its spacious sixteen galleries feature changing exhibitions and an outstanding permanent collection, including Texas furniture, American paintings from the eighteenth century to the present, and pre-Columbian art.

There is approximately 66,000 square feet of exhibition space in the entire complex, which includes seven ancillary historic buildings. The renovation created display galleries in twin, four-story towers joined by a glass catwalk overlooking the downtown San Antonio skyline on one side and the San Antonio River and San Antonio's northern suburbs on the other. The large, glass elevators were specially constructed and give an X-ray of the galleries during their trips.

The Museum of Art has a well-planned and organized changing exhibition program. It brings new shows from all over the world as well as from other museums. Donations and purchases are constantly adding to the permanent collection, which includes work of such eminent American artists as Edward Hicks, Alvan Fisher, Samuel Lovett Waldo, Henry Inman, Thomas Birch, Ezra Ames, Jasper Francis Cropsey, Worthington Whittredge, Alfred Thompson Bricher, Thomas Moran, Gilbert Stuart, James Peale, Rembrandt Peale, Charles Wilson Peale, Jeremiah Theus, and William Dunlap.

Late nineteenth- and early-twentieth-century American artists include John George Brown, William Merritt Chase, Thomas Hill, Robert Henri, Ernst Lawson, and Richard

Celso Navarro House and Log Cabin, Witte Museum

Diebenkorn. Sculpture is not neglected. Coppini, Borglum, and Umlauf are among those represented. In addition there is a 2 1/2-acre sculpture garden.

San Antonio Museum of Transportation

One of the largest exhibits of the modes of transportation of the past is on display in HemisFair Plaza. Some of the material was displayed at the Witte Museum years ago. Many automobiles and other vehicles of the past have been added and either restored or maintained in mint condition.

A treasure from the past is a fire engine steam pumper. Purchased in 1881 for the San Antonio Fire Department, it roared down city streets for twenty years until all horse-drawn equipment was abandoned for gasoline-powered vehicles. One fireman drove the three horses, and two others swung and clung to the back of the machine gleaming with brass, copper, and nickel and glistening with valves and pipes.

One of the vehicles representing mass transportation in an earlier day is an 1875 twenty-passenger mule-drawn trolley car. It was the last mule car ever to operate in San Antonio and was presented to the museum on April 29, 1933, the last day of the streetcar operation in San Antonio.

The automobile collection, antiques and classics, began with a Richard Brazier French car—the third automobile in San Antonio. Also on display are an Oldsmobile, Ford, Duesenberg, Auburn, Rolls Royce, Pierce Arrow, Stutz, and a couple of presidential cars.

Other exhibits include a 1939 miniature train that a Dr. Herff had built and run on a circular track. The cars are large enough that people could sit on top of the cars and be pulled around the track. There are early bicycles, some of them made in San Antonio in backyard shops. Horse-drawn carriages and even a pony cart are on display.

McNay Art Museum

192

(Marion Koogler) McNay Art Museum

(Marion Koogler) McNay Art Museum (6000 North New Braunfels Avenue) is not a "treasure house of art," if that term suggests a warehouse stacked with random acquisitions; it is, rather, a shrine religiously dedicated to discriminating taste. Here you will find hardly any work that is bad, and very little that is mediocre.

The choice of modern French paintings is a joy to the connoisseur. No less stunning is the collection of medieval art housed upstairs.

The building and collection were bequeathed by Mrs. Marion Koogler McNay, herself a painter, who died in 1950. The painters best represented belong to the first generation of postimpressionists. There is also a remarkable head of Christ by El Greco. Among the paintings on permanent exhibition are works of van Gogh, Braque, Cézanne (2), Chagall, Degas, Dugy (4), Gauguin (3), Matisse, Modigliani (2), Picasso (3), Renoir, Rivera, Rouault (3), Rousseau, Soutine (2), and Toulouse-Lautrec. Many others are represented, all by choice examples of their work.

Besides French painting, Mrs. McNay collected watercolors, with emphasis on American watercolorists: Winslow Homer, John Marin, and dozens more are here.

There is a collection of Indian and Spanish arts and crafts from New Mexico: *santos*, rugs, and blankets.

The medieval art, housed in the north wing, upstairs, is the gift of Dr. and Mrs. Frederic Oppenheimer and was put on exhibition here in 1956. Stone statuaries, mainly early Gothic, and a stone-carved tabernacle from an ancient church are displayed on the loggias connecting the galleries

The first gallery is devoted to fourteenth- and fifteenth-century Flemish and Italian panel painting and sculptures of the school of Troyes. Artists represented include Jan Gossaert of Mabuse, Alvise Vivarini, Van Dyck, and Joos van Cleve. The prize of the whole collection, perhaps, is the double panel carved by Albert Bouts, with "Moses and the Burning Bush" on one side and "Herod and the Golden Fleece" on the other.

The second gallery is paneled in oak taken from a fifteenth-century château in France. Here ecclesiastical carvings and sculpture are exhibited. The furniture includes a Flemish church stall, Gothic and Venetian chests, benches, and Cromwellian chairs. The galleries are decorated throughout with chalices, French embroidered panels, velvet and embroidered chasubles, and tapestries.

Gifts to the museum in 1973 by the Estate of Tom Slick of San Antonio include three pieces of sculpture by Dame Barbara Hepworth, two paintings by Georgia O'Keeffe, and the monumental Picasso oil of 1954, *Portrait of Sylvette*. The print collection includes masterpieces by

Entrance hall at the McNay Art Museum

McNay Art Museum Tobin Wing: upper level

195

Picasso, Braque, Manet, Matisse, Toulouse-Lautrec, and others.

The Lang Galleries, opened in 1973, house a distinguished collection of modern sculpture, modern French paintings, and American art.

The Adele and Jack Frost Wing, opened in 1975, contains three galleries, which lead to the Santos Gallery via a handsome stairway illuminated by Gothic stained glass.

The Great Gallery in the Emily Wells Brown Wing displays monumental canvases and is used for lectures, concerts, and receptions.

A series of five galleries in which changing contemporary art exhibitions are presented is upstairs.

The Jerry Lawson Print Gallery was donated in 1982 to exhibit the McNay's collection of graphic arts, pre-eminent in the Southwest. Master prints by Goya, Toulouse-Lautrec and other nineteenth- and twentieth-century artists are available.

The Tobin Wing opened in 1984. The upper level houses approximately eight thousand volumes from the library of Robert L. B. Tobin. His collection consists primarily of the theater arts, including hundreds of rare books, stage models, and costume designs, which are displayed on a rotating basis. A spiral staircase leads to the museum's extensive Fine Arts Research Library on the lower level. Visitors are invited to use its resources Tuesday through Friday from 9:00 A.M. to 5:00 P.M. Librarians are available for assistance.

The museum is situated on twenty-five acres of spacious grounds. Dominating the south lawn is the large *Asteriskos* by Tony Smith, presented by the Catto Foundation. Dominating the main New Braunfels Avenue entrance is the Koehler Fountain. This entrance leads to the parking area.

The gardens are landscaped. Some are Japanese in character, with lily ponds, bridges, and arbors set about with Oriental tomb figures and other antique statuary.

Buckhorn Hall of Horns, Fins, Feathers, and Hall of Texas History

Buckhorn Hall of Horns (Lone Star Brewing Company, 600 Lone Star Boulevard) is the world's largest and choicest display of horns.

This famous collection was moved, in 1957, to its present spacious and inviting home from the old Buckhorn curio store at West Houston and North Flores streets, mecca of tourists for two generations. Only since the move has it been possible to see the amazing array of horns in an appropriate setting. The roomy halls built especially to house these exhibits provide the ideal background: plenty of space, rough-sawed pine walls with a driftwood finish, indirect lighting, painted scenes of wildlife. The collection is said to include at least one specimen from every kind of horned animal. Its longhorn steer heads and horns are unequalled for number and variety.

The collection was started in 1884 by Albert Friedrich, who became proprietor of the celebrated Buckhorn Saloon in 1887, and it has been added to ever since by gifts from all over the world. The Buckhorn, established first in 1887 on Dolorosa Street, was moved in 1890 to the southeast corner of West Houston and Soledad streets, where a shop still shows the interior design of the saloon. No schnapps emporium in all the rowdy history of San Antonio was more respectable than the Buckhorn. Never a dead body was dragged out by the heels through its swinging doors, but many a body, more or less alive, was chucked out. Friedrich, a high-strung man, as might be expected of a superb hunter, tolerated no nonsense. He would not have any chairs in his place, because he did not want his customers to dawdle over their drinks. For his cowboy friends he kept a couple of lockers behind the bar: in one he stashed their revolvers until they were ready to leave town; in the other he put their wallets. He thus protected them, in a measure, from the perils of gunplay and from the danger of getting rolled in the fleshpots of the sinful city.

The old Buckhorn Saloon has been reproduced here and is set off to one side so as not to be in the path of the children who come to see the Hall of Horns. The original bar was scarred and battered; it has been replaced with a facsimile. The back bar is the original. Mirrors with carved ebony cupids and other furnishings are authentic period pieces.

The approach to the Hall of Horns is by way of a gallery; its walls are gay with vivacious murals representing scenes in old San Antonio by Texas artist Louise Clairmont: some of them were drawn from rare photographs.

Off this gallery to the right is a roofed area open at two sides: a sort of breezeway, with facilities for the festive barbecue. Longhorn specimens, all shapes and sizes, are arrayed here on the rafters, and there are groupings of other horns. Quaint machines from the original Buckhorn, intended to convulse the customers while extracting nickels from them, stand along the walls, which are hung with amusing signs and pictures made of rattlesnake rattles. In one of them the national emblems of the United States and Mexico are intermixed: the eagle holds a serpent in his beak, but his talons clutch arrows.

The Hall of Fins was completed in 1966. Here one will find a cypress-paneled hall that has over one hundred specimens of marine life ranging from a palm-size piranha to a 1,056-pound black marlin. Fish specimens are displayed dramatically to reflect their environment, from fresh water as well as salt-water seas. Visitors to this famous

Buckhorn Hall of Horns: North American Hall

exhibit contribute to the fish stories that are often told there. In addition, there is a large variety of sea shells, some rare, plus other very interesting memorabilia.

Entering the Buckhorn Bar from the breezeway, to the right is the Boar's Nest: a collection of some 150 modern, classic, and antique firearms and prized hunting trophies, acquired from Mrs. John I. Moore of San Angelo, Texas, whose late husband won fame as an international conservationist, hunter, and expert marksman. On permanent display are a musket dating back to 1776, bench-rest rifles, flintlocks, commemoratives, powder horns, knives, pistols, ammunition, and medals. This entire room is now the home of the complete Moore collection.

From the Boar's Nest, back through the Buckhorn Saloon, one can begin to view in the Hall of Feathers some of the hundreds of birds from all over the world on display in diorama fashion. They can be viewed from two sides, which allows the mind's eye to capture the awe-inspiring array of colors and uniqueness of each specimen. The flora in each diorama suggests the natural habitat of each bird and, with the use of artificial and natural lighting, these birds seem almost lifelike. Some of the outstanding specimens are the Lady Amherst's pheasant of Asia, the magnificent crested pigeon of Australia, and the lovely cotinga from South America. Another rare specimen is the quetzal, which was worshipped by the Aztec Indians as the god of the air. The Aztecs raised these beautiful birds for the tail feathers used as ornaments of dress. Included in the collection of birds is the only known pair of passenger pigeons in the world. They are hermetically sealed in a glass-bubble enclosure in perfect splendor.

As you enter the Hall of Horns, you see a ceiling studded with hundreds of deer antlers. This entrance leads to the Asiatic Hall. Among the trophies is a sacred sheep of India with four horns. Dioramas in front of the different sections represent animals from each continent in their native habitat.

A huge mounted gorilla steals the show in the African Hall. He was shot in 1913 by a German big-game hunter, who relates the story of the kill in Katzenjammer English on a plaque that hangs here: "The male gorilla was esteemed to be about 25 years old. He had not yet got a wife himself. No mark or trace of a companion was found."

In the European Hall is a set of giant antlers from a prehistoric elk whose bones had been preserved in the peat bogs of Ireland. The antlers were known to weigh upward to ninety pounds with a maximum spread of twelve feet. This animal was believed to have been extinct eleven thousand years ago. Here is also a nine-foot-long ivory tooth, or tusk, from the narwhal whale of the Arctic Ocean, which has been referred to as the unicorn of the sea.

From the European Hall you enter the Toepperwein Gallery, named for Adolph (Ad) and Plinky Toepperwein, the world's greatest sharpshooting team. One of Ad's greatest feats of shooting was in 1907 when he shot at 72,500 2 3/4-inch wooden blocks thrown into the air over a period of ten days and missed only 9. He accomplished remarkable trick shooting that has never been equalled. Other memorabilia of his, including some of his targets and rifles, are on display in this room.

The North American Hall bristles with the heads of countless deer, mountain goats and mountain sheep, a walrus, and bulls that were killed in the arenas of Mexico. Here are several heads of the javelina—the wild hog of Texas and northern Mexico.

Among the mounted animals are a lion and his mate, a black bear with cub, and a horse that belonged to silent-screen star William S. Hart.

The glory of the exhibit, of course, is the Texas room in the center. It is crowned by the fabulous chandelier, weighing almost three tons and bristling with more than four thousand horns, which adorned the old Buckhorn Saloon. Here, too, is the celebrated deer head with seventy-eight points, champion of the world.

"Old Tex," another champion, is a stuffed steer with a horn spread of more than eight feet. He stands, in a realistic setting of brush-country thorns, before a Texas bluebonnet scene painted by the late San Antonio artist Porfirio Salinas. Opposite, Salinas depicted a Texas autumn scene; it is fronted by a mounted deer standing in hill-country growth.

The credit for such a fabulous collection and the many specimens and exhibits that have been added since it was relocated in the Lone Star Brewery property belongs to Lone Star's founder and chairman of the board, Harry Jersig. Of inestimable value are the contributions of the talented husband-and-wife team, Fritz and Emilie Toepperwein, artists, curators, and historians, who designed and laid out the entire museum complex.

Hertzberg Circus Collection

Hertzberg Circus Collection is housed in the former San Antonio Public Library (210 West Market Street). Bequeathed to the library by the late Harry Hertzberg, this priceless collection of circusana contains more than twenty thousand exhibits of circus life. Among them are rare and ornate handbills and posters, many photographs and mementos of great circus names: aerialists, clowns, and freaks. There is a gaudily decorated ticket wagon. One of the two rooms is given over to an exact replica in miniature of the Big Top, with all the animals, and even such details as tiny buckets for watering the elephants—everything reduced to scale.

Hertzberg Circus Collection: Tom Thumb's carriage

Particularly intriguing are the relics of Tom Thumb and his wife. The personal belongings of the famous midgets—their miniscule but smartly equipped coach, his violin, even a fragment of their wedding cake—are all here.

San Pedro Park

San Pedro Park (San Pedro Avenue, between West Myrtle Street and West Ashby Place, west to North Flores Street), site of the storied San Pedro Springs, which ceased to run in 1950, is of historic rather than immediate interest.

Here is San Pedro Playhouse, whose front is a replica of the vanished Market House, which gave its name to Market Street in the 1850's; a swimming pool, a baseball field, and tennis courts are also part of the park.

But its glory is in its past. At the once lovely springs, in 1718, the

Spanish governor of Texas, Martín de Alarcón, staged the ceremonies founding the town of Béxar, as it was first called.

San Pedro Park is said to be the second-oldest municipal playground in the United States, the oldest being Boston Common. The site lay within the eight leagues of land granted to the town by the king of Spain about 1734. According to this title, every inch of the grant that was not specifically vested in some private person remained the property of the community.

Among the most valuable of these properties, of course, were the headwaters of San Pedro Creek and the San Antonio River. Incredible as it may seem, the city fathers sweated to get rid of these assets. The head of the river, perhaps the most beautiful spot in Texas, was quietly put on the auction block and speedily snapped up by one of the city fathers; and if it had not eventually fallen into the hands of the enlightened George W. Bracken-ridge, today there would be no Brackenridge Park.

In 1846 the site that is now San Pedro Park was offered, free of charge, to the United States Army for a military post. Only the army's disapproval of the overlooking heights of Tobin Hill prevented acceptance of the gift.

In 1852 the city engineer, F. Giraud, recommended that the city reserve for public purposes a plot around the springs. On November 8 this was done, and San Antonio had its first real park. Already, according to the *Memoirs* of Mary A. Maverick, the springs were a favorite resort for families. A few years later the park was leased by J. J. Duerler, a born landscape artist, who, with the help of his strapping boys, made it a place of enchantment.

By 1855, William Muller advertised in the *Express* that he was "prepared to accommodate all who will call on him at the San Pedro Springs with the best quality of wines and liquors as well as meals to order. He has engaged a good Band of Musicians for harmony music, to play every Sunday at his place." And Edgar Braden advertised "regular conveyances" to carry parties to the springs and back at the rate of 25 cents for each person.

Political rallies were held in the park; here Sam Houston, in 1859, made one of his eloquent pleas against secession.

Sidney Lanier, in 1872, was delighted with the place. There was the pavilion, where little girls were taught to waltz by a German dancing master. There were a bathhouse, a museum with a collection of stuffed animals and curios, a tropical garden with giant cactuses and exotic flora. In the natural grove was a marvelous grapevine arch. There were tame fawns to pet, and, in the zoo, a huge affectionate bear would shamble to meet its keeper, reaching out its forearms for an embrace. A Mexican cougar liked to have his head scratched.

The bear pit still can be seen: it

is the stone cell under the more recent bandstand. A legend has grown up that this was originally the outlet of a tunnel from San Fernando Cathedral. Another legend says the little stone tower with the embrasures in it is the remnant of a Spanish fort. It looks Spanish, right enough. But it may have been built later for protection against Indians, who were still killing men in the vicinity of the park into the 1860's.

In 1878 the first mule car in San Antonio bounced from Main Plaza to the springs.

The numerous small ponds and lakes that the Duerlers built in the park were so connected by small covered waterways with the headsprings that they were always supplied with pure water, in whose clear depths were seen rare fish sporting among the ferns. Large catfish, the color of the blue water, swam slowly about in the large lake made in the bed of the creek. "In this lake [says Gould's *Guide*, 1882] are several romantic little islands, which can be visited by means of the pleasure boats which are kept here. The shores are well wooded and the banks are covered to the water's edge with beautiful aquatic plants. Here the tropical banana grows wild and waves its long and broad leaves in the delightful breeze. On the eastern shores of the lake is a pecan grove, and under the noble trees are tables and benches."

With the acquisition of Brackenridge Park, in 1899, San Pedro was neglected. In the late 1950's some improvements were made.

Other Parks

Friedrich Park

Friedrich Park (21480 Milsa Road off IH 10 just south of Boerne) has many wilderness trails.
Open: Wednesday through Sunday, 9:00 A.M. to 5:00 P.M.

McAllister Park

McAllister Park (Jones Maltsberger Road north of Loop 410) is the largest city park. Playing fields and hiking and biking trails are available.

Olmos Park

Olmos Park (Devine Road and Alamo Heights Boulevard) is a picnic ground with typical Texas flora along Olmos Creek. There are several baseball/softball and soccer fields.

Roosevelt Park

Roosevelt Park (Roosevelt Avenue and Simpson Street) is a picnic ground in a beautiful pecan grove on the San Antonio River and on the line of ancient Concepción Ditch. A swimming pool is also available.

Woodlawn Park

Woodlawn Park (West Cincinnati Avenue) boasts more varied recreational facilities than any other park in the city. It has an expansive lake, with boating and fishing, a large swimming pool, and all sorts of courts. The city recreation department conducts classes in folk-dancing, drama, and ceramics here.

Golf and Tennis

There are five public golf courses in San Antonio; four are city owned. There are also a number of private golf clubs. The public courses are:

Brackenridge Golf Course (Broadway at Millrace Road).

Willow Springs (202 Coliseum Drive).

Riverside Golf Course (Riverside Park at 9315 Nelson Road).

Olmos Basin Golf Course (7022 McCullough).

Pecan Valley Golf Course (4700 Pecan Valley Drive).

The Parks and Recreation Department operates about one hundred tennis courts spread all over San Antonio. They are available first come, first served. Phone P&R for reservations. Clubs, schools, other organizations, and private individuals have scores of other courts.

11

Halls of Learning

Only since 1950 has San Antonio had ample and varied institutions of higher learning. One hundred years before that, when it was already an old town, it had no schools to speak of. In the intervening century, a number of small, sound schools were established. Most of them grew slowly. Few made any pretensions to the loftier flights of learning.

Earlier, the Spaniards had shown a languid interest in training the young. The first mention of an effort to start a school was in 1759, when the bishop of Guadalajara came here, over a fearful distance, to confirm, in the old San Fernando parish church, 430 persons. In 1789 a man named José Francisco de la Mata tried to start a school for the boys of the town, who, he complained, were running around as vagrants, "engaged in such vicious pursuits as games with ropes and arrows." But why should these young cowboys and Indians have been expected to molder in a

schoolroom, when their fathers, even those of the *ayuntamiento*, or municipal council, could hardly sign their own names?

In 1803 young José Francisco Ruiz, who at twenty-two had just returned from college in Spain, was set up by the town council as schoolteacher in his father's house on Military Plaza (the same house now removed to Witte Museum). Ruiz later became the second signer of the Texas Declaration of Independence (March 2, 1836). His career as teacher seems to have been short.

Under the Mexican regime (1821–1836) more energetic efforts to provide schooling came to little or nothing. In 1828 a school for English-speaking children was set up by one McClure, no doubt for children of the American colonists who came here seasonally to escape the malaria of the coast. There was also a school for the Spanish-speaking, in the parish church. Neither lasted long.

The Republic of Texas actually set aside lands for a public school system. But this provision was not taken advantage of until 1853. Then four primitive schools were opened: two (one for boys, one for girls) on either side of the river. This, it is said, was the first free public school system in Texas.

In the 1850's, too, the first good private schools were founded, by Catholic orders from France: the Ursuline Academy, for girls (1851), and St. Mary's, for boys (1852). The German colony founded the German-English School, for both sexes, in 1858. Many girls and boys of "good family" were sent to Episcopal schools in Seguin, thirty-five miles east of San Antonio.

The public schools were out-classed and did not offer serious competition until late in the nineteenth century. The first high school was opened in 1879. Meanwhile, several good private schools had been started; some of them flourish to this day.

Boys—never girls—of "good" family were sent to college in the East, finances permitting.

Not until after 1950 did the institutions of higher learning in San Antonio grow large enough to edify the cultural life of the city. Since then they have grown rapidly, with splendid new campuses.

The Alamo Community College District's three two-year colleges are widely scattered. Trinity University is a Presbyterian school. The University of Texas at San Antonio and the University of Texas Health Science Center are state institutions. St. Mary's University, Incarnate Word College, and Our Lady of the Lake University are Catholic.

The Catholic colleges were established by French missionary orders. Jean Odin, first bishop of Galveston, laid the foundations for present-day St. Mary's University when he sent a group of Marianist brothers to start a school for boys on the rugged frontier that was San Antonio in 1852.

The second bishop of Galveston (after 1862), Claude Dubuis, induced members of two French orders, the Sisters of Charity of the Incarnate Word and the Congregation of the Sisters of Divine Providence, to brave the wilds of Texas in the 1870's. The first of these orders eventually founded Incarnate Word College; the second, Our Lady of the Lake.

The University of Texas at San Antonio

In May, 1970, the Board of Regents of the University of Texas System accepted a gift of approximately six hundred acres of wooded land located sixteen miles northwest of the center of San Antonio to serve as a permanent site for the University of Texas at San Antonio (UTSA) campus (6700 North FM 1604 W).

206

The major purpose of UTSA is to respond, in a climate of intellectual freedom and with academic programs of the highest quality, to the educational needs of its multiple constituencies. Through programs of a multidisciplinary character, UTSA strives to eliminate the isolation of disciplines and to reflect the integral nature of societal issues and problems.

The UTSA library holds over 325,000 volumes, extensive microform collections, 2,500 current periodicals, and a depository of local, state, and federal documents. The special collections and rare books focus on western Americana and on Texas and Mexico, especially during the period of the Republic. The various collections include the John Peace Collection, donated by the former chairman of the University of Texas Board of Regents for whom the library building is named; the R. D. Warden collection of western Americana; the Sons of the Republic collection of Spanish-Mexican books and documents; and the Ralph H. Cameron collection of architectural materials.

The UTSA Center for Archaeological Research is one of the departments that is in the public eye, the area around San Antonio being so historic. The Texas state law requiring a "dig" prior to excavation in a historic site has unearthed and recorded a great deal about Indian life, colonial buildings, and early Texas life.

The University of Texas Institute of Texan Cultures

Open: Tuesday through Sunday, 9:00 A.M. to 5:00 P.M. Closed: Thanksgiving and Christmas.
Admission: free.
Parking: $1.00.

This is a separate component of the UT system and not a branch of UTSA. In the semantics of the political legislation setting it up for the HemisFair in 1968, it was not to be a museum, but do not be surprised if you find it one of the better museums in the country.

The institute is very busy behind its exhibits. The well-equipped shops design and make the exhibits, including traveling exhibits. Every August it presents a four-day Texas Folklife Festival. This has about 6,000 participants and 100,000 or more visitors. The festival includes music, dance, food, crafts, and traditions of the Texas pioneers.

The Institute of Texan Cultures is a communications center of Texas subjects charged to tell the authentic story of Texas and its people with films, filmstrips, slide shows, tapes, publications, and traveling exhibits used in classrooms and a variety of public places. It is a repository of pictures that are copied from libraries, private collections, museums, newspaper morgues, and elsewhere, to be used in books, periodicals, exhibits, and audiovisual productions.

Institute of Texan Cultures

208

Institute of Texan Cultures

The University of Texas Health Science Center at San Antonio

The University of Texas Health Science Center at San Antonio has become an outstanding, nationally known institution for health care training. A part of the University of Texas System, but a completely separate institution from UTSA, the 1.7-million-square-foot Health Science Center is located on a 100-acre campus in the South Texas Medical Center. There are five component schools: medical school, dental school, graduate school of biomedical sciences, school of nursing, and school of allied health sciences. Total enrollment now exceeds 2,300 students.

The medical school was the first on the scene and, indeed, was the first University of Texas institution in San Antonio. The school was authorized by the Texas Legislature in 1959. In 1961 the San Antonio Medical Foundation donated one hundred acres of land in the South Texas Medical Center for educational facilities. The school originally was named the South Texas Medical School, but in 1967 the Legislature authorized the present name: the University of Texas Medical School at San Antonio.

The University of Texas Dental School at San Antonio was authorized by the Legislature in 1969 and signed into law by Governor Preston Smith in ceremonies in front of the Alamo on June 5 of that year. Using medical school facilities, the school opened in 1970 and graduated its first class of 14 students in 1974. Construction of a separate four-level building to adjoin the existing facility was completed in 1975, in time to admit 152 entering dental students per class.

The Graduate School of Biomedical Sciences, which furnishes basic science resources for the other component schools, also offers programs leading to master's and doctorate degrees in biochemistry, cellular and structural biology, microbiology, pharmacology, and physiology. Postdoctoral certificate programs in some dental specialties are also offered.

The School of Allied Health Sciences offers three programs in dental auxiliary training and, together with UTSA, bachelor's degree programs in medical technology, physical therapy, and occupational therapy.

Students in the School of Nursing are accepted for the final two years of a bachelor's degree program as well as for a master's degree program.

A doctor of pharmacy degree is offered jointly by the Health Science Center and the College of Pharmacy at the University of Texas at Austin.

Bexar County Hospital District facilities—the 540-bed Medical Center Hospital adjacent to the university and the Brady/Green Community Health Center downtown—are primary teaching facilities. The 760-

bed Audie L. Murphy Memorial Veterans Hospital in the South Texas Medical Center is another primary teaching institution.

A new library building opened in 1982. It houses more than 144,000 books and journals, has a computerized card catalog, and provides computerized bibliographies in many biomedical fields. Open to the public, the library is an important resource in Central and South Texas.

The Health Science Center receives more than $30 million in research and training grants, contracts, and awards. Future plans include a University-Industry Cooperative Research Center, which will contain a Center for Molecular Targeting, an Institute of Biotechnology for basic research, and a clinical research facility, all of which will be significant catalysts in San Antonio's biotechnology future.

The Health Science Center represents approximately one-third of the total medical complex. There are about six more hospitals and

University of Texas Health Science Center

several medical office buildings or laboratories in the South Texas Medical Center. Patients come from all over the world to these modern facilities.

National Autonomous University of Mexico

The cultures of Mexico and Latin America are shared through university-level instruction in San Antonio by a branch of the National Autonomous University of Mexico (Hemis-Fair Plaza). The National University,

oldest institution of higher learning in the Western Hemisphere and one of the world's leading universities, opened its Permanent Resident School in 1972 in downtown San Antonio.

Spanish-language classes, from beginning through advanced and translation, are offered through lectures, class work, and a modern audiovisual language laboratory. The curriculum in Latin American studies also includes history, art, and literature of Latin America in the pre-Hispanic, Colonial, and modern periods.

Course work in San Antonio may be combined with other courses at the university's main campus in Mexico City to lead to a master's degree in Latin American studies. All courses taught in the Permanent Resident School are fully accredited and transferable to other institutions.

Mexican Cultural Institute

Open: Monday through Friday, 9:00 A.M. to 6:00 P.M.; Saturday and Sunday, 10:00 A.M. to 5:00 P.M.

This public exhibition area was also established in 1972 by the Mexican government to display and bring together the cultural ties between the people in Mexico and the United States.

Alamo Community College District

The Alamo Community College District consists of three public two-year colleges. They offer a full range of arts and sciences courses preparing students for transfer to four-year colleges.

San Antonio College (1300 San Pedro), the largest two-year college in the state, has a flexible schedule, including evening hours and weekends. It has technical programs for job skills and continuing education programs for life-long learning. Courses by television are also offered.

St. Philip's College (2111 Nevada), established in 1898 as a sewing school for girls, has grown into a large, modern campus facility. It offers occupational-technical programs in three divisions: industrial, health careers, and business. St. Philip's also offers programs in hospital management and health careers.

Palo Alto College (Loop 410 and Palo Alto Road) was opened in 1985. In addition to the arts and sciences, it provides job training in technical programs, such as business technology, telecommunications, agribusiness, and retail merchandising.

Incarnate Word College

Incarnate Word College (4301 Broadway, at Hildebrand Avenue) is a stimulating educational environment for men and women. Offering thirty-seven undergraduate degrees ranging from all facets of the fine arts to science, nursing, and business, the college also offers ten master's degree programs, including the M.B.A. and masters of education and arts. The Incarnate Word College has an excellent academic reputation, and three thousand of its alumni enhance San Antonio's health care, teaching, business, and cultural enterprises.

The school primarily serves the Bexar County population with 85 percent of its students from the local area. Incarnate Word College is committed to helping students fund a college education and provides extensive financial aid. This is part of the mission of the school as determined with its founding in 1881 by the Sisters of Charity of the Incarnate Word. Though it is a Catholic college, people of many different backgrounds call the campus their home. The sisters also own and operate Santa Rosa Hospital, the largest Catholic hospital in the United States. The facilities of this hospital have been used by Incarnate Word College to develop an outstanding program in nursing, medical, and health services, courses that lead to the bachelor of science degree.

History: Incarnate Word

In 1897 the reverend mother of the Sisters of Charity of the Incarnate Word was driving in a carriage about the outskirts of San Antonio, accompanied by two sisters. For the nearly twenty years since their arrival from France, they had conducted their schools in makeshift quarters. Now they were seeking a permanent home.

Out a country road that is now traffic-heavy Broadway, they came upon a spot that enchanted them. Alighting from their carriage, they searched among themselves and found a medal of St. Joseph. This they furtively hid under a fence on the property, petitioning that protector to help them get the desired land for their own. Then they drove home to ask their priest how they might help St. Joseph with his task. Things began to work out. The property belonged to Colonel George W. Brackenridge, wealthy banker and philanthropist, who about this time had decided to sell his fancy show place on the river. He agreed to sell, however, only on the condition that the order buy his entire holdings— nearly three hundred acres, mostly wild and undeveloped land. He offered the tract, with his home and all its furnishings, for $125,000. To the poverty-stricken order, this was a stupendous sum.

But the sisters accepted the offer, and for the first few years, until the red brick Mother House could be built, they used the colonel's former homestead as a convent, complete with its rare silver and napery, ornate carvings, and dining room lined with tanned elephant hide.

As the land increased in value, small parcels were disposed of. When the sisters sold a tract for a residential site, across Broadway, they insisted on one stipulation to protect their privacy: no building ever to be erected was to face the convent. For years, this stipulation was strictly observed. But, after the passing of decades, a store, a service station, and the like sprang up on Broadway. The sisters did not protest: by now the Mother House and most of the other buildings were veiled by the leaves and branches of oaks and elms.

Our Lady of the Lake University

Since the institution (24th and Commerce streets) started in 1911, its programs have expanded to include thirty-two areas of specialization. Five different bachelor's degrees and five different master's degrees are offered. For greater access to its program, the university's scheduling alternatives include summer and interterm sessions, extensive evening offerings, a Weekend College, and occasional telecourses and off-campus courses and programs.

The academic programs of the university are organized into a College of Arts and Sciences and three professional schools: the School of Business and Public Administration, the School of Education and Clinical Studies, and the Worden School of Social Service.

As part of Lady of the Lake University's community service and research functions, it maintains the Harry Jersig Center, providing diagnosis and therapy for communication and learning disorders, day schools for special education students, and clinical counseling, and the St. Martin Hall Campus Demonstration School, providing model curricula for early childhood through the eighth grade.

History: Our Lady of the Lake

Our Lady of the Lake College was founded by the Sisters of Divine Providence, which originated in France. The college has its antecedents in two of the first American establishments of the French order, both in Texas: at Austin (1866) and at Castroville (1868), a village settled by French and Alsatians, twenty-five miles west of San Antonio.

For more than a quarter of a century, the Sisters of Divine Providence based their educational work in the Southwest at Castroville. In 1896 the order moved to San Antonio for a more central location. But the foundations for a college had already been prepared while the congregation was still in Castroville. Normal courses, as they were called then, were offered to train the sisters to teach in the parochial schools. The order saw to it that its teachers and schools conformed to the increasingly stiff requirements of the State Board of Education.

In 1975 the college became Our Lady of the Lake University of San Antonio.

Trinity University

Trinity University (715 Stadium Drive) is, says its bulletin, a "coeducational Christian college of the arts and sciences," with an annual enrollment of more than 2,700, and an additional 867 graduate students. It is controlled by the Texas Synod of the Presbyterian Church, U.S.A.

One of the oldest colleges in Texas, Trinity was founded in 1869 at Tehuacana; it was moved in 1902 to Waxahachie and in 1942 to San Antonio. The move to the present splendid campus, on a rocky height overlooking the city from the north, was made in 1952.

Trinity offers a general education program in four major areas: arts and letters, humanities, social sciences, and natural and mathematical sciences. The university offers forty-three undergraduate majors in twenty-five departmental and three interdisciplinary programs. Trinity is affiliated with the Institute of European Studies to help pursue studies for a semester or a year abroad in a different environment. An honors program was established in 1981 by the Trinity faculty as a challenge for exceptionally talented undergraduates.

The Trinity Campus

Trinity's imposing campus had its dramatic start in 1951, when architects O'Neil Ford and Bartlett Cocke tried out for the first time in history the Youtz-Slick construction method, fairly common today but revolutionary then. By this method, as reported in the *Architectural Forum*, concrete floors and roof slabs for multistory buildings were "poured on the ground, one atop another, like layers in a cake, held apart only by a waxy coating. Then, one by one, the concrete slabs were jacked up on steel columns to their proper height."

The Trinity campus is built upon a splintered rocky bluff which used to be an ancient rock quarry. This broken site was considered a difficult one to build on and, therefore, relatively valueless. But the architects were enthusiastic. Said the *Forum*:

They refused to operate on it with bulldozers or dynamite to make it normally habitable; . . . instead they kept it rough, unregenerate, unsubdued; . . . on the irregular terrain, *each building form and position was shifted until it seemed to fall in place naturally. There is no cliffhanging.*

In a part of the United States where an ornate Spanish tradition lingers fondly, the Trinity buildings themselves are architecturally modest. But their effect is not, for the architects' preservation of the lacerating site adds interesting romantic sauce. The simple structures are inherently involved in the rich natural variations of the campus land; they cannot stay aloof. And to the vertical crags and gullies of the land the sweeping dominant horizontals of the neat stacks of lifted slabs add their visual order—to arrange, balance and bind the architectural composition. The architects have succeeded also in pulling off an economic paradox in marrying these two seemingly incompatible conditions—the inexpensive buildings and the rough land. In combination, low-cost buildings and low-cost land multiply one another's value.

St. Mary's University

St. Mary's University (One Camino Santa Maria) is the oldest institution of higher learning in San Antonio. Degrees are awarded by the School of Humanities and Social Sciences; the School of Science, Engineering, and Technology; the School of Business Administration; and the Graduate School. The School of Law offers the Juris Doctor degree.

From the first plans in 1894 for an administration building to the completion of the new law library in 1984, thirty-two buildings have been erected on St. Mary's University campus.

The late Rev. Louis J. Blume, S.M., inaugurated an ambitious program, which included the planning, financing, and construction of a handsome new Law Center, a three-story Academic Library, the Moody Life Science Building, the Richter Math Engineering Building, the Computer Center, and the Central Power Plant.

During Fiesta Week one of St. Mary's most unusual and successful fund-raising events is its annual "Oyster Bake."

History: St. Mary's

The first three intrepid Brothers of the Society of Mary, from France, clambered wearily out of a stagecoach from Galveston in the spring of 1852. Their first school was in some dingy rooms over a livery stable on the west side of Military Plaza.

In 1855, ground was broken for the buildings which were to house St. Mary's College (as it was called) and which, with considerable alterations, were occupied by the School of Law until 1968. By 1860 the large stone edifice on College Street was the pride of the city. Except during the Civil War, the college enjoyed a steady growth.

By 1894 the buildings had become overcrowded, and the board-ing students were moved to a new location, surrounded by cactus and mesquite and far from the fleshpots of the town. This was called St. Louis College. In 1916 the football coach was Second Lieutenant Dwight D. Eisenhower. In 1923 all advanced classes were moved there; the school took the name of St. Mary's College, becoming St. Mary's University in 1927.

The old buildings on College Street were used for high-school classes and became known as St. Mary's Academy until 1931, when Central Catholic High was built, and the law classes were moved there. The original building has been preserved and is now La Mansión Motor Hotel.

These austere walls enclose the scene of a struggle, not violent like some battles that have been fought close by, and not bloody, but long-drawn-out and heroic.

The heroes—and the victors, surely—of this quiet, unceasing conflict were the little group of men from France. They had in their charge the first good school for boys in the city of San Antonio, and they had to cope not only with the rude and strange hardships of the frontier but also with the native sons, who often showed a sizable streak of the Old Ned.

To sum up the long war in a few words, we might say that the brothers were determined to make Christian gentlemen out of wild young Texans who were, many of them, just as determined to be themselves.

That the brothers won out, by and large, is evident from the fact that for several decades former students of St. Mary's dominated local business and civic affairs. Sometimes all candidates for an office would be St. Mary's men.

At this point St. Mary's Street was called Rincón (bend), and a garden of flowers and vegetables grew on the site of the college before it was built. The brothers, too, cultivated a garden—so lovingly that it became a show place, known as the "French Garden." There were grape arbors going down to the river. Let us hope that some of the grapes were put to the pleasant uses of France. The only beverage served at the school, we are told, was water from the San Antonio River—not the least of the privations that the poor brothers had to endure. There was also cornbread three times a day. The only stove in those early days was in the study room; teachers and students wrapped themselves in blankets and huddled about it when northers howled.

St. Mary's was known as the "French School," and the woods near Mission Concepción, which had been deeded in perpetuity to these Brothers of the Society of Mary by Bishop Odin, were known as the "French Woods." The brothers were always addressed as "Monsieur," a French custom, instead of "Brother," although English and Spanish, not French, were the official languages of the school.

At Concepción (which was not restored as a church until 1887), the old mission gardens were cultivated—perhaps the same gardens that, according to a visiting prelate in the eighteenth century, produced a grape as fine as the best in Spain.

Thus, a suave Gallic seasoning was added to the Spanish–Indian–German–Anglo-American mixture in this polyglot rim of the frontier.

It is interesting to note that Bishop Odin's intention in founding the school was to serve the needs of Spanish-speaking people. A great many of them did attend, from San Antonio and from Mexico. St. Mary's was an early practical workshop for understanding between the so-called races. Games were played in either English or Spanish.

One of the tasks that the brothers imposed on themselves was to learn Spanish. But that was no trouble at all, compared with the vagaries of English, which they denounced as a "barbarous language."

That discipline was strict at old St. Mary's all accounts agree. The brothers, we are told by an alumnus, were "thorough, hard as nails, but just." They also "stood for an awful lot."

One of them had the trying habit of reading aloud, as part of the daily teaching program, out of a book which he kept in his desk and which the students considered intolerably dull. A bright boy solved the problem, for a while, at least, by concealing a live crawfish from the nearby river in this desk. The proper moment arrived: the teacher raised the lid of the desk, closed it promptly.

"We played many a trick in those days," a graduate remembers, "but we always had to pay for it."

No person so impressed his stamp of character on the college as did Brother Charles Francis, its principal builder, who came in 1854 and was director for twenty years after 1866. The embodiment of zeal and common sense, he was the main architect of the school's success.

Nothing escaped him. He seemed to be all over the place. He read the weekly marks every Monday and could be expected to step into any class at any hour and carry on the recitation. And—most disconcerting of all—he never failed to be on hand at the morning and afternoon recesses, when the entire 300 or 400 pupils were let loose in the school yard for a quarter of an hour. His single presence kept them in reasonable check.

He also watched over the boarders during their meals and walked up and down the dining room, keeping a sharp lookout for faults of etiquette. A chart hung at one end of the room, with the principal "Don'ts" stenciled in big letters. Any boy who broke a rule had to copy the whole chart, once or twice or oftener, depending upon the gravity of his offense.

Scholastic standards were high. At least one graduate was admitted to Harvard without examination. The emphasis was mainly on science, but drawing was a popular course. And no wonder: the drawing instructor, for many years up to 1894, was Théodore Gentilz, perhaps the finest of early Texas artists. (See under Alamo Library, Chapter 3.)

San Antonio Art Institute

The San Antonio Art Institute (on the grounds of McNay Art Museum) stems from the old Millrace Studio in Brackenridge Park built in 1885. Gutzon Borglum, the famous sculptor, decided to use the place while making his model for the Trail Drivers Association Memorial. Borglum made his headquarters here for ten years until he left in 1934 for his monumental task of carving the faces of four United States presidents on Mount Rushmore.

In 1937 he turned the place over to the late Ellen Schulz Quillin, director of the Witte Memorial Museum. With the support of Josephine Kincaid, Mary Aubrey Keating, Ellen Quillin, and the San Antonio Art League, the school continued on a limited basis until 1942, when the Board of Directors of the Witte decided to close it for the duration of the war.

Mrs. Marion Koogler McNay then offered to provide quarters for the school on her estate and announced that she would bequeath her entire large home to the city to be used as an art museum. Charles Rosen became the first director of the new school when it opened October 15, 1942.

The school continued under the aegis of the San Antonio Art League until 1962, making slow but definite progress in spite of crippling financial limitations. Since then it has operated as an independent organization under its own

Board of Trustees, enjoying a close relationship with the Marion Koogler McNay Art Museum. The present faculty is composed of trained teachers with academic degrees. All have their master of fine arts degrees and are recognized artists in their own fields.

An addition to the Art Institute in 1975 and another 50,000 square feet scheduled for completion in 1986 will help, with the outstanding faculty, to provide the facilities for making this an independent College of Art—the first in the Southwest.

The Art Institute offers instructions in studio art and art appreciation. Classes are designed for beginning, intermediate, and advanced students. Field trips, workshops, exhibitions, and lectures by visiting artists supplement the program. Students may enroll full- or part-time. There are no formal requirements to enter the nondegree activities.

The Art Institute has acquired prestige from the distinguished

artists who have been associated with it as teachers and as students. Artists and scholars of high standing are brought in to lecture. Students benefit from the permanent and loan exhibits at the McNay Art Museum and from the excellent library.

Southwest Research Institute and Southwest Foundation for Research and Education

The Southwest Foundation was established in 1941 by Tom B. Slick. In 1947 he added the Southwest Research Institute to the organization. Tom Slick was an oil man interested in all phases of science, real and simulated. Some of his projects included: concrete slabs poured on the ground and then lifted for various floor levels, two or more expeditions searching for the Abominable Snowman, the institute of Inventive Research to promote researched or submitted inventions, and the Mind Science Foundation to delve into extrasensory perception.

Tom Slick died in a small-plane crash, returning from a Canadian hunting trip, October 6, 1962. These organizations have grown and perhaps changed their format but they still represent the seed planted by Tom Slick.

Southwest Research Institute

Southwest Research Institute (6220 Culebra Road) is the third largest among eight independent, nonprofit, applied research and development organizations in the country. It is eight miles west of downtown San Antonio on 471 acres.

It has two thousand employees in more than 1 million square feet of laboratories, workshops, and offices. At any given time the scientists and engineers can be working on more than fifteen hundred pro-

jects in the physical sciences and engineering disciplines. Due to security, tours are limited to groups that have interest affiliation in the Institute's research.

Southwest Foundation

This biomedical research center (West Loop 410 and Military Drive) encompasses 912 acres containing 195,000 square feet of laboratory space, library space, an animal hospital, and specially designed facilities to accommodate three thousand nonhuman primates and four thousand research animals of other species. Visiting is limited but some of its large baboon colonies can be seen from Loop 410.

The Southwest Foundation for Biomedical Research staff consists of approximately 40 research scientists and 190 technicians and other staff members who are actively engaged in full-time research into the

detection, cause, cure, prevention, and elimination of disease.

The Argyle

The Argyle (934 Patterson Avenue, Alamo Heights), a distinguished landmark on the heights overlooking San Antonio from the north for more than a century, has been converted into an exclusive club for sponsors of the Southwest Foundation for Research and Education and their friends. It is not open to the public.

There was already an old stone house on the spot when Colonel Charles Anderson built his home here. The colonel was a gentleman who raised fine horses; two of his famous studs were "Jehoshaphat" and "Nebuchadnezzar." He also had hunting parties at his home, which was in 1859 in the midst of wild-game country. Among his guests, Albert Sidney Johnston and

Robert E. Lee are said to have slept here.

Anderson was a rabid Unionist and a friend of Sam Houston. In the fall of 1860 he made an antisecession speech in front of the Menger Hotel. His life was threatened by a proslavery order known as the "Knights of the Golden Circle." One story has it that he left town disguised in women's clothes. Anyhow, he left, and became a prominent politician up North.

The Argyle was so named by a Scotsman because the view reminded him of his native hills. It was successively a ranch, a stagecoach inn, and after 1893 a hotel, under the management of Alice O'Grady, whose meals made it so famous she was persuaded to publish her recipes in a book.

An effort has been made to restore the building, rescued as late as 1955 from an uncertain fate, to its original simplicity. Each of the six upstairs suites has for a motif one of the six flags (French, Spanish, Mexican, Texas, Confederate, United States) that symbolize the sovereignties which have claimed Texas.

Catholic Archives

(2718 West Woodlawn)
Open: Monday through Friday,
8:30 A.M. to 4:30 P.M.

In the fall of 1973, Archbishop Francis J. Furey initiated a new department to work out of the Catholic Chancery. The project was to develop an archival facility where all existing Catholic records and historical material in the possession of archdiocesan authorities could be made available to researchers. To this department has been entrusted the assignment of sorting out and cataloging thousands of manuscripts dating back to the sixteenth century —papers and records from the earliest mission period through the modern, social justice era.

The Catholic Archives occupies quarters in the Chancery Building (constructed 1983), including a beautifully designed research library, a microfilm department, and work areas. The task of taking inventory, cataloging, and putting into retrievable condition literally millions of pages of important records was done years ago by a team of volunteers. Now the records are kept up to date by the trained staff.

The Research Library has increasingly attracted national attention from serious researchers who find entirely new fields of historical documentation from previously untouched sources.

12

Army and Air Force

Of the places covered in this chapter, the most worthwhile to the visitor with general interests will be the Quadrangle at Fort Sam Houston, which has charm as well as historic value. The others are included in this list because of their over-all importance rather than because of any particular appeal.

Changes and developments in these installations are rapid and often sweeping. Visitors should consult the information offices at each base for up-to-date information.

Visitors to air force bases must stop at the gate and receive the guard's recognition before entering.

The following order is for the convenience of those who want to see *all* the bases. By following Military Drive from U.S. Highway 90W to Loop 13 on the east, it is possible to get a quick view of the air force bases (except Randolph) without entering any of them.

Fort Sam Houston

Quadrangle

(Grayson Street entrance)
Open: daily, 9:00 A.M. to 6:00 P.M.
Admission: free

Military Museum

(North New Braunfels to Wilson and S4)
Open: Wednesday through Sunday, 10:00 A.M. to 4:00 P.M.
Admission: free.

Medical Museum

(North New Braunfels to Stanley and Connell)
Open: Monday through Friday, 8:00 A.M. to 11:30 A.M. and 12:30 P.M. to 4:00 P.M.
Admission: free.

Lackland Air Force Base

(Highway 90—entrance on Military West or Highway 13)

History and Traditions Museum

Open: Monday through Friday,
9:00 A.M. to 6:00 P.M.
Admission: free.

Kelly Air Force Base

In the southwest part of the city. It is a working, or repair, air base and parts are "restricted" or "controlled."
Best access is via Gen. McMullen Drive or Gen. Hudnell Road.

Brooks Air Force Base

(6 miles southeast of downtown San Antonio, on Southeast Military Drive, exit I 37)

Museum of Aerospace Medicine

(Hangar 9: Edward H. White II Memorial Museum)
Open: Monday through Friday,
8:00 A.M. to 4:00 P.M.
Admission: free.

Randolph Air Force Base

(19 miles northeast of downtown San Antonio, by U.S. Interstate 35N; turn right at Pat Booker Road) Tours, including the "Taj Mahal" elevator, can be arranged through the Public Affairs Division.

San Antonio has been a military center for over two centuries and a half—or since 1718, when the king of Spain's viceroy in Mexico sent soldiers and a Franciscan friar to found here a fort and a mission.
It was an outpost against menacing Indians for a century and a half.
It was of strategic importance, and the scene of frightful carnage, in the Mexican revolution against Spain and in the Texan revolution against Mexico. There have always been barracks and soldiers in San Antonio except for a brief time during the precarious days of the Republic of Texas (1836–1845). Then a band of some fifteen Texas Rangers held in check thousands of hostile Indians, and, on occasion, Mexican troops.
For more than a century, this has been the principal bastion, lookout, and training post of the United States Army in the Southwest.
In the fall of 1845—the year Texas joined the Union—Colonel

William S. Harney inspected San Antonio with a view to establishing a United States Army supply depot here and occupied the ancient barracks then on Military Plaza. Troops were temporarily encamped on two sites at the same time: present-day Brackenridge Park and Mission Concepción. In 1846, the year of the Mexican War, some 2,800 volunteers from the northern states and Texas were trained here by General Wool at various camps around the city, including San Pedro Springs. General Wool marched the troops into Mexico in September, 1846, where they joined General Taylor's army.

The first permanent military facilities were set up in the church and part of the convent of the Alamo, rebuilt from ruins, in 1849/50. For the next thirty years this was a quartermaster's depot, used for forage, camp and garrison equipment, and part of the work shops.

San Antonio, in the 1850's, was headquarters and supply center for a line of frontier forts that stretched south to the border and west to New Mexico.

Military offices and barracks were moved about the town, from one privately owned building to another. In the 1870's the city donated ninety-two acres of land as a site for a permanent military post. This was the beginning of Fort Sam Houston, called, until 1890, Post of San Antonio.

The government payroll has long been the mainstay of San Antonio's economy.

In modern times, San Antonio has become a great air force center, with bases covering thousands of acres, employing and training thousands of uniformed personnel and civilian workers.

Fort Sam Houston

Fort Sam Houston is the oldest military unit still operating in San Antonio. Since the completion of the Quadrangle (1878), it has been, except for two short periods, headquarters of the military establishment for this area of the United States. It occupies over 3,000 acres, with more than fifteen hundred buildings.

In addition to Post Headquarters, the principal activities at Fort Sam Houston are Headquarters Fifth Army, Brooke Army Medical Center, Health Services Command, Academy of Health Sciences, and the U.S. Modern Pentathlon Training Center.

The Quadrangle

One of the most picturesque spots in San Antonio is the old Quadrangle of Fort Sam Houston, built between 1876 and 1878, with its

In the Quadrangle, Fort Sam Houston

stern, massive walls, its ninety-seven–foot medieval clock tower (originally a water tower with a tank on top; the clock replaced the tank in 1882), its pond and greensward, the swans and ducks, the deer and peacocks.

The Quadrangle was actually built for defense. There were no doors or windows in the outside walls, only small loopholes near the top. Rooms open on the inner court. Entrance is through a sally port in the south wall (Grayson Street).

When Geronimo, the Apache chief, was confined here with his band in 1886, some of the braves decided to climb the tower to the top. The clock chimed, and the braves came scrambling down in disorder.

Staff, Artillery, and Infantry Posts

The second unit built here (1881) was the Staff Post, fifteen sets of large two-story residences of stone, west of the Quadrangle, at Grayson and Pine streets. Typical mansions of the 1880's, designed by architect Alfred Giles, they were built to house the commander of the Headquarters, Department of Texas, and his staff. The hospital, built in 1886, has been converted into the Sam Houston Guest House.

The third unit (1886–1894) was the Infantry Post, east of North New Braunfels at Grayson Street. The twenty-six sets of spacious brick quarters accommodated the line officers, and the long barracks at the eastern slope of the parade grounds quartered eight companies of troops. These were the first permanent barracks built here. The parade grounds were eliminated in 1948 when duplexes were built there. A plaque on building No. 688 (Apt. E) proclaims that First Lieutenant and Mrs. Dwight D. Eisenhower lived there in 1916. The troops had formerly been quartered in town, beside the river,

which was considered an unhealthy location, both because of the damp and because some of the men would drink heavily, then take a swim, and a number drowned. The removal was therefore, in some degree, a health measure.

The fourth unit (1905-1911) was the Artillery and Cavalry Post, its contoured road lined with spacious brick homes across the parade grounds from the Artillery and Cavalry barracks.

These four units, along with the main post chapel (Gift Chapel) and portions of the pentathlon stable area, were given National Historic Landmark status May 15, 1975. The entire area includes approximately four hundred acres.

U.S. Army Health Services Command

U.S. Army Health Services Command (HSC) provides health services for the army within the continental United States, Alaska, and Hawaii. Under the direction of HSC is the Academy of Health Sciences, which conducts most of the army medical department's training of officers and enlisted personnel. All army medical department officers come here to take the basic orientation course. All enlistees going into the medical service receive the base health service course here. In association with certain civilian institutions, graduates of the academy courses can receive degrees. Qualified personnel receive master's degrees in preventive medicine, nurse anesthesiology, health care administration, and physical therapy. Students who participate in any of the seventy courses, primarily for enlisted personnel, upon completion can receive college credits, transferable to civilian colleges.

Brooke Army Medical Center, under the direction of HSC, is one of the largest teaching and patient care hospitals in the army. Attached to the medical center is the

Institute of Surgical Research, which has attained international recognition for outstanding research and treatment of severe burns. Specialized teams fly from here throughout the United States bringing seriously burned patients to Brooke for specialized, intensive burn treatment.

Military Assistance to Safety and Traffic (MAST) is a program designed by the Departments of Defense, Health and Human Services, and Transportation to rapidly move injured civilians from the surrounding community to hospitals when immediate medical care is required. Army helicopters, pilots, and medical corpsmen are used to transport accident victims and emergency patients.

MAST began at Fort Sam Houston in July, 1970, when the 507th Medical Company (air ambulance) was the first unit chosen to test the innovative, lifesaving program by the Department of Defense. The program has been so successful that it is continuing on an indefinite basis. Not only has the program been of incalculable value to citizens around and in San Antonio, but it also has enabled the medical specialists and the air ambulance crews to maintain their skills.

The U.S. Modern Pentathlon Training Center trains athletes in the five sports of the Modern Pentathlon: riding, fencing, shooting, swimming, and cross-country running. National and international competitions are conducted here, and the training center selects teams to compete in the Pan American Games, the Pentathlon World Championships, the International Military Pentathlon Championships, and the Olympic Games.

Brooke Army Hospital was named for Brigadier General Roger Brooke, one-time chief of the station hospital at Fort Sam Houston, who had a distinguished career.

History: Fort Sam Houston

The ninety-two acres of land for the original government post were donated by the city in 1870, 1871, and 1875. The Quadrangle, begun in 1876, was occupied in January, 1878, by the U.S. Quartermaster Depot, which had formerly been in the Alamo. But it was not until 1890 that the whole post, by then much enlarged, was named after General Sam Houston, victor of the Battle of San Jacinto in the Texas revolution against Mexico, first president of the Republic of Texas, and governor of the state (1859–1861).

On September 10, 1886, Geronimo, the Apache chief, was brought in as a prisoner, along with his warriors, their squaws, and their papooses. They were encamped, under guard, in the Quadrangle, for over a month.

In 1898, Fort Sam Houston again got national attention when Colonel Leonard Wood arrived to make preparations for the encampment and training of the "Rough Riders," who were then being recruited by Theodore Roosevelt for the war against Spain. The actual training was done at Riverside Golf Park, on the south side of town. Roosevelt arrived on May 15, and the regiment departed for Cuba on May 29.

In 1910, the first beginnings of the great air force center that San Antonio now is were made by Lieutenant Benjamin D. Foulois, who unpacked, from seventeen boxes, the first airplane ever owned by the United States Army. It was a biplane, bought from the Wright brothers in 1909, a contraption of bamboo poles and canvas fitted around a gasoline engine—a wheelless, pusher-type stick and jenny, swung off the ground from a monorail. The first flights were successful: a height of 150 feet was attained. As a result of these experiments, the Aviation Section, Signal Corps, was established in 1914. In 1915 Captain Foulois built the first permanent airdrome at Fort Sam Houston. It housed the entire United States Army Air Corps—six planes. In 1916 this force took part in the wild-goose chase after Pancho Villa, over the mountains of Mexico.

In 1916, too, an encampment of seventeen thousand National Guardsmen was here, called Camp Wilson. In 1917, during the First World War, a huge cantonment, Camp Travis, was spread out here.

In the Second World War, experiments conducted by the Second Infantry Division, under the command of General Walter Krueger, resulted in the present triangular form of the infantry division. The first airborne maneuvers were conducted here in 1942. Three infantry divisions and a wide variety of corps and service-force units trained here.

Thousands of troops and inductees had been processed through the Fort Sam Houston Reception Center when it closed in 1953.

Camp Bullis

Camp Bullis (18 miles northwest of San Antonio, off U.S. Highway 87), a subpost of 28,000 acres, is used for training reserves, National Guard, R.O.T.C., air force, and regular army troops.

Kelly Air Force Base

Kelly Air Force Base is one of the world's greatest repair and supply bases for planes. Much of the base is controlled.

Kelly is the largest single employer of civilians in the Southwest. Because of its government wage scale and other benefits, it has been a boon to the economy of

San Antonio. Especially grateful are its numerous Spanish-speaking employees, who have made a song (actually a polka) about it: "No te acabes, Kelly Field." Freely translated, this could mean "Please don't peter out, Kelly Field."

The Air Logistics Center is the major organization at Kelly.

The Hangar

One of the most arresting sights in San Antonio is at Kelly: a giant airplane hangar of revolutionary design, one of the largest in the world. Engineers from all over have come to Kelly to see the stupendous building, a mile in circumference—so huge that eleven football games could be carried on there at the same time.

Constructed at a cost of $13 million, the building has a 250-foot unsupported section at its center. Its massive 672-ton rolling doors are large enough to permit easy entry of the air force's largest intercontinental bombers.

Within the hangar, the aircraft production line and the shops unit are housed under the same roof.

Air force ships fly into Kelly from all over the world for servicing jobs that may include retreading the tires, manufacturing the Plexiglas canopies, and overhauling the engines. It is the sole repairer of the C-5A Galaxy airplane and engine, the world's largest aircraft. The base also has a two-mile runway designed for landing the C-5A and other large aircraft, such as the C-141, B-1, and B-52 bombers.

Kelly is also headquarters for the Air Force Electronic Security Service, Commissary Service, 433rd Tactical Aircraft Reserve Wing, and 149th Tactical Fighter Group of the Texas Air National Guard.

History: Kelly Air Force Base

Kelly Air Force Base was named for Second Lieutenant George E. M. Kelly (born in London, England), who died in a crash at Fort Sam Houston on May 10, 1911—the first army aviator to lose his life while piloting a military aircraft.

As a result of this accident, flying activity in the San Antonio area was suspended for several years.

Kelly began as an aviation depot and pilot training school in 1917. The oldest continuous military aviation base in Texas, it was one of the first in the United States.

Virtually all the Air Force commanders who received their pilot wings before World War II were trained at Kelly. Charles A. Lindbergh received his flight training here. Jimmy Doolittle was stationed here when he made his famous "dawn to dusk" flight in 1922, spanning the continent for the first time in daylight hours. Billy Mitchell and Hap Arnold were once familiar figures here.

Since the inception of the air force, Kelly has grown in size and importance. During World War II the flying-school activities were transferred elsewhere and Kelly is now best known as one of the world's largest aircraft supply and overhaul depots. It covers 3,924 acres with a perimeter of 19 miles.

Since 1956, Kelly has housed a squadron of the Air National Guard, installed at a cost of over $1 million.

Lackland Air Force Base

Lackland Air Force Base is known as "The Gateway to the Air Force." It is the largest air force base in the United States in terms of population, which exceeds 33,000 during peak periods.

All male and female recruits must take their basic training at Lackland's Basic Military Training School, as must all Air National Guard and Air Force Reserve enlistees.

USAF School of Applied Aerospace Sciences

The largest of its kind in the air force, the school offers approximately seventy-five different courses of instruction. Thousands of new security policemen, cryptographic technicians, recruiters, academic and military training instructors, and social action counselors are trained annually by the school's five departments. The school is also responsible for training all dogs and dog handlers assigned to Department of Defense agencies.

Also at Lackland is the Air Force Officer Training School, which has commissioned almost sixty thousand air force officers since it was organized here in 1959. Approximately 70 percent of the trainees entering the school have no prior service; the balance are active-duty airmen who possess college degrees in areas needed to fill air force specialties.

The Defense Language Institute, English Language Branch, trains young men and women from many parts of the world who come to Lackland for English-language training.

Wilford Hall U.S.A.F. Medical Center, the largest air force hospital in the world, provides specialized medical training and care. The nine-story medical center was constructed in 1957 and dominates the base. It receives patients from around the globe.

History and Traditions Museum

Opened to the public in 1956, the museum houses exhibits showing the progress of military aviation. On display are a skeleton of a Jenny (JN-4) aircraft, armament and navigational aids, and an assortment of more than twenty aircraft engines, including the Hispano-Suiza, a Le Rhone rotary, and a Liberty 12. The actual wind-tunnel plane model used to develop the first American jet aircraft—the Bell P-59—is shown.

Three-dimensional color dioramas depict the first military flight, the first flying school, the first round-the-world flight, and other historic events.

Parked in various areas throughout the base are more than fifty aircraft on static display. These include the B-17, P-63, F-82, F-104, F-80 (the first jet), and many others.

History: Lackland Air Force Base

Until 1942, Lackland was a desolate, mesquite-covered bombing range on a hill above Kelly Field. Planned by the late Brigadier General Frank D. Lackland, pioneer commander of Kelly Field, it took the name of San Antonio Aviation Cadet Center after the bombing of Pearl Harbor touched off an enormous expansion, a thousand buildings springing up.

Here ground training was provided for more than a third of the nation's fliers. At the high point of operation, in August, 1943, the base had a military population of more than 31,000. It was named Lackland Air Force Base in July, 1947.

After the war in Europe ended, the base began the huge task of separating and reassigning the flow of combat veterans. Within six months, more than thirty thousand air force personnel were separated here. Of this number, four thousand had been prisoners of the Germans.

Brooks Air Force Base

Brooks Air Force Base is of historic and growing importance.

The first oil production ever reported in Texas (forty-nine barrels for the year 1886) was on the George Dullnig ranch, near Brooks. A marker was placed on the south side of Southeast Military Drive, east of Goliad Road, in 1956.

School of Aerospace Medicine

Brooks is the site of the free world's finest aerospace medical research center.

During July, 1959, the School of Aviation Medicine became the principal activity at Brooks. Founded in 1918, at a small army airfield on Long Island (Mitchel Field), New York, the School of Aviation Medicine was transferred to Brooks on June 30, 1926, and remained there for five years before being moved to the newly activated base at Randolph Field in October, 1931. There it remained for more than a quarter of a century before being returned to Brooks in 1959.

On October 1, 1959, the school was incorporated into the newly established Aerospace Medical Center, which represented the initial step toward the placement of the management of aerospace medical research, education, and certain clinical practices under one command. Two years later it was designated the Aerospace Medical Division.

Formal dedication of the $40-million-dollar complex of modern buildings occupied by the division headquarters and the USAF School of Aerospace Medicine was made on November 21, 1963, by President John F. Kennedy.

Brooks became the location of another unit of the Air Force System Command on July 1, 1968. Designated the Air Force Human Resources Laboratory, the newly formed organization is now part of the Aerospace Medical Division.

Every aspect of flight medicine is examined at the School of Aerospace Medicine. The giant twenty-foot human centrifuge at the school aids in medical research as a high-G training device. In addition to research, the school provides training for flight surgeons, flight nurses, and other medical personnel involved with operational flying units.

The mission of the school is three-fold: (1) to furnish latest educational techniques to air force personnel in the field of air medicine; (2) to carry on a vast network of research projects, which cover such a variety of problems as air sickness among flying crews, aircraft accident proneness, sealed cabins for space flight, treatment of injuries from cold, and noise hazards from jets; (3) to engage in the special practice of aviation medicine.

Medical officers from all over the world have been among the students of the school. Through the exchange of advanced aeromedical knowledge with the officers, and the exchange of duty tours between our medical officers and those of friendly countries, all students are assured a thorough introduction to world-wide aeromedical problems and procedures.

The Museum of Aerospace Medicine

The Museum of Aerospace Medicine (Hangar 9: Edward H. White II Memorial Museum) was opened June 30, 1970. The hangar, built in 1918, was the ninth hangar in a row of sixteen and is one of the oldest in the air force. In 1967, when the air force planned to demolish the hangar because it was a potential fire hazard, a group of San Antonians petitioned the air force to spare it, resulting in its being temporariliy leased to the Bexar County Historical Survey Committee (now the Bexar County Historical Commission), which obtained funds for the restoration. Mr. and Mrs. Harry Jersig were instrumental in conducting the campaign and personally subsidized much of the effort to restore Hangar 9 to its original condition. It is dedicated to and named for air force Lieutenant Colonel Edward H. White II, who was born at Fort Sam Houston and was the first American to walk in space. He lost his life in 1967 in the

Hangar 9, Brooks Air Force Base

tragic space-capsule fire at Cape Canaveral. The museum houses a special display on Ed White.

Also on display are military uniforms related to aviation from the First World War to the present, including the Gosport tube and space helmets. Approximately 60 percent of the displays pertain to aerospace medicine.

History: Brooks Air Force Base

Founded in December, 1917, Brooks Field was named for Cadet Sidney J. Brooks, Jr., who was killed that year on a training flight from Kelly Field.

Brooks's first mission was to train men as instructors in the Gosport system of flying instruction. This was a simple and unique system: a speaking tube between instructor and student carried to the fledgling airman words of caution and encouragement.

In May, 1919, the first balloon and airship school was opened at Brooks, where it stayed until 1922, when a primary flying school was established. Among the famous flyers trained here were Charles A. Lindbergh, Claire Chennault, Thomas D. White, Nathan F. Twining, and Curtis LeMay. The first mass parachute drop anywhere was demonstrated at Brooks when paratroops and supplies were dropped from aircraft on April 28, 1929.

Brooks became the center of activity for observation aviation in late 1931, when the primary flying school was transferred to Randolph. Advanced pilots and combat observers for the Second World War were trained here.

In the Korean War, the 182nd Fighter-Bomber Squadron of the Texas Air National Guard was organized and trained at Brooks. After flying six thousand sorties in Korea, the unit was returned to state control in June, 1952.

An era in aviation history ended on June 23, 1960, when the last takeoff from Brooks runways was made. All flight operations were discontinued on the base after a period of forty-two years of service to the army and the air force, and all aircraft was reassigned to other bases in the local area.

Brooks had entered into a new era of aerospace medicine.

Randolph Air Force Base

Randolph Air Force Base, better known as Randolph Field, is the most famous, though not the oldest, training school for flyers in the United States.

With its much-photographed tower (called the "Taj Mahal" by cadets), its fame as the "West Point of the Air," and its identification with the "Flying Cadets" of the 1940's, Randolph's name has a glamor that no other airfield can boast.

It is headquarters of the Air Training Command.

The "Taj Mahal" and the Missing Man Monument, Randolph Air Force Base

History: Randolph Air Force Base

The base, built on land donated by citizens of San Antonio in 1928, was named after Captain William M. Randolph, who was killed that same year in a crash at Gorman, Texas, while assigned to Kelly. It was dedicated in June, 1930.

Randolph's colorful history has closely paralleled the growth of air power—from the PT-13's of aviation's early days to modern jets.

During the first decade of its operation, and until the air force began a tremendous expansion in 1939, Randolph was the largest primary and basic school of the air.

Randolph-trained pilots, a select group of some five thousand, formed the nucleus of a great air armada built up during the Second World War and again during the Korean War.

They led the raids over Tokyo; they flew the Hump in China-Burma-India; they bombed Berlin, Italy, and North Africa; they manned the planes that flew under the United Nations flag in Korea.

In 1943/44, when the need for pilot instructors was most critical, some fifteen thousand pilots learned here the techniques of training others to fly.

By 1950, when the now-obsolete B-29 was based at Randolph, the school was training crews to operate as a unit, rather than teaching individuals to fly.

Randolph Air Force Base is now the home of the 12th Flying Training Wing. In addition to its flying training missions, the wing plays host to the Headquarters Air Training Command, Headquarters Air Force Manpower and Personnel Center, Headquarters Air Force Recruiting Service, Air Force Instrument Flight Center, and Office of Civilian Personnel Operations.

Randolph has a primary base mission of pilot-instructor training. The pilots learn the techniques of teaching students to fly all sizes and types of aircraft.

13

A Chapter on Churches

The churches of San Antonio that are of outstanding interest are, of course, historic, and many, therefore, are Catholic. These are treated in other chapters, as follows:

San Fernando Cathedral

See Chapter 6.

The Missions

See Chapter 7; for additional history, Chapter 2.

The Alamo

Not regarded as a church, but see Chapters 2 and 3.

Besides the historic churches listed above, the following are treated, for special reasons, in other chapters:

St. Joseph's Church

Catholic, in Chapter 8.

Guadalupe Church

Catholic, in Chapter 9.

Villita Church

Nondenominational, in Chapter 5.

Chapel of the Miracles

See Chapters 2 and 9.

Catholic Churches

(Other than Historic)

Shrine of the Little Flower

Shrine of the Little Flower (southwest corner Zarzamora Street and Kentucky Avenue) is an imposing edifice built in 1930 at a cost of half a million dollars. The statues are from Spain, the Stations of the Cross from Germany, the marble altars from Italy. White marble tablets on the walls are inscribed with the names of donors from all over the world.

St. Peter Claver Church

St. Peter Claver Church (northeast corner Nolan and Liveoak streets), a tiny gem of a chapel, built in 1888, was the first Catholic church for Negroes in western Texas and the first church in the United States to be named for St. Peter Claver, Jesuit missionary who worked among African slaves in South America and who was canonized in 1888. The church, as well as the adjacent school and an order (Sister-Servants of the Holy Ghost and Mary Immaculate), was founded for the benefit of the Negroes by Mrs. Margaret Murphy, widow of a mayor of Corpus Christi. She dedicated her life and fortune to the service of the race after hearing Father Richard Maloney, a native of Ireland and pastor of St. Mary's Church, deliver a sermon denouncing the southern custom of restricting Negroes to a few seats in the rear of the congregation.

Lourdes Grotto Sanctuary

Lourdes Grotto Sanctuary (on the grounds of the seminary, De Mazenod Scholasticate, 285 Oblate Drive) is an exact replica of the famed Shrine of Lourdes in southern France.

Protestant Churches

Travis Park Methodist Church

Travis Park Methodist Church (southwest corner Travis and St. Mary's streets) is the direct successor of the first Methodist congregation in San Antonio. The church was built on its present location in 1883 and has been many times remodeled, without losing its original charm.

The first Protestant sermon in San Antonio was preached by John Wesley DeVilbiss in April, 1844. He rode in with another young minister, John McCullough, a Presbyterian, and an escort of Jack Hays's Texas Rangers from Seguin, for the Indians were hostile. About fifteen people attended the services at the county clerk's office, then on Commerce Street. They sang "Jesus, Lover of My Soul." DeVilbiss preached; McCullough closed with a prayer. They left town two days later.

But DeVilbiss returned in 1845 and preached in the parlor of the Veramendi House, then on Soledad Street. The innkeeper, an Italian, fixed up the room in a neat and proper manner for divine service, with a clean white cloth on the table, a pitcher of water, comfortable seats for the assembly. He also placed on the table a bottle of port. When DeVilbiss asked him to take it away, the innkeeper remonstrated: It would greatly improve the quality of the sermon; the priests in Italy would not think of preaching without the assistance of good wine. Besides, this was the very best wine.

DeVilbiss preached, without the assistance of wine, several times, and the next year, 1846, he was stationed in San Antonio. He had some trouble getting a place to preach. He finally obtained the use of the Courthouse (the Spanish *casas reales*, the Council House of bloody memory) on the east side of Main Plaza. He made pews and a pulpit with his own hands. There was one great annoyance. Just as he would start preaching, a large noisy crowd led by Americans would gather in the plaza and engage in cockfighting.

About this time "some friend" reported to Hays's company of Texas Rangers that DeVilbiss had denounced them in a church publication as a mean, contemptible set of men. DeVilbiss protested that he had not written the article. But the rangers were furious. They plotted to duck him in the river.

He heard of the plot, invited the rangers to attend services Sunday, and established his innocence. Some of them became regular attendants, and the cockfighting ceased—anyhow, it was moved away from the plaza.

In the hope of building a church, DeVilbiss bought a lot on Villita Street (just across the alley from the Cos House) and made a trip to the northern states in quest of funds. He bought a good bell at Cincinnati. On his return, he set the bell up at La Villita. He "wanted the people to see that we had made a start." He would swing it lustily, then cross the river and meet his congregation in the Courthouse a quarter of a mile away.

Meanwhile his old friend the Presbyterian, McCullough, had bought a lot on Commerce Street and was building an adobe house on it. He persuaded DeVilbiss to turn over the building material he had bought, with the understanding that the church would be used by both congregations. This arrangement worked smoothly. But toward the end of 1847 DeVilbiss discovered, to his consternation, that the title to his lot in La Villita was no good. In 1848 he took another post.

Not until 1853 did the Methodists build their own church, on Soledad Street. In 1860 they counted 55 white members, 20 Negroes. In 1883 the first unit of the present church was opened, with 237 members.

First Presbyterian Church

First Presbyterian Church (northeast corner of Fourth Street and Avenue D) is the direct successor of John McCullough's tiny church once on Commerce Street, which was used until 1860.

"It was of adobe, and was one long room," wrote Vinton James. "When church services were over we boys, concealed behind the fence, would place a large dead snake in a coiled position on the sidewalk, and about the time the home-going crowd passed we would give the string attached to the snake a violent pull, which caused a panic among the ladies."

John McCullough had opened this, the first Protestant church in San Antonio, in 1846. He opened a day school and, in his own words, "continued it for three years without molestation, and to the gratification of the citizens." He was not so fortunate with his church, however:

You can have no idea at present of the difficulty of getting a foothold for the gospel in San Antonio in those early times. I was persecuted, slandered and insulted. Every effort was made by ungodly Americans to induce me to leave. The town was overrun by a devilish set of men and gamblers. I had occasion to rebuke them publicly in the pulpit and recommended a Vigilance Committee to execute law and keep order. For this and other causes I was threatened with violence and subjected to daily danger.

The gamblers would gamble and rowdy all night and sleep most of the day. They kept up a continual shouting during the night, back and forward between the Alamo and Main Plaza, and disturbed my sleep so that for several months I got very little rest. I took occasion to give them my sentiments from the pulpit. This gave them mortal offense.

Among McCullough's enemies was the murderous John Glanton, who, according to an old newspaper account, "quarreled with a man on one of the plazas, struck him over the head with a long horse pistol such a blow that the barrel was broken in two. Then he dashed down the street at a fearful pace to his home, right next to the Presbyterian school. When the minister, possessor of the only plug hat in town, put his head out of the win-

240

dow to locate the desperado, the latter perforated the tiara with his little gun, so for many years the only plug hat in San Antonio had more holes in it than are *au fait*."

Another time six or eight desperados went heavily armed to McCullough's house to murder him. He saw them approach and knew their design. He went into the strongest room, barricaded the door as well as he could. The only weapon he could find was a hatchet. With that in hand he stood by the door. They fired through it six or eight balls. Two grazed his head; two cut his clothes at the side. This was more than even the stout heart of McCullough could take. He left San Antonio in 1849 and never came back.

In 1860 the Presbyterians laid the cornerstone for a large and, considering the epoch, elegant edifice on the northeast corner of West Houston and North Flores streets, which was finished in 1865, right after the Civil War. It stood proud-ly until 1907. Later the former church buttresses flanked a liquor store and a hot dog emporium, but all traces vanished about 1980.

First Baptist Church

First Baptist Church (202 Fifth Street), a huge structure with a huge membership, is the oldest of the many Baptist churches in the city.

The Baptists got off to a late start. In 1861 their church, opposite the Veramendi House on Soledad Street, had only thirteen members. Ten years later they built the First Baptist Church on the southeast corner across from Travis Park. Wrote Mrs. Charlotte Jones:

The first Baptist minister came in the fall of 1855, traveling on horseback. With him he brought his personal possessions: his horse, saddle and a pair of rather worn saddlebags. One side of the saddlebags contained his wearing apparel, Bible and hymn book, and the other side was devoted to the commissary department: a small tin cup and a piece of bacon and a hardtack. He had long white ringlets and black laughing eyes. He carried a green umbrella that protected him from the burning rays of the sun. As he got to Main Plaza he halted and inquired, "Is there any Baptists in this town?" He was directed to a store, where the merchant [Enoch Jones] told him he could find lodgings at his wife's hotel; she was a Baptist. To a clerk, the merchant said, "Show the stranger up to the house and tell my wife this is a Baptist preacher." The parson thanked him, shouted "Eureka!" and was proceeding to the door when his gaze fell upon his faithful steed, footsore and weary; turning to the merchant with a troubled expression, he said, "This is my horse, and he is a Baptist, too."

He remained in town a week, preaching at the Courthouse on Military Plaza every night.

The first baptizing was done in the San Antonio River in 1857. Pious merchants donated lead, which was sewn into the hems of ladies' skirts to keep those garments from rising in the water.

St. John's Lutheran Church

St. John's Lutheran Church (302 East Nueva Street) was the first congregation of German Protestants in San Antonio. Its beginnings go back to 1852, when its founder, P. F. Zizelmann, arrived without friends, shelter, or funds for food. He was greeted by a tipsy reception committee of one, with a Nassau accent:

"You're a greenhorn, ain't you?"

"I'm a Lutheran pastor."

"Then I suggest you go back wherever you came from. We've got too many preachers as it is."

But Zizelmann did preach next day, to an audience of fifteen, including children and Negroes. He organized classes and was about to start a church, when illness overtook him. Four years later he returned, founded a congregation in 1857, built the first small church in 1860. The Civil War intervened; when the fifth anniversary was celebrated, only seven members were present. The rest had been drafted or were in hiding or had been killed trying to escape to Mexico. Most Germans were Union sympathizers. But after the war the church flourished. In 1875 a tower was added, topped by a steeple with a rooster for a weather vane. St. John's became known as the "rooster church." The nickname persisted even after the vane had been discarded and a new church built. The present structure dates from 1932. The educational building, once a hotel, dates from 1875.

St. Mark's Episcopal Church

At first sight, St. Mark's Church (315 East Pecan Street), with its graceful English Gothic lines, appears to be one more building whose design was lifted straight out of the Old World.

But if the style is English, the church has, nevertheless, a personality all its own.

For one thing, it has many close ties with the history of San Antonio and of Texas. A list of the parishioners, beginning with the then Colonel Robert E. Lee, would include an impressive number of men whose names are outstanding. Lee was a member of St. Mark's before the Civil War, before the church was built.

The church was built on historic soil—lands that formerly belonged to the ancient Mission of San Antonio de Valero, whose church is now the Alamo—and the cream-colored limestone walls came from quarries hacked out in Spanish times.

Its bell was cast from a cannon which had been found near the outer wall of the Alamo by Samuel A. Maverick, who had built his home at the northwest corner of the old mission quadrangle (now Alamo Plaza) because he wanted to live in view of the place where his comrades had died. He would have died with them if he had not been their envoy, before the siege, to represent them at the Convention that declared the independence of Texas. Perhaps this is the meaning of the inscription on the bell, which reads, in part, "I too have been born from works of death to words of life through Christ's eternal merit." Of course, the phrase applies to the bell itself, too.

The bell also bears the Texas Star, with the word *Alamo* in the center and the dates 1813 and 1836. Apparently Maverick was somehow sure that the gun had not been used at the Battle of the Alamo—that it had been buried by the revolutionists who took San Antonio from the king of Spain's soldiers in 1813. "Being about to march against an approaching army of royalists," wrote Dean W. R. Richardson, "they spiked all the cannons in the city except a few field pieces which they took with them into battle. A number of the guns were buried and the rest were run into the river." Just how the dean, or Maverick, identified this particular gun, we are not told. The dean says positively that it "bore no part" in the battle of 1836. He also says that a third date, 1876, is on the bell. Anyhow, it hangs in a belfry that is well-nigh inaccessible.

St. Mark's has the mellowness of those special places which have evoked the deepest emotions of a great many lives.

The cornerstone was laid in December, 1859. The walls, which had been partially reared when the Civil War stopped all work on the building, turned quite gray from exposure to the weather, and strangers often mistook them for the ruins of a Spanish mission. Work was not resumed until 1873. Meanwhile, the first rector, the Reverend Lucius H. Jones, had died, and in 1868 the Reverend W. R. Richardson became rector. Better known as Dean Richardson because he held the office of dean when the church was, for a time, designated as a cathedral, he was rector until 1906—almost forty years.

The first services were held on Easter Day, 1875.

Dean Richardson, surely, did more than anyone else to give the church its personality and its peculiar beauty. The effect of cool, spacious repose which greets you in the interior, the broad, low, mullioned windows, the general grace of the plan, are no doubt the work of Richard Upjohn, who was also architect for Trinity Church in New York.

But the dean himself designed all the glowing memorial windows, which give the church warmth and color. He also stenciled with his own hand much of the ornamentation that was once on the walls and ceiling. This, unfortunately, has since been removed. He is even said to have carved the pulpit.

He was an imposing figure, with his flowing beard, like one of the ancient prophets. But there was nothing of the Jeremiah about him. He was a humorous, tolerant man, given to puns and charitable deeds.

His salary was at one time $100 a month, and not even then was it always forthcoming. He never asked for it. Instead, he would drop in for dinner at his parishioners' homes. One of them remembers how he loved to sit and rock while he talked. "He would rock until he had traveled nearly all the way around the room."

He was especially proud of his boys' choir, of which he said, "Some look well, some sing well, and some just fill up space." A Chorister Library Association was organized for the boys' mutual improvement, by which it was hoped (in 1882, that was) to "supplant the trashy 'Boys Weeklies' and dime novels by works and papers of a healthier tone, and thereby to cultivate a higher taste in literature."

Perhaps no man who ever lived in San Antonio has had so much influence on so many people. Among them was the famous surgeon Dr. Hugh Young. As a child he once nearly drowned in the San Antonio River. He was rescued, and his father was so overjoyed that "he placed a stained-glass window in St. Mark's Cathedral, depicting Pharaoh's daughter fishing Moses out of the water." Of the dean he wrote (*A Surgeon's Autobiography*): "He was undoubtedly one of the finest characters I ever met, and his literary and artistic abilities were outstanding."

In 1949 a tower was added, with a six-ton carillon, in memory of Albert Steves, Jr., by his family. Lyndon and Lady Bird Johnson were married here.

St. Paul's Episcopal Church

St. Paul's Episcopal Church (1018 East Grayson Street) has the same pleasing Gothic style that other San Antonio churches of its period show. It was built in 1884 with funds supplied by a Philadelphia lady who had heard of the difficulty that the ladies of the army post, so remote from town in those days, had in getting to church.

St. Luke's Episcopal Church

St. Luke's Episcopal Church (11 St. Luke's Lane) is an interesting example of modern church architecture, by the late Henry Steinbomer. It was built in 1956. The impressive stained-glass window is by Cecil Casebier; like Steinbomer he is a resident of San Antonio.

Jewish Congregations

Temple Beth-El

Temple Beth-El (211 Belknap) was organized in 1874. The first temple was built in 1875 on the east side of Travis Park. The present one dates from 1933.

Agudas Achim Congregation

Agudas Achim Congregation (1201 Donaldson Avenue) was founded in 1885. The first meeting place was in a rented hall at North Flores Street and Main Avenue, where the Torah had to be removed for Saturday night dances. The first building, of wood, was at Aubrey and Guilbeau streets.

14

Seasons and Evenings

April
Fiesta San Antonio

(Check newspapers for daily calendar)

February
Livestock Exposition and Rodeo

(Coliseum, 3201 East Houston Street)

April, October
River Art Show

September–May
Symphony Season

Concerts

June–August
Summer Festival

This chapter deals with events that occur just once a year or during certain seasons in the year. Since some of these events will interest some people but will leave others quite cold, the varied attractions and celebrations have been listed in categories, without regard for their position in the calendar. We begin with the Fiesta San Antonio, in April, the most popular of all.

Fiesta San Antonio

Each year, during the week which includes the date April 21, the anniversary of the Battle of San Jacinto, when Texas won its independence from Mexico in 1836, the town is decked out for a spring festival. More than half a million people, including nearly the whole population and many out-of-town visitors, take part, if only as spectators.

The Parade of the Ugly King starts the festivities on the afternoon of the previous Saturday. Monday features a solemn pilgrimage in memory of the 187 men killed at the Alamo. The Battle of Flowers Parade is on Friday and the last event, the Fiesta Flambeau Parade, is on Saturday.

The Fiesta rollicks along through the week, with something going on all the time and something to suit almost everybody's taste. New events are annually added, and old ones that have proved to be duds are discarded. Until around 1950, the whole program centered about the Battle of Flowers Parade, on Friday afternoon, the first public appearance of the queen.

For the Fiesta has a queen—and a king, too, though their paths scarcely cross. The king is chosen from among the Texas Cavaliers and is crowned at a ceremony Saturday evening in front of the Alamo. The Cavaliers are businessmen who rank in the higher echelons and who get themselves up during Fiesta Week in smart blue-and-red uniforms. The king rides in parades, attends parties, and visits charitable institutions. He is invariably a married man, and his picture is taken for the papers with his progeny grouped around him—none of them, Heaven forbid, owing the gift of life to the queen, who is a young unmarried girl.

The queen is chosen on Christmas Day before Fiesta by the Order of the Alamo, a society composed of young men who belong to the older wealthy families, the country-club set. The queen's identity is supposed to be a carefully guarded secret, and, as a matter of fact, not more than a few thousand citizens do know her name before she makes her first appearance at the coronation ceremonies on Wednesday evening at Municipal Auditorium, along with her princesses and duchesses, all dazzling in bejeweled sumptuous robes with long trains and escorted by the town's most eligible male catches.

Tickets for the coronation are expensive; the show is not for the common herd, who do not get a chance to see the queen until she rides on a gorgeous float in the Battle of Flowers Parade on Friday.

This parade was the original event of the Fiesta, which at first was called simply "The Battle of Flowers."

River Pageant

The festive part of Fiesta Week begins on Monday night with a parade of decorated barges on the San Antonio River, downtown. It is a jolly occasion. The crowd finds odd perches along the riverbank. Some bring picnic suppers. The illuminated floats, on scows, are likely at any minute to get fouled on some projection—thereby adding to the merriment.

The king makes his first official appearance in this pageant. The royal barge descends the stream to the Arneson River Theatre, at La Villita, where he disembarks and is escorted to his throne on the stage.

A Night in Old San Antonio

The visitor at Fiesta time who enjoys an atmosphere of relaxed gaiety, or who may be curious to know what holiday street life was like in this venerable city between 70 and 170 years ago, should spend at least one evening at "A Night in Old San Antonio."

The plazas and patios of La Villita, the old Spanish suburb, with their borders of banana plants, tropical vines, and flowers, are decorated for the occasion with colored lights and paper roses. Pink and green and yellow festoons, hung crosswise, flutter over Villita Street, as in Mexican towns on fiesta days. As in Mexico, too, the walks are lined with booths. There is even a Mexican market, where an *escribano* (public letter-writer) takes down letters on a battered typewriter, where bouquets and love charms are sold, and where steaming tacos and tamales, among other savory dishes, are served up over charcoal braziers in the flickering glow of cast-iron lanterns.

Everywhere is music: Spanish songs by serenaders in big braided sombreros, with guitars; hillbilly ballads, intoned by a nasal tenor in cowboy boots, accompanied by fiddle and banjo. A small German band, on a gallery overlooking the beer garden, where customers sup on frankfurters and sauerkraut, tootles out waltzes and polkas.

Even the casual visitor to the "Nights" will discover that San Antonio's background is a colorful patchwork of Spanish and Mexican and German cultures, bordered with a swatch of the old American Frontier West.

Costumes of all sorts invade La Villita for the Nights: the stovepipe hat, fashionable togs of the nineties, Spanish silks with high comb and mantilla, the white cotton drawers and sash and *huaraches* of the peon, short Bavarian pants with open vest and Tyrolese hat with feather, the besequined red and green skirt of the *china poblana*, the sunbonnet of the trail driver's womenfolk, the ranger's Stetson.

Pungent aromas pervade the air: coffee, garlic, chilis, the special tang of German or Chinese or Mexican food. A grinning multitude weaves its way back and forth between yipping vendors of lovebirds, of pretzels, of carnations; steps around ducks and geese and woolly lambs on leash, past children piled high in a goat cart. A burro, its long ears signaling thanks, chews on a proffered cigarette, accepts a nip of beer. Always the crowd grins, all evening.

The first Night was staged by the San Antonio Conservation Society, whose members do the planning and most of the work, shortly after the Second World War. From a small bazaar-type, ladies-club affair, it grew, nurtured by the imagination of a few women and the toil of many, until it became so popular it had to be spread out over Fiesta Week.

Battle of Flowers Parade

This, the oldest event of Fiesta Week, attracts thousands of spectators, who line the four and one-half miles of parade route hours in advance.

The name is anachronistic, for there is no battle (except sometimes behind the scenes, over whose float should go where) and fresh flowers are scarcely practical decorations any more, in a parade that lasts over two hours. (They do have a few.)

It is a rewarding spectacle, however, for those who love parades. The floats are lavish and colorful; schools and civic organizations participate; there are dozens of bands, thousands of marching youngsters, the United States Army and Air Force with a great display of military might, the king in a gaudy uniform straight out of musical comedy waving from a gilded coach drawn by blond palomino horses, and, as a climax, the queen and her court borne on a succession of resplendent floats in gorgeous and indeed costly robes.

Fiesta Flambeau

This illuminated Saturday night parade became part of Fiesta Week in 1948. To encourage its growth, the participation rules were lax, but it grew so popular and large that it became unwieldy and the regulations had to be tightened. It is still a very unusual and spectacular parade. The cars and floats are outlined or flooded with lights furnished via batteries or generators. Most of the band members have small flashlights shining from their boots, cuffs, and so on. It reminds one of a commercial testing the life of batteries.

Fiesta Flambeau calls itself "America's Foremost Illuminated Night Parade," and splendiferous effects are achieved with colored lights on floats and battalions of marching boys carrying flaming torches.

Fiesta Background

The idea of having a Battle of Flowers in San Antonio seems to have occurred to any number of people about the same time. But it was the news that President Benjamin Harrison was going to honor the city with a visit on April 20, 1891, that put the idea into action. As his visit would be on the day before the anniversary of San Jacinto, it seemed like a wonderful chance to combine entertainment of the distinguished guest with celebration of the most glorious day in Texas history.

The suggestion was first made in the *Express* of April 8. On April 13 the paper published a description of a flower carnival in Mexico City. That same afternoon a number of prominent ladies met at the San Antonio Club and mapped out plans for the fiesta. One of the ladies had seen the flower battle in Mexico. Another had seen a similar fete in France. Elaborate plans were made, and there was great ex-citement on the eve of the president's visit.

But, unfortunately, on that day it rained cats and dogs, as the saying goes. So the parade had to be called off, and only the more eminent citizens and politicians felt it necessary to stand in the soaking downpour in order to get a look at the president. He was not much to look at, we are told.

"He was just a little shrimp with a beard and a top hat," said a San Antonio artist who had just arrived from Germany then and expected the president of the United States to be a man of imposing build.

But the parade was held anyway, on April 24. It was a rousing success. The *Express* reported:

At 5 o'clock the starting point on Nacogdoches Street was a busy scene. The last finishing touches were being given to the carriages. The marshals and gay cavaliers and damsels pranced about on gaily decorated horses. The bicyclists prepared to mount, and over all the police officers cast a watchful eye.

About 5:30 the signal was given and the military band and equestrians heading westward got in motion. The mounted police officers were already in front clearing the way. As they reached Alamo Plaza a hum of expectancy rose from the spectators. Presently the mounted cavalcade came in view. By twos they passed, the ladies attired in becoming habits and their gallant squires white-trousered and gay with roses and smiles.

Next came the bicyclists, the majority mounted on "safeties." Among them rode a young lady "who with becoming self-composure wheeled gracefully in line to the admiration of thousands."

Then came the carriages, lavishly adorned with real flowers, chosen to match the horses' colors. The occupants shaded their faces with parasols or with fans decorated with flowers.

Fiesta San Antonio coronation

A burst of applause greeted the first float, which was drawn by four festooned horses, covered with "many a fold of white lace work," and contained "a wealth of buds that dazzled the beholder." The "buds" were little girls dressed in immaculate, loose-flowing white costumes. "Their little heads were protected with close-fitting sunbonnets, which set as in a frame their delighted faces."

The procession moved down Houston Street to Navarro, thence to Commerce Street and Main Plaza and back along Commerce to Alamo Plaza. There it divided in two files going around the park in opposite directions, and for a full hour, while the band played, the carriages passed and repassed one another, and a fusillade of flowers was kept up.

While this Battle of Flowers was going on, we are told, good horsemanship prevented many an accident. The only disagreeable feature of the event was the presence of young hoodlums, who picked up blossoms and pieces of laurel from the ground and flung them about with no regard for consequences, even singling out as their favorite target the tender little buds with the delighted faces.

After the brilliant success of the first festival, it was naturally decided to repeat it every year. With each repetition the affair became more elaborate.

Old-timers tell us that the fiesta was a much cozier occcasion in the early days, when everybody knew everybody else. That may be so, but there seem to have been a good many neighborly squabbles in those days.

There was a terrific row over the first queen appointed in 1896. She was a beauty from Austin. Some patriotic San Antonians objected to being ruled over by a foreigner. Later there was a fuss made about the participation of fire engines in the parade. And for some time a quarrel raged about the place of "commercialism" in the festivities.

Indeed, we are inclined to suspect that it may not have been always just the hoodlums, gamins, and street urchins who, in the Battle of Flowers, were tempted to hurl the thorny stem of the rose instead of the petals.

Those ancient feuds are now nearly all forgotten, of course.

But there was one occasion that seems to linger in the memory of witnesses: the time the beautiful and vivacious lady who was president of the Battle of Flowers that year decided her rightful place was at the head of the procession.

It so happened that the Belknap Rifles, a distinguished association of juvenile militiamen, had received orders to lead the parade. Their commander, Robert B. Green, was a fearless and determined man, undaunted even by the imperious beauty of the lady president.

Ladies of high social standing were not generally addicted to swearing in those days—not even in the privacy of their boudoirs. The lady president, however, proved to be an exception.

The air crackled. It seemed to thicken with sulphurous fumes.

But the Belknap Rifles led the parade.

In 1900 crass commercialism ran rampant. There was no Battle of Flowers, only a "Trades Parade," which was apparently nothing to write home to mother about. The great event of the "Carnival and Street Fair," as the celebration was called that year, was the reception of the king and queen and their knights and ladies, who were loaded into a Pullman car at a small town south of San Antonio and greeted, on their arrival, with tremendous fanfare. An *Express* reporter described the occasion:

As the train rolled into the station amid the aerial jubilations of fluttering flags and flying colors and the lusty shouts of an assembled multitude of 10,000 people, light battery K of the First Artillery, U.S.A., fired a royal salute, and all the whistles in town, locomotive, factory, laundry and what not, took up the din, and threw the atmosphere into myriad harsh, earsplitting waves and ripples, which made dogs stand on their hind legs and howl and bronchos snap inch ropes and buck.

In the part of town known as "Chihuahua," continues our reporter, a rumor had been circulated that the king and queen, arriving from the south, were authentic descendants of ancient Aztec rulers, and the enthusiastic populace of that section turned out en masse to welcome their compatriots.

Sidewalks, plazas, parks, and windows were jammed with representatives of all races and nations along the route from the depot to Alamo Plaza, "where the royal procession terminated, in front of the San Antonio Club, on the balcony of which the welcoming ceremonies took place. Alamo Plaza, as seen from this balcony, was a sea of faces, a flare of colors and a wilderness of flowers, and there was heard a din of racket and a confusion of music."

The next night there was a "grand illumination" of Commerce Street, "which is not unlike a child's dream of fairyland." The street was "flooded with manifold lights of different colors." And the people were so fascinated they "played about them like moths fluttering about some feeble, flickering flame."

"The joy of the small boy as he revels in that cream of all toys, the tin horn, is unspeakable, indescribable. Commerce Street is wild with this music. Nothing except a few cow bells could add to the horror of it."

There were also amusements for more mature tastes, such as the show on Main Plaza which offered "the can-can dance, alias hoochie-koochie," and Kichi the Wild Man.

On Alamo Plaza, Esau the Egyptian regaled his customers by letting rattlesnakes bite him. Then he retaliated by eating the reptiles alive. To start with, he snapped off their heads.

A novelty of the next festival was the appearance of three automobiles. The *Express* said:

This was the first time the horseless vehicle has figured in a flower pageant. They followed the artillery without a balk, rather a remarkable performance for automobiles. . . .
The storming of the Alamo, which marked the close of the pageant, was a pretty conclusion to the beautiful display. After the vehicles and floats had circled the plaza, they drew up before the old battle-scarred mission-church and threw their floral offerings at its front.

The parade of 1902 was pronounced "by those competent to judge, the finest of all that have been given. It was distinguished, first of all, by the absolute absence of advertising features." (Here was a complete reversal: crass commercialism utterly vanquished!) "Elegance, elaborateness of design, tastefulness and beauty were the distinguishing features of the long line of color that swept through the city."

"The floats of the German societies, representing the months of the year, received compliments all along the line." After these floats came phaetons, victorias, and tally-hos, and then the automobile division. "Five of the horseless carriages, all gorgeously resplendent in bright colors, called forth exclamations of wonder and surprise as noiselessly they rolled past an awe-inspired multitude."

The automobiles were followed by a bicycle brigade, "made up chiefly of little girls and boys," and, at the very rear was a wagon drawn by a dog and occupied by a tiny dog; "the whole was covered with flowers."

A main attraction, in 1902, was the Horse Show, at San Pedro Park, which was attended by all the "best" people. Advertisements warned, "It wouldn't do for you to say you hadn't been there."

The festivals of 1902 and 1903 had neither king nor queen. There was no accepted method of choosing royalty; each organization wanted to have a hand in it. To put an end to this chaos, the Order of the Alamo was founded in 1909. It has chosen the queen ever since. In 1911 the Fiesta San Jacinto Association was organized by the Chamber of Commerce to co-ordinate all the societies interested in the Fiesta. In 1926 the Texas Cavaliers were founded, and the next year chose their first king.

Except in war years the Fiesta has been held continuously.

Livestock Exposition and Rodeo

For nine days each year in mid-February the San Antonio Livestock Exposition and Rodeo is held at the huge Coliseum and the city streets are gaudy with cowboy clothes, some of them the genuine article.

The Exposition, inaugurated in 1949 by San Antonio businessmen, attracts large crowds, mainly people who have a professional or amateur interest in livestock, and youngsters who like rodeos and "Western" outfits and carnivals.

The show starts with a "Western" parade downtown. The rodeo performances feature first-rate riders and ropers, and the star is some famous figure from the horse operas of television or the movies.

For the professional cattleman, there is an Auction Sale of Fat Animals, which draws exhibitors from all over the country.

The Wool and Mohair Show is

254

the only annual state-wide fair of its kind.

The Horse Show has hundreds of entries in its three divisions: quarter horse, Appaloosa, and cutting horse.

Other attractions are the Calf Scramble, with boys from all over Texas competing, a rabbit show, farm and ranch machinery displays, military and wildlife exhibits.

Paintings and Crafts

Interest in graphic arts and in handicrafts makes San Antonio a lively place for painters, ceramists, and the like.

The town has a tradition of good painting. The work of the Germans Hermann Lungkwitz and Karl von Iwonski; of the Frenchmen Théodore Gentilz and Edward Grenet; of the Spaniard José Arpa and his nephew Xavier Gonzales; of the Onderdonks, father (Robert J.) and son (Julian)—most of them well represented in local galleries and libraries and homes—gives the artist of a later day a solid background and a diversity of schools. Several of the younger painters are making themselves known.

Societies devoted to art flourish. Exhibits are numerous and varied.

The San Antonio Art League sponsors a "San Antonio Artist of the Year" show, a local artists' show, and a fund-raising "Art Jamboree" where artists have a chance to hawk their wares.

The River Art Association stages two jolly shows on the San Antonio River banks: one during Fiesta San Antonio (the week of April 21); the other in October.

The Texas Watercolor Society raises several thousand dollars, in prize money, for its annual show, which subsequently travels all over Texas.

The Southwest Craft Center has an operating gallery for artists and then once a year holds a large crafts sale, which also exhibits their accomplishments.

The Western Art Show, held during the February Rodeo, has grown to monstrous size and includes many of the leading western artists.

For the serious artist or the dilettante, there are excellent classes at the San Antonio Art Institute and the Southwest Craft Center, and also under the aegis of several professional artists.

There are many art galleries in San Antonio representing outstanding local and out-of-town artists. Several are in La Villita and the Coppini Academy at 115 Melrose, and others are scattered about the city.

Music

San Antonio can no longer claim, as it did before the First World War, to be the second leading musical town of the South (the first was New Orleans). Its activity then was owing to the dominance of German

255

intellectuals. With the absorption of this element into the general population, musical life has been fostered mainly by certain organizations and in the colleges. It is perhaps fair to say that since then more talent has been brought in from the outside and less has been developed here. There has also been an increasing emphasis on quality, at the expense of widespread participation.

At least two attempts to form a symphony orchestra were made here previous to the First World War. These ultimately came to nothing.

In 1939 a group of local musicians and amateurs employed a refugee from Hitler's Europe, a distinguished conductor, Max Reiter, to direct them in four concerts. This was the beginning of the San Antonio Symphony Society. Reiter died in 1951 and was succeeded by Texas-born Victor Alessandro. The orchestra, composed for the most part of talent from outside, now

plays a season lasting from September through May. The symphony plays in the revitalized Aztec Theater. The Aztec was built in the heyday of the glorified movie houses and served well for years. In the 1960's and 1970's, when so many of the theaters bit the dust, the Aztec struggled along.

The Symphony Society has labored over the years to bring fine music to San Antonians. One problem was the lack of a home. For years the symphony performed in the Municipal Auditorium. It was too large and acoustics were bad; many unsuccessful cures were tried. The orchestra finally moved to the theater in the HemisFair area. Again, this did not work out due to a number of reasons.

Now the Symphony Society has joined with the Aztec Theater so that the orchestra can have its own rehearsal hall and a theater of its own to schedule to its own advantage.

The symphony occasionally goes

on the road. Another project is free concerts given in each of the city voting districts.

The Saturday night symphony programs are a San Antonio social event where everyone comes to see and be seen. Quite a few even listen.

The San Antonio Chamber Music Society sponsors four concerts each year at the Incarnate Word College auditorium, engaging the best available ensembles in this country, Europe, Japan, and elsewhere. It is necessary to buy subscription tickets for the whole season.

A variety of concerts, given mostly by talented young performers, are sponsored by the Tuesday Music Club, founded by Mrs. Eli Hertzberg in 1901. The club, which has done much to bridge the gap in musical culture left by the decline of the German societies, has its own clubhouse, with an excellent library and a small auditorium, on North St. Mary's Street, near Brackenridge Park. The club also helps promising young musicians.

Theater

The theater got off to a rattling good start, back in the 1850's, when a lovely girl in her teens, later known to the world as Ada Isaacs Menken but born Dolores Fuentes, a Texas Mexican, graced the boards in San Antonio.

In 1892 there was "cockfighting every Sunday, and first-rate theater every day in the week," to quote that sophisticated world traveler Richard Harding Davis.

With the coming of the movies, professional theater definitely went into the doldrums; at this writing there is as yet no sign that it will soon rise again.

A group of businessmen bring in many of the shows currently on tour: ballet and other dance groups, Broadway productions, and concert artists.

The encouraging signs in the theater here are seen in the emergence of regional and local groups outgrowing the status of amateur.

San Antonio's Little Theater (SALT), chartered in 1925, is now Theater San Antonio at San Pedro Playhouse and one of the most successful in the land. In a season its performances are seen by some twenty thousand people. About two hundred nonprofessional actors and more than five hundred backstage workers produce plays and one elaborate musical comedy each year. Most of these productions are shown at San Pedro Playhouse (in San Pedro Park). There are numerous good dinner theaters at HemisFair Plaza, Fort Sam Houston, and the colleges.

Less portentous, but sound entertainment, is the Fiesta Noche del Río or "Party Night on the River." The evening begins with a gondola ride, starting from Commerce Street Bridge, and winds up at Arneson River Theatre, where a program of authentic Mexican music and dancing is given from mid-June through August.

Ballet

The San Antonio Civic Ballet was founded in 1960 by the well-known dance teacher and choreographer Ruth Russell Matlock, with Josephine Shields Neal and Amory Oliver. Since that time ballet seems to have been infused into the art scene of San Antonio. Ballet classes take place at various locations. Ballet performing companies visit San Antonio, but the city also always seems to support one or two companies of its own. These organizations start, fade into history, or are rejuvenated to perform again. Some of them include the San Antonio Ballet Company, Festival Ballet, and Ballet Folklórico.

15
Fiesta
Mexicana

The events listed below are not "shows." They are not intended to be public entertainment. With the exception of a single performance of the *Pastores*, they are not, properly speaking, "tourist attractions."

Some of these observances are dying out; some may be hard to find. But for the convenience of those who are interested in Latin drama and Indian color, here is the chronological index to the events in this chapter:

Los Pastores

December 24–February 2

Blessing of the Animals

January 17 (or nearest Sunday)

Pésame

Good Friday

Cinco de Mayo

May 5

Mexican Independence Day

September 14–16

Columbus Day

October 12

Day of the Dead

October 31–November 2

Guadalupe Day

December 12

Las Posadas

December 16–24

To know San Antonio is to understand that this is a town essentially Mexican—or, if you prefer, Latin—and that the way to see the town at its liveliest and gayest is to take part in one of the *fiestas* of this folk.

In these *fiestas*, with the exception of a few severely religious rites, nobody is merely a spectator: everybody takes part.

There are two kinds of *fiestas*, secular and religious. But often the two are intermingled.

To see the secular *fiestas*, you have only to drop in at La Villita on any of the evenings described. Usually there are three days of celebration for each holiday.

The most popular of these occasions are on (and around) the following national holidays, which are described below: May 5, September 14–16, and October 12.

The principal religious festivals are also described briefly below. For a more thorough and detailed account—also a masterly description of the September 16 jubilation—the reader is referred to *The Silver Cradle*, by Julia Nott Waugh, a beautifully written book about the cycle of ceremony in the year of the San Antonio Mexican.

At the dances held at La Villita to celebrate both secular and religious events, ordinary street or evening clothes are worn. The visitor may also wear either.

On special occasions all the splendid heritage of the past is renewed. The adornments of a more romantic era are put on again, and both men and women appear in the traditional costumes of old Mexico, full of grace and glowing color. Swift young feet retrace the measures of exhilarating dances centuries old. A favorite is the national dance of Mexico, *jarabe tapatio*, which comes from away down in Jalisco. The *jarabe* is danced to many different tunes, but it always winds up with an especially rousing one, known as the *dianas*. These are strains of triumph and are played on occasions when some action merits applause—as when a bullfighter has done something exceptionally brave and elegant.

Any dance that has its origin in Latin America is likely to find favor, and these young people dance with equal spirit the rumba, the samba, and the tango. Their costumes may come from any section of Mexico or South America; but the *china poblana* dress for women, accompanied by the *charro* outfit for men, is the national costume of Mexico and so preferred.

Although Puebla is near the east

coast of Mexico, the *china poblana* ("Chinese Lady of Puebla"), in the *fiestas*, is coupled with the *charro*, whose costume originated in the state of Jalisco, on the Pacific slopes. The *charro* is essentially a horseman and a gentleman cowboy. He wears a tall, peaked hat of felt or rabbit hair, a short jacket, tight pants embroidered to taste, stitched boots, and as much delicately tooled leather in one place or another as he pleases. He carries over one shoulder a serape, or blanket, brilliant in color.

There is always music, laughter, and color in any merrymaking of the Latin folk, masters of the joyous arts.

The Charro Societies

While many Mexican customs are disappearing, or have disappeared, there has been a vigorous revival of late in San Antonio of the ancient riding and roping arts of the *charro*.

The first *charro* association in San Antonio was organized in 1947. Since then at least three rival clubs have flourished. They hold *charreadas*: riding and roping exhibitions and bloodless bullfights (with two-year-old bulls). The *charros* take part in parades and civic ceremonies.

The Piñata

Another Mexican custom that is not disappearing but is spreading to the non-Latin people of Texas is the festive *piñata*. It used to be a specialty for Christmas and birthdays and was for the delight of children only. But it has become so popular it may be introduced at any party.

The *piñata* has come a long way since Aztec times. Before Cortés smashed Moctezuma's empire to smithereens, the priests of the war god Huitzilopochtli—a monstrous idol with feathered headdress, necklace of skulls, and scepter in the

A piñata

form of a snake—invented the *piñata* as a vessel for offerings. They took an earthen pot, filled it with treasures and delicacies, covered it with fine woven feathers and brilliant plumes, and stood it on a pole in the temple. When the time came for the sacrifice—which was the Aztec New Year—a priest walloped it with a club, and the gifts all spilled out at the idol's feet.

The Christian padres taught the conquered Indians jollier uses for the *piñata*. But it is still made in very much the same way: a clay pot filled with goodies and covered with bright-colored paper curlicues and streamers.

The *piñata*, in Texas at least, is now made in a charming variety of shapes: a boat, a bull, a rooster, a boy on a burro eating watermelon—anything that appeals to the fancy of the maker—including, of course, Santa Claus.

At Christmas or birthday parties the *piñata* is always the climax. Child after child, blindfolded, is whirled about and turned loose to bat wildly in the supposed direction of the *piñata*, which dangles at the end of a rope stretched across a clothesline (or a limb). An adult holds the end of the rope and jerks it this way and that, just out of reach, until finally some child whales it, and everyone rushes for the good things that spill out.

Los Pastores

(December 24–February 2)

For the general public there is just one chance to see this pageant of the Christmas *fiesta*. It is given, usually the first Sunday after Christmas, at Mission San José under the auspices of the San Antonio Conservation Society. It begins about 7:00 P.M.

One of the few really medieval spectacles that have survived in the Southwest since the day of the Spaniard is the mystery play called *Los Pastores* ("The Shepherds")— about the celebrated journey that some shepherds once made to adore the Infant Jesus in Bethlehem.

Each year the first performance of the play is given at Guadalupe Church (see Chapter 9), and it is repeated any number of times between Christmas Eve and Candlemas (February 2), and even later, at other Catholic churches and in private backyards. But for the stranger there are no accommodations at these performances: no place to sit.

At San José a lantern is lighted over the mission gate. Within the walls the scene is set. Bleachers are placed about a long rectangle in front of the majestic church. At one end of the rectangle is a manger full of golden straw; at the other, a canvas enclosure with a great gaping mouth painted on it, red, with fangs. This is the mouth of Hell, through which the devils make their entrances and exits. Between Hell and Bethlehem the play goes on.

Los Pastores

It begins with a procession of the shepherds, wearing short trousers, bright ornamented jackets of silk or satin, and broad-brimmed, cocked, beribboned hats. Each carries a staff, which is adorned with jingling bells, paper flowers, and Christmas-tree ornaments. This is the chorus. They accent their songs by shaking the staffs, which tinkle.

The heroes and heroines of the drama are enacted by little children dressed in white, symbol of purity. There is the winged Archangel Michael, who announces to the shepherds the birth of the Messiah. The Virgin Mary and St. Joseph have rather static roles: their place is beside the manger that dominates the scene throughout; the Christ Child is represented by a doll, which has been blessed. The real heroine is the young girl Gila, who acts as a guide to the shepherds on their way to Bethlehem. Her part in the allegory is that of Good Conscience pointing the right way through the pitfalls and snares of a world infested with scheming devils on the prowl.

The devils—there are seven of them—have by far the most dramatic and flamboyant and sought-after parts. Their masks, usually of tin, painted vermilion, with real hogs' tusks and deer's antlers added, are fearsome, homemade creations in which the imagination is allowed to run absolutely nightmare-wild.

Two comic characters are Bartolo, the lazy shepherd, and the Hermit, a caricature of a friar (or possibly of St. Anthony, Abbot) in a Franciscan robe, with a great rough beard, a lofty sanctimoniousness, and a low IQ, which makes him easy prey to the machinations of the devils.

The devils are hell-bent on keeping the shepherds from ever reaching Bethlehem. They clash their swords together and make a solemn, evil pact. Then they proceed to torment the shepherds in ways that make for comedy, some of it low.

The climax is reached when Archangel Michael, a little boy in white satin who proclaims the innocence of his soul, stands, flashing his sword, with his foot on the throat of the prostrate Archfiend Lucifer. He thereby puts an end to the tricks and stratagems of the devils, who have had things pretty well their own way up to that point.

The shepherds, having overcome all difficulties, kneel before the Christ Child in the manger, attended by Mary and Joseph, and, one by one, offer Him gifts.

No performance of the *Pastores* would be complete without Mexican food. At the mission, long tables are laid out for the crowds. There is the smell of cinnamon chocolate and of tamales kept hot over charcoal braziers in copper pots and clay bowls. *Buñuelos*, festive Christmas dainties from Spain, are paper-thin pancakes dipped in sizzling-hot oil, dipped again in syrup, and served piping.

For a detailed and delightful account of *Los Pastores*, see Chapter 3 of Julia Waugh's *The Silver Cradle*.

Blessing of the Animals

(January 17 or nearest Sunday)

This observance takes place some time during the afternoon in or near various Catholic churches.

On this, the feast day of St. Anthony, Abbot, you may, if you are lucky, see a number of people in family groups bearing in their arms, or towing on leashes, dogs and cats of many breeds and sizes, washed, brushed, anointed with perfume. You may see also a rabbit, a goat, a parakeet, a bowl of goldfish. The late folklorist John A. Lomax claimed he saw an old woman bring an egg to be blessed.

The Blessing of the Animals is a prayer by the priest, asking protection and good health for the animal so that it may serve its master. The custom is dying out. Not long ago it was observed in many churches of the city, and the streetcar company allowed people with animals to ride free on that day.

There has been a recent revival of the tradition, however, by the San Antonio Charros. For some reason they have chosen the feast day of St. Anthony of Padua, and on the nearest Sunday to June 13 the horsemen gather in full regalia with their families at San Fernando Cathedral for an early mass, then repair to their ranch, where a priest blesses their horses and the pets of their children.

Pésame

(Good Friday)

At Guadalupe Church, after the regular Good Friday services, the parishioners hold a Pésame (Condolences) to the Blessed Virgin Mary.

The ceremony is a very touching one during which a live tableau consisting of the Blessed Virgin Mary and three other women—one holding the nails, one holding the shroud, one holding the crown of thorns—stand in front of the church, while the priest and members of the congregation reflect on Mary's sorrows as portrayed through the scripture. The most beautiful part of this ceremony is the sorrowful songs that are soloed by one or another parishioner. The ceremony generally begins at 7:00 P.M. and lasts an hour.

Formerly, on Good Friday at the Guadalupe Church a quiet but beautiful ceremony, the Descent from the Cross, was enacted. To abridge the moving description by Julia Nott Waugh (in *The Silver Cradle*, Chapter 5):

. . . there appear in the front pews of the nave twelve Jews—figures with draped heads and flowing garments, blue and yellow and gray and crimson, lavender and green and cream and rose, below which are revealed blue jeans and worn shoes. These are the apostles . . .

. . . The eleven apostles (Judas has passed forever from the scene) move to take the dead Christ down from the cross. . . . Out into the pale light of late afternoon the procession passes. The priests have departed from the scene. This is an expression wholly of the people.

. . . There is only a bare beaten yard bordered by church and school and the poor homes of poor people. Around this unlovely space they move, a line of silent figures carrying their dramatic burden.

Cinco de Mayo

(May 5)

Celebration of this national holiday generally goes on for three days. An elaborate three-evening function, called "La Feria de las Flores," held at La Villita under sponsorship of the Lulacs (Loyal Union of Latin-American Citizens), is notable for beautiful women and gorgeous costumes.

It was on May 5, 1862, that the most brilliant victory in Mexican history was won, over invading French troops, at the city of Puebla, by the greatest military leader that country has produced, General Ignacio Zaragoza. Although it is not a matter of common knowledge, he was born in the village of La Bahía, now a ruin, near the present town of Goliad, Texas. His father, an army officer, happened to be assigned to that post. His mother was a Seguín, of the well-known San Antonio family, for whom the town of Seguin is named.

Cinco de Mayo is one of the two most-celebrated Mexican secular holidays, the other being September 16.

Mexican Independence Day

(September 14, 15, and 16)

The great national holiday of Mexico spreads over three days of authorized rejoicing, although for some reason the official designation for the whole affair is *diez-y-seis de septiembre*, "Sixteenth of September"; it is equivalent to our Fourth of July. The nearest weekend is annexed too, so there are five or six big days in a row. The ardent patriot who celebrates with libations of ardent spirits is likely to build up what is spoken of in hushed awe as a Father Hangover, which may last for as many days more.

The festivities in San Antonio are manifold and include programs of speeches, concerts, and dances at places as widely separated as Municipal Auditorium, Plaza de México (at the junction of San Pedro and Main Avenue), the Mexican Consulate, Cassiano Park (on the West Side), and, of course, La Villita.

Some of these goings-on are delightfully described in Chapter 7, "Honor to the Cura Hidalgo," of Julia Nott Waugh's *The Silver Cradle*.

September 14 is officially the "Day of the Charro," a recent designation; it is in honor of the national costume, and the local societies of *charros* make the most of it, with roping and riding exhibitions, parades, and dances.

September 15 is unofficially the day of the yell. On September 15, 1810, at 11:00 P.M. in the town of Dolores, state of Guanajuato, Mexico, the Mexican revolution against Spain got off to an explosive start with the famous *grito* (yell) of Dolores, when the parish priest Miguel Hidalgo stood on the balcony of the municipal palace and shouted: "Death to the *gachupines*, and long live the Virgin of Guadalupe!" Now, on the same date, at the same hour, the president of Mexico stands on the balcony of the National Palace in Mexico City and, mindful of friendly relations with the people of Spain (*gachupines* to the unfriendly), mindful also of the anticlerical bias of Mexican governments since 1911, shouts "Long live Mexico!" And the shout is repeated from lesser balconies of lesser dignitaries all over the country, and from the stage of the Municipal Auditorium in San Antonio, Texas.

Columbus Day

(October 12)

A civil holiday, Columbus Day is celebrated by the Spanish-speaking peoples of both North and South America as the "Día de la Raza," or "Day of the Race." Though this holiday is called "Day of the *Race*," its emphasis is entirely on the spiritual heritage of the Spanish-speaking community.

It occurred to President Hipólito Irigoyen, of Argentina, that the only thing un-Spanish about the discovery of the Americas was Columbus's Italian birth. About 1915 he launched the idea of Columbus Day. It has taken hold not only in North and South America but in Spain as well, though it is celebrated on a different date there. Festivities at La Villita emphasize this solidarity of Spanish-speaking people.

Day of the Dead

(October 31–November 2)

On the closing day of October (Hallowe'en) and the first and second days of November (All Souls' and All Saints') the Spanish-speaking people of San Antonio go to the cemeteries to visit with their dead. These are holy days, when mass is said in the Catholic churches.

Mass is said outdoors, too, in the San Fernando cemeteries. The oldest and smallest, San Fernando No. 1 (two blocks south of Guadalupe Street, on Colorado Street), has the weathered tombstones of many old families. It was the third Catholic cemetery in San Antonio; the first was the tiny churchyard of San Fernando (now the cathedral); the second was excavated to build Santa Rosa Hospital. When San Fernando No. 1 became crowded—many of the dead there are now forgotten, and flowers on their day are few—the vast San Fernando No. 2 was opened. It is there that you find the crowds—and the flowers (west on Guadalupe Street to Castroville Road at Cupples Road).

The people flock by thousands to the graves of their dead, to decorate them with the flowers of the season: glowing marigolds, all shades of zinnias, tawny and deep-purple and white chrysanthemums, red cockscomb.

They make of the occasion a *fiesta*, solemn, yet merry.

For a month before, the variety stores will have offered gaudy funeral wreaths. Well ahead of the holidays El Mercado and various entrepreneurs stock up on blossoms. The Belgian gardeners, whose fields of flowers have been cultivated south of San Antonio since the 1880's, but who have moved ever farther from town to make way for expanding Kelly Air Force Base, will have prepared a $100,000 crop that will be harvested for the dead.

The people stream to the cemetery throughout the daylight hours, early and late. They come in Cadillacs, bearing tributes arranged by the florist. They come in aging jalopies, in ancient carts drawn by spavined mules, all laden with flowers and children and picnic baskets.

Outside the cemetery walls are the sights and smells of a Mexican *fiesta: cabrito* (young goat) roasting over charcoal, tamales for sale, coffee steaming in kettles. There are merry-go-round rides for the children.

The decking of the graves is a pleasant ritual. Children run back and forth to the hydrants, fetching water in painted cans. Grandmother is settled in a comfortable chair, and around her the decoration proceeds, with frequent family consultations. Sometimes a name is spelled out in flowers, sometimes a word: PADRE. Friends pause and admire the artistry.

When the sun is high, lunch baskets appear and picnic lunches are set out. The decorating done, the children grow sleepy. The older people are quiet and contemplative. In years gone by, they would sit all night amid the flickering candles on the graves. But it is no longer permitted. In country cemeteries you can still see the candles lighted. Toys are left on the graves of children, sometimes a lipstick or high comb on a young girl's grave. In earlier days food was left for the dead. But not any more—not in San Fernando No. 2.

The acres of piled flowers catch the last light as the families gather up their baskets and their babies, and leave their dead in peace.

Guadalupe Day

(December 12)

The Virgin of Guadalupe is, of course, the patron saint of Mexico, and this is her day. She is said to have appeared to the Indian Juan Diego on the Hill of Tepeyac, near Mexico City, in 1531. For proof she left him with roses and her image miraculously stamped on his *tilma*, or cotton mantle.

At Guadalupe Church the day starts with the singing of the "Mañanitas" at 4:00 A.M. People begin gathering at the front of the church, singing traditional and original songs in honor of the Virgin of Guadalupe. Various mariachi groups, usually sponsored by different families, sing and play for the

Virgin. In the past few years, the church doors have been opened and the different groups come up before the Virgin's altar to serenade her. A mariachi mass celebrating the appearances at Tepeyac begins at 5:00 A.M. It is followed by tamales and coffee. By 7:30 A.M. people begin leaving for work or to go back home.

On the nearest Sunday, most Mexican parishes celebrate on a grand scale, with a colorful concelebrated mass in the HemisFair Convention Arena. All the various mariachi groups and choirs perform, while folk dances are integrated into the performance of the mass itself at various times. This archdiocesan-wide celebration was begun by Bishop Patricio F. Flores, the first Mexican American ever to be consecrated to the episcopacy, in 1970. This Guadalupe celebration has now become a yearly event.

Las Posadas

(Conservation Society, December 14; Guadalupe Church, December 24)

The custom known as *posadas* ("shelters") commemorates the journey of Mary and Joseph to Bethlehem. Small lanterns over doorways or swaying from trees indicate the places where this ceremony is to be held. A cheerful sight to come upon, in an obscure street of the city, on one of the nine evenings before Christmas, is a group of people walking along singing and bearing candles or lanterns.

Nine families join in the ceremony. The family chosen to be first appears before the house of the second family, singing Christmas carols. They ask for shelter, and it is refused them, so they move on to the next house, which may be some distance away or just next door. The second family goes with them. The performance is repeated. The

group of singers increases at each *posada* they seek. Curious onlookers join in the march, and by the time the ninth house is reached, the group may have become quite a crowd. Everybody is admitted, refreshments are served, and prayers are recited by the assembled company before a manger scene (*nacimiento*) or improvised altar.

The *posadas* are repeated on nine evenings, the last time on Christmas Eve. This last celebration, in a holiday atmosphere, is a merry one. The celebrants attend Midnight Mass at the nearest church, then return to the home of the host, where quiet festivity prevails till dawn.

The Conservation Society, in conjunction with the Paseo del Río Association, conducts the yearly "Fiesta de las Luminarias" (Feast of the Lights) along the San Antonio River. It is a procession of persons carrying lighted candles, and at the conclusion of the procession *las posadas* take place.

Christmas at Guadalupe Church begins with *las posadas* in and around the church itself. Guadalupe Church has a very beautiful and complicated melody structure for its *posadas* which is not used in other churches in San Antonio. After the *posadas*, the children are treated to a *piñata* in the church yard.

Beginning about 7:30 P.M. the *pastorela* begins in the parish hall. It generally lasts until 11:00 P.M., at which time the Christmas concert begins in the church. This may consist of choral, orchestral, or brass-band Christmas music. At midnight the *pastores* line up for the procession that begins the Midnight Mass. The first ceremony is the *acostamiento* of the child Jesus in the empty crib by the main altar. This is done by the girl who portrays the Blessed Virgin Mary. The mass follows and is ended by all the members of the congregation coming to the front and kissing the figurine of the Christ Child. During this adoration period, the *pastores* sing their traditional songs.

The *nacimiento*, or manger scene, will be found in most Mexican homes at the Christmas season. Besides the small wooden or clay figures of the Christ Child, Mary, Joseph, the Wise Men, the ox, the ass, and the lamb, an astonishing variety of characters may be introduced, depending on the whim or imagination of the artist. Some *nacimientos* are elaborate. A peculiar homemade snow, a mixture of resin and other ingredients, forming a thick liquid, is blown in the form of bubbles over the scene and acquires, when dry, a hard luster that, reflecting light, makes a fine shimmering.

16

Food, Mostly Fiery

Of the several peoples who have made their mark on San Antonio, the Mexican has contributed most— has made the single original contribution—to the arts of cookery.

You can get German food here that is prepared according to recipes handed down in families for generations. But it is pretty much like German food elsewhere. The Germans have added something to the Mexican dishes, however: their chili con carne and enchiladas are richer, blander.

The native dishes of San Antonio should not be confused with the Mexican dishes from below the border, even when they are called by the same name. Aside from the two kinds of tortillas (corn and flour), there are other differences. Restaurants in or near El Mercado, as well as other parts of San Antonio, serve a sort of combination of northern Mexico and Texas cooking. One gourmet dish is *cabrito*, consisting of very young, tender, baked kid (goat).

Genuine Spanish food, in the taste of Spain, is of course something else again. It can be found here, however.

A thriving Italian colony has produced a number of restaurants serving the traditional foods. Some of the cooks are Mexican, though; there may be an extra piquancy to the spaghetti sauce.

Perhaps the best-known restaurant in San Antonio is French, but in the New Orleans tradition.

There are, of course, numerous good American-style eating houses. The larger hotels hire excellent chefs.

Evolution of the Brimstone Bowl

The one thing that comes from San Antonio, Texas—and from nowhere else—is chili con carne.

But that is a Mexican dish, you say. How strange, then, that it is not found in Mexico. Or in New Mexico, either. The word *chili* (spelled thus) is an Aztec word for the wonderfully varied species of the *Capsicum frutescens*, a plant bearing seed pods of singular piquancy, native to the lands along the Caribbean Sea and the Gulf of Mexico. The Aztecs used these peppers in cooking (the Spanish word for them is *chiles*, spelled thus) and they used them in cooking the Spaniards who fell into their hands before the Conquest was complete: the luckless *conquistadores* were carved up by blood-smeared priests on the platforms atop the graded temples of stone, and the warm cuts were tossed to the howling multitude below. Then each family man carried his prize off to the dear ones at home, who basted the roast with a sauce made of *chiles*. So says the chronicler Bernal Díaz del Castillo. This was not, however, anything like the chili con carne that we know; it was probably a version of the classic *mole poblano*, concocted for festive occasions by the Aztecs and by their descendants to-day, who make it with chicken or turkey. What they call "chile con carne" is simply cooked meat with a sauce poured over it. What Erna Fergusson, the interpreter of New Mexico, in a book that purports to be a collection of recipes handed down by ancient families, calls by the same name is a stew, like the original Texas dish. But it is made without any liquid, and the recipe calls for a quart of ripe tomatoes and a pint of ripe olives! Now, chili con carne is a poor man's treat, a savory disguise for tough beef. Who in ancient New Mexico had ripe olives? This sounds like the perversion practiced Up North, where the Yankee tosspot who lurches from his unsteady couch after a fluid evening and cries out for "chillee cahn corny" is resuscitated with a bland goo tasting of tomatoes and sugar.

There were no tomatoes in Texas when chili con carne was invented by the Mexicans of San Antonio a long time ago, but lots of tough beef. And there was *chile ancho*—the

Chiles

Chili stand on Military Plaza, about 1882

broad red *chile* despised as coarse-flavored down in Mexico—and cumin-seed and garlic and wild marjoram. An American colonist in Texas, J. C. Clopper, who visited San Antonio in 1828, gives us our first description of the dish:

When they have to pay for their meat in market a very little is made to suffice a family; it is generally cut into a kind of hash with nearly as many peppers as there are pieces of meat—this is all stewed together. [The women made the tortillas, he said, which served as spoons, and] with which they all dip into the same dish of meat & peppers prepared as above, one spoon not lasting longer than to supply with two mouthfuls when a new one is made use of. Very few families are supplied with the common necessary kitchen & household utensils, not even with chairs, sitting on skins spread upon the earthen floors of their dwellings.

Ripe olives, ¡mi sombrero!

Sidney Lanier came to town in 1872 and wrote about the colorful street life and the squalor of the Mexican slums. If there had been chili stands on the plazas then, surely he would have described them. Nor did Edward King mention them in his "Glimpses of Texas" (published in *Scribner's*, January, 1874); but he does show that the piquant pod of the Aztecs was already well started on its conquest of the white man's palate:

From Military Plaza it is only a few steps to one of the Mexican quarters of town, sometimes called "Laredito." There the life of the Seventeenth Century still prevails, without any taint of modernism. Wandering along the unpaved street in the evening, one finds the doors of all the Mexican cottages open, and has only to enter and demand supper to be instantly served; for the Mexican has learned to turn Ameri-can curiosity about his cookery to account.

Entering one of these hovels, you will find a long, rough table with wooden benches around it, a single candlestick dimly sending its light into the dark recesses of the unsealed roof; a hard earth floor, on which the fowls are busily bestowing themselves for sleep; a few dishes arranged on the table, and glasses and coffee cups beside them. The fat, swarthy Mexican mater-familias will place before you various savory compounds, swimming in fiery pepper, which biteth like a serpent; and the tortilla, a smoking hot cake, thin as a shaving, and about as eatable, is the substitute for bread. This meal, with bitterest of coffee to wash it down, and liquid dulcet Spanish talked by your neighbors for dessert, will be an event in your gastronomic experience. You will see many Americans scattered along the tables in the little houses of Laredito.

In 1877, Harriet Prescott Spofford wrote in *Harper's*: "Little tables are spread [on Military Plaza] where the market people get their rolls and chocolate and bit of pastry."

No chili? But elsewhere she says: "At almost any hut you can get Mexican refreshment, if you wish it, that will make you malodorous for days."

In 1879 Thomas Allen, visiting San Antonio, painted Military Plaza, showing what looks like a chili stand, cauldron and all.

Not until 1882, when Gould's *Guide* was published, do we find a reference to chili stands on the plaza: "Those who delight in the Mexican luxuries of tamales, chile con carne and enchiladas, can find them here cooked in the open air in the rear of the tables and served by lineal descendants of the ancient Aztecs."

Evidently, then, Americans first took to "Mexican" food in the 1870's; they were served in homes and not on the plazas. The first chili stands on Military Plaza must have appeared about 1880. The first Mexican restaurant, it seems, was opened by a Madame Garza (listed in the city directory of 1889) on West Dolorosa Street, across San Pedro Creek. Says Frank H. Bushick (in *Glamorous Days*):

She was a fine-looking Spanish woman who served the best Mexican food in the city. She always had on hand chile con carne, frijoles, tortillas, gallina. . . . Perfect order was maintained at Madame Garza's and the best people of the city were her patrons for years and years. Her success was followed by later restaurants up town conducted by shrewd Americans.

One fascination that Madame Garza's place had for the "best people," besides food, was its location on the very rim of the Red Light District. It was frequented by pimps, gamblers, and courtesans as well as by the best people. The two worlds had a rare opportunity to study each other over a bowl of chili.

Not until the 1890's did the chili queens reign over Military Plaza. In 1892 Richard Harding Davis was here, and he writes in *The West through a Car Window*, "At night the men sit outside their hotels and the plazas are full of Mexicans, and their outdoor restaurants and the lights of these and the brigandish appearance of those who keep them are unlike anything one may see at home."

In 1895, O. Henry, who was then William Sydney Porter—that is, nobody—used to come frequently from Austin on the pretext of business. He would dine outdoors on chili when he could not rate a free lunch. The chili queen he writes of is an old crone with the complexion of a canteloupe. One of his boozier stories, "The Enchanted Kiss," has praise for "the delectable chile con carne . . . composed of delicate meats minced with aromatic herbs and the poignant *chili colorado*."

When Stephen Crane was in town that same year, a chili queen, says Frank Bushick, pinned a rose on him.

On Military Plaza and later on Alamo Plaza and still later on Haymarket Plaza, and in the more and more numerous restaurants, chili had become a prime attraction for tourists. Droves of Yankees returned with tingling tonsils to their frozen haunts. They had, indeed, become, in their outlandish way, addicts of the brimstone bowl. Thus, says Bushick, "In New York and many other northern cities can be found pseudo-Mexican restaurants serving nondescript imitations of the dishes which have made the Mexican restaurants of San Antonio famous. At the world's fair in Chicago in 1893 the eye was greeted with a sign in front of a booth on the grounds: 'The San Antonio Chili Stand.'"

San Antonians who visit Mexico, he notes, can hardly wait to get back home where they can find the "Mexican" food they are accustomed to.

But the making of chili—the

method of extracting the pulp from the pods, the right combination of spices—was quite beyond the American housewife until German-born William Gebhardt put out the first commercial chili powder in 1896, at New Braunfels. He moved his factory to San Antonio two years later, and in 1908 put out the first canned chili con carne.

Thus, the Mexican food that originated in San Antonio, Texas, has become a household staple throughout the United States and New Mexico—has even found its way into Old Mexico. But chili con carne, like many another strong character, in the process of making itself popular has made itself insipid. Not long ago the ordeal by chili was practiced even as the badger game and the snipe hunt, as a measure of reprisal for Appomattox. Prize-awarding, chili-making contests are held all over Texas. They are often fund-raising events, and if your insides are burned in testing the finished product, that is just incidental and free.

A Note on Sources

A guidebook has no place for foot-notes. Besides, the sources that have been tapped to get the materials for this book run into several hundreds, not counting newspapers or manuscripts. It would obviously be impracticable to list them all. For the gratification of those readers who would like to read further, and for the confusion of those critics who snipe from the musty back rooms of libraries, a few of (1) the most illuminating and (2) the most controversial sources will be listed under the numerals of the chapters in which they are used. Some of these sources, identified in the text, will not be cited here.

An enormous amount of the information that goes into all the chapters concerned with developments since the Civil War has been gleaned from tattered files of the *San Antonio Express*. A good deal of this material made a second appearance in the *Express* during the years 1947–1949, when the author was a regular contributor to its Sun-

day magazine. Portions of those articles have been rewritten for this book.

The material for this book was gleaned over the years from various sources. A great many of these facts were hidden away. Now they have been collected, and these major depositories are recommended: Bancroft Library, University of California, Berkeley; Barker Texas History Center, University of Texas at Austin; Yale University Library, New Haven, Connecticut; Daughters of the Republic of Texas Library at the Alamo, San Antonio, Texas.

Recommended Reading

Nearly all the books listed below or cited in the text are out of print. Some can be found in only a few libraries. Two outstanding exceptions are:

San Antonio

277

Waugh, Julia Nott. *The Silver Cradle*. Austin: University of Texas Press, 1955.
A beautifully written book about the ceremonial and holiday life of San Antonio Mexicans.

Green, Rena Maverick, ed. *Samuel Maverick, Texan*. San Antonio, 1952.
Family papers more exciting than a novel; they include the *Memoirs* of Mary A. Maverick, a classic of Texas literature and the best personal account of life in San Antonio ever written (previously published in an imperfect edition, 1924).

Other Helpful Books about San Antonio, Listed Chronologically

Gould, Stephen. *The Alamo City Guide*. New York: McGowan & Slipper, 1882.

Corner, William. *San Antonio de Bexar: A Guide and History*. San Antonio: Bainbridge and Corner, 1890.
Included is much of Sidney Lanier's "In San Antonio de Bexar: A Historical Sketch," but not all of it.

History and Guide of San Antonio, Texas. N.p., n.d. [Published in San Antonio, 1892.]
Very rare.

Chabot, Frederick Charles. *With the Makers of San Antonio*. San Antonio: Artes Gráficas, 1937.

Federal Writers Project in Texas. *San Antonio: An Authoritative Guide to the City and Its Environs*. San Antonio: Clegg Company, 1938.

James, Vinton Lee. *Frontier and Pioneer: Recollections of Early Days in San Antonio and West Texas*. San Antonio: Artes Gráficas, 1938.

Bushick, Frank H. *Glamorous Days*. San Antonio: Naylor Company, 1940.

Hagner, Lillie May. *Alluring San Antonio through the Eyes of an Artist*. San Antonio: Naylor Company, 1940.
Interesting sketches of old houses.

Johnston, Leah Carter. *San Antonio: St. Anthony's Town*. San Antonio: Librarian Council, 1947.

Woolford, Sam, and Bess Woolford. *The San Antonio Story*. San Antonio: Joske's of Texas, 1950.
Includes an excellent bibliography, which should be consulted by those interested in pursuing any phase of San Antonio's later history.

Pioneer Flour Mills. *100th Anniversary, Pioneer Flour Mills*. San Antonio: Privately printed, 1951.
Best printed assortment of San Antonio pictures.

Curtis, Albert. *Fabulous San Antonio*. San Antonio: Naylor Company, 1954.

Habig, Marion A., O.F.M. *San Antonio's Mission San José*. San Antonio: Naylor Company, 1968.

Habig, Marion A., O.F.M. *The Alamo Chain of Missions*. Chicago: Franciscan Herald Press, 1968.

Burkholder, Mary V. *The King William Area*. San Antonio: King William Association, 1973.

Other Sources, by Chapters

1

The letters of Sidney Lanier and the complete sketch "In San Antonio de Bexar," excerpted in William Corner's guidebook of 1890 (see above), are included in the Centennial Edition of Lanier's works, published by Johns Hopkins Press (Baltimore, 1945).

2

For the Spanish period, the author has studied manuscripts in the archives at Mexico City and at Austin and San Antonio, including the large collection of transcripts from the archives of Spain, Mexico, and scattered libraries that is at the University of Texas at Austin.

Photostatic copies from the Archivo San Francisco el Grande, whose originals are in the Biblioteca Nacional, Mexico City, have been preferred in checking certain translations; among these translations are some published in the 1930's as *Preliminary Studies of the Texas Catholic Historical Society*; they include the diaries of Fray Damián Massanet and Domingo Terán (1691–1692); of Fray Ysidro Espinosa (1709 and 1716); of Domingo Ramón (1716); of Juan Antonio de la Peña (1721/22).

Two translations by Fritz Leo Hoffman, which cover the founding of San Antonio, were not checked: his *Diary of the Alarcón Expedition into Texas, 1718–1719, by Fray Francisco de Céliz* (Los Angeles: Quivira Society, 1935) and his "Mezquía Diary of the Alarcón Expedition into Texas, 1718," *Southwestern Historical Quarterly* 41 (January, 1938).

Documents used for the early history of the Alamo are included under 7.

3

All available printed and manuscript sources have been consulted in preparing this chapter. The narrative of Enrique Esparza is condensed from a single story in the *Express*, May 12 and May 19, 1907. The account of Mrs. Dickinson is compiled from a dozen places. In the later history of the Alamo are allusions to *Texas in 1837*, ed. Andrew Forest Muir (Austin: University of Texas Press, 1958); and *William Bollaert's Texas*, ed. W. E. Hollon and Ruth L. Butler (Norman: University of Oklahoma Press, 1956).

4

The initial sentence under 1, 2, and 3 applies also to this chapter.

The "book published in 1883" is *On a Mexican Mustang through Texas*, by Alex E. Sweet and J. Armoy Knox.

The passage about Moses Koenigsberg is condensed from his *King News* (Philadelphia: F. A. Stokes, 1941).

7

This chapter is based mainly on manuscripts. Some of the most valuable are in the Archivo San Francisco el Grande (see 2, above) and include the reports of Fathers Fernández de Santa Ana (1740), Ciprián (1749), and Ortiz (1745 and 1756—this last has apparently never before been used), and Governor Barrios (1758). The following reports in published translations have been checked with transcriptions of originals in the University of Texas archives: Fray Gaspar Solís (1767/68), Fray José Francisco López (1785), both in the *Preliminary Studies* mentioned above; Fray Juan Augustín Morfi, *Indian Excerpts from Memorias*, trans. Frederick C. Chabot (San Antonio: Naylor Company, 1932).

The "romantic novel" about San José is *The Daughter of Tehuan*, published in German by one of the Benedictines who lived at the mission about 1860, P. A. S. Hoermann; it is without merit.

8

The alumnus of the German-English School whose manuscript is quoted is Gretchen Rochs Goldschmidt.

13

The bibliography on local churches is unbelievably long and consists of innumerable pamphlets, obscure books, and unpublished reports, all to be found in the San Antonio Public Library.

Index

Murphy, Margaret, 238
Músquiz, Ramón, 74, 94, 95

National Autonomous University
    of Mexico, 211–212
Navarrete, Angel Martos, 122
Navarro, Celso, 188
Navarro, José Antonio, 172–173,
    188
Navarro Street Bridge, 76, 90, 110
Neal, Josephine Shields, 257
Neill, J. C., 72–73
"Night in Old San Antonio, A,"
    106, 108, 248–249
Norton, Russel C., 163
Núñez, Father Miguel, 18

O. Henry (William Sydney Porter),
    157, 274; and Commerce Street
    Bridge, 98–100
Oconor, Hugo, 133
Odin, Bishop Jean, 124, 206, 218
Oge House, 164
O'Grady, Alice, 221
Olivares, Father Antonio, 8, 12–13,
    16
Oliver, Amory, 257
Olmos Golf Course, 204

Olmos Park, 203
Olmsted, Frederick Law, 41, 96,
    153, 156
Onderdonk, Julian, 187, 255
Onderdonk, Robert J., 187, 255
Oppenheimer, Dr. and Mrs.
    Frederic G., 193, 196
Order of the Alamo, 247, 254
Ortíz, Father Francisco Xavier,
    16, 19
Our Lady of the Lake University,
    141, 159, 206, 214

Pages, "Monsieur," 23–24, 110
Palo Alto College, 212
Paseo del Río, 89, 101–103, 109,
    268
Pastores, Los, 173, 258, 261–263
Patrón, Father Agustín, 18
Pecan Valley Golf Course, 204
Pefferkorn, Father Henry, 159
Pentenrider, Erhard, 187
Pérez, Ignacio, 123
Pésame, 173, 264
Pike, Zebulon M., 17, 26–27,
    123
Piñata, 260–261
Pioneers, Trail Drivers, and Texas

Rangers Memorial Building,
    178, 189
Plaza de las Islas. *See* Main Plaza
Plaza de México, 265
Plaza House, 44, 114
Plaza Juárez, 104, 106
Polk, Edward, 163
Porter, William Sydney. *See*
    O. Henry
Posadas, las, 137, 268–269
Potter, Reuben M., 76, 94
Pryor, Ike T., 163
Public Library, 167, 200

Quadrangle, the, 222, 224–225,
    226, 227
Querétaro, college of, 16, 18, 21,
    22
Quillin, Ellen Schulz, 186, 219

Ramón, Domingo, 12
Randolph, William M., 236
Randolph Air Force Base: access
    to, 223; history and description
    of, 231, 234–236
Read House, 45
Reiter, Max, 256
Richardson, Dean W. R., 243–244

"Tom Thumb," 201
Torres, José, 171
Trail Drivers Association Museum, 178, 189, 219
Tranchese, Father Carmelo, S.J., 173
Travis, William Barret, at the Alamo, 73-74, 78, 80, 93, 94; killed, 80
Travis Park Methodist Church, 238-240
Trinity University, 206, 214-215
Trolley buses, 125
Tuesday Music Club, 256
Turner-Halle (Turner Hall), 156
Turnverein, 156-157
Twiggs, David E., 45, 115
Twining, Nathan F., 234
Twohig, John, 31, 188

Umlauf, Charles, 184, 191
U.S. Army Health Services Command, 226-227
U.S. Arsenal, 126
University of Texas at San Antonio, 160, 206-207
University of Texas Health Science Center, 206, 210-211
Upjohn, Richard, 243

Ursuline Academy, 206, 255
Ursuline Convent, 35, 124

Valero, Marquis of, 13, 122
Vásquez, Rafael, 31
Veramendi House, 30, 85, 239, 241
Villa, Pancho, 228

Washington Street, 153, 164-165
Waugh, Julia Nott, 31-35, 174, 176, 259, 263, 264, 265
Webb, Walter Prescott, 2
Western Art Show, 255
White, Edward H., 223, 233-234
White, Thomas D., 234
Willow Springs Golf Course, 180, 204
Witte, Alfred G., 186
Witte Museum, 177, 180, 219; described, 184-188; historic houses at, 188, 190, 205
Woll, Adrian, 31
Wood, Leonard, 64-65, 227-228
Woodlawn Park, 180, 204
Wool, John E., 224
Wueste, Luisa, 187
Wulff, Anton Friedrich, 157, 162

Yanaguana, Indian camp, 7
Young, Dr. Hugh, 244
Yturri-Edmunds home and mill, 151

Zacatecas, college of, 16, 18, 24, 140, 141
Zaragoza, Ignacio, 265
Zizelmann, Rev. P. F., 242
Zoological Gardens, 177, 180, 184

Picture Credits

The sources of the illustrations in this book are shown below.

Barker Texas History Center, Texas Collection, University of Texas at Austin: pp. 15, 28, 29, 44

Barnes, Charles M. *Visitor's Guide and History of San Antonio, Texas.* San Antonio, 1913: pp. 72, 84

Brooks Air Force Base Information Office: p. 232

Buckhorn Hall of Horns, Lone Star Brewing Company: p. 198

Daughters of the Republic of Texas Library: pp. 173, 262

Fort Sam Houston Information Office: p. 225

Harper's Weekly, May 19, 1888, supplement: p. 67

Hendel, Richard: pp. 135, 148, 150, 260

James, Ted: pp. 5, 14, 32, 50, 51, 64, 168

Le Gwin, Jean, and Lynne Herndon: pp. xx, 88, 101, 103, 106, 107, 108, 109, 115, 120, 128, 136, 144, 145, 146, 149, 159, 162, 164, 165, 166 *left,* 174, 271

Long, Charles J.: pp. 104, 125, 163, 171, 235

Marion Koogler McNay Art Museum: pp. 194, 195

Mathis, Walter N.: p. 166 *right*

Menger Hotel: p. 158

O. Henry Memorial Museum: p. 99

Old San Antonio. © 1968 by Express Publishing Co. Property of Express-News Corporation: pp. 42, 43, 46, 47, 53, 57, 59, 66, 119

Randolph Blue Print Company: pp. 54-55

San Antonio Chamber of Commerce: pp. 92, 93, 181

San Antonio Conservation Society: p. 172

San Antonio Convention and Visitors Bureau: pp. 3, 83, 102, 112, 192, 208, 209, 251, 276

San Antonio Museum Association: pp. 183, 185, 187, 190

Texas Highway Department: pp. 68, 73, 121, 130, 133, 142, 152, 179

Thrall, Herman S. *A Pictorial History of Texas . . .* St. Louis: N. D. Thompson & Co., 1879: pp. 9, 10, 36, 37, 75, 79, 80

University of Texas Health Science Center at San Antonio: p. 211